The Flexible Enterprise

How to Reinvent Your Company, Unlock Your Strengths, and Prosper in a Changing World

David Gewirtz

JOHN WILEY & SONS, INC.

New York • Chichester • Brisbane • Toronto • Singapore

*To all my customers and all my clients. Without you
there would be no enterprise.*

—David Gewirtz

This text is printed on acid-free paper.

Copyright © 1996 by David Gewirtz
Published by John Wiley & Sons, Inc.

Library of Congress Cataloging-in-Publication Data:

Gewirtz, David.
    The Flexible Enterprise : how to reinvent your company, unlock
your strengths, and prosper in a changing world / by David Gewirtz.
        p.   cm.
    Includes bibliographical references (p.).
    ISBN 0-471-07235-4 (alk. paper). — ISBN 0-471-07246-X (pbk. :
alk. paper)
    1. Reengineering (Management)   2. Small business—Management.
3. Diversification in industry.   I. Title.
HD58.87.G49   1996
658.4' 063—dc20   95-37312

Printed in the United States of America

10 9 8 7 6 5 4 3 2 1

Preface

It is change, continuing change, inevitable change, that is the dominant factor in society today. No sensible decision can be made any longer without taking into account not only the world as it is, but the world as it will be.

—Isaac Asimov, 1978

Change is a tangible force of nature. Whether it comes in the form of erosion, evolution, entropy, or an economic action by a competitor, change is unavoidable. In business, numerous outside forces compel change. Whether it's the sudden drop in list price from a competitor, the introduction of a revolutionary new device that changes your market, the collapse of a previously secure business channel, or the fickleness of your customers, change is inevitable. Your relationship with the force of change will define your future. You can tap into this most elemental of forces, and use change as a tool to shape your business.

In most businesses, there is a detrimental though perfectly understandable tendency toward rigidity. It takes enormous effort and investment to make a business operational and profitable. Once you've got it working, why change? Change requires new training, new products, new investments, new sales techniques, and, above all, new risks.

On the one hand, we've got the entropic inevitability of change. On the other hand, we've got a highly reasonable philosophy best articulated by "If it ain't broke, don't fix it."

Our paradox lives in the age-old story of the unyielding force pressing against the immovable object. In the world of business, the unyielding force takes the form of external pressures, whether from customers, competitors, government, or acts of nature. That leaves the rigid business enterprise as the immovable object. However, this is not a battle of equals. When faced with the pressures of external change, the business (your business?) will budge.

If your business is rigid, like the dried-out old stick in the Japanese proverb, the unyielding force will eventually cause your business to break. On the other hand, if your business is flexible, like the supple branch of a living tree, your business will bend to outside pressures, but rarely, if ever break.

Being flexible and responsive to outside pressures is important if your business is to survive. But you must still retain the ability to chart the course of your own destiny. Rather than changing your business solely due to outside influences, you can and must drive change creatively from within. You can leverage off those things you do exceptionally well—your strengths—to redefine your company. You can harness change as a proactive, planned, creative activity driven from inside yourself and your business.

Creating the Flexible Enterprise requires reinventing your business from the inside out with these steps: Identify your strengths; eliminate weaknesses; search out new opportunities; reposition appropriately; evaluate; and repeat. By being "strength driven" rather than technology, market, or sales driven, your company can work to maximum benefit within its own capabilities rather than pin all its hopes on the slim chances of attracting an outside "savior" or reacting with conventional approaches that have failed time and time again.

Reinventing your business from the inside out is a strategy that will help you manage growth and make your company work for the long haul. Best of all, everything you need to drive the change is within your grasp—your own strengths and the strengths of your company, your motivation, your willingness to change, and the tactics and principles described in this book.

HOW TO GET THE MOST OUT OF THIS BOOK

This book provides more than a description of how to change; it also provides a methodology for handling change again and again, while each time improving the foundation of what works. Reinventing from the inside out is a powerful way to incrementally effect positive change that benefits the company, its management, and its owners more than it hurts. And it's the only way that takes into account real-world constraints of business owners and managers rather than blue sky theories and the assumption of an infinite cash war chest.

This book is targeted at owners, senior managers, and investors in small companies with revenues of $1 million to $20 million. Most of my experience comes from learning the hard way with my own technology companies. These lessons can benefit any manager in any small business.

The book is divided into three parts: Dynamics of Change, the Art of Reinvention, and Strategies and Tactics for Change.

Part I: Dynamics of Change

Part I will help you explore the business dynamic that is change. It opens with a detailed case study from my company's past that will help put business change into stark perspective.

Part II: The Art of Reinvention

While change can happen on its own, the successful business manager will guide and coach the reinvention process. Successful reinvention isn't just a matter of downsizing and delayering. Rather, reinvention is like an art form seeking a sense of synthesis, a balance of strengths, opportunities, and challenges. In Part II, you'll learn how to take control of change and use it to your advantage.

Part III: Strategies and Tactics for Change

If Parts I and II are the theory of the Flexible Enterprise, Part III is the practice. In these chapters, you get tactics, hints, and ideas for transforming your organization. We'll look at all the important aspects of your organization—products and services, marketing, sales, cash management, operations, people management, and even positioning, planning, and managing your life in harmony with the business.

If you're impatient and unwilling to take the time to learn the dynamics of change, start with Part II and learn about the importance of strengths, and then go on to your specific interest areas within Part III. But remember: To really master this process for the life of your business, you need to understand the underlying forces driving change. So I recommend you do, sometime, read Part I with care.

ACKNOWLEDGMENTS

The Flexible Enterprise largely reflects my experience growing and transforming the company that's the main character of this book. In the years since I struck out on my own, literally hundreds of people have become members of the extended family that was once Hyperpress and is now Component Software. Among them, of course, are those who believed in me and the company. These people deserve special mention and thanks:

- My parents . . . who from thousands of miles away, accepted the reality of my need and drive to do things my own way—even if it meant I gave up a cushy executive's job at one of the country's largest software firms.
- Jim Connor . . . who many times thought I was totally out of my mind—and then left his own important job to help us get through a pretty tough year. Jim's unique perspective has influenced my thinking and strategy throughout the history of the business. His friendship has been priceless as I struggled through good times and bad.
- Dan Shafer and James Paul . . . who put their trust in a wet-behind-the-ears entrepreneur with no office or products. Dan and James created the first two packaged products offered by the company and have continued to be mentors, contributors, advocates, sounding boards, and friends.
- Merrie Brown, Mary Medoff, Toni Erickson, Linda Lou Lehman, George Forrester, Matt Kwan, and Shannon Delfino . . . who

were among my first employees and who are all my own personal heroes. These people went way beyond the role of employee and were founders, if not in name, then in spirit.

- Denise Amrich . . . who's been heavily involved in more recent times and who's made strong contributions to the company, as well as substantial editorial contributions to this book.

- Tom Peters . . . who, while he and I have never met, has served as a virtual board of directors. His books have provided me with invaluable advice, wisdom, comfort, and the occasional dressing down.

There are many others who've made important contributions to the company. Although there's not enough room in this book to acknowledge everyone who's been there for me and the company, there's certainly enough room in my heart and head to remember and thank you all.

Contents

PART I

Dynamics of Change

CHAPTER 1

The Winds of Change: A Case Study

In the future, everyone will be world-famous for 15 minutes.

—Andy Warhol, Stockholm, 1968

Sweat was dripping down my back. I was thankful my suit was dark blue so that no one could see the puddles of perspiration under my arms. The hall was packed with more than a thousand people. In five minutes, my presentation was due to begin.

The next hour would determine the fate of my company. If my presentation failed, our last, greatest chance to keep the company afloat would be destroyed. We would be forced to close our doors, lay everyone off, and join the unemployment lines.

But, if my presentation succeeded, we'd have a real chance at the brass ring.

Standing on the speaker's dais, another droplet of sweat landed squarely in my eye. I shared the stage with the big names in technology: Intel (creators of the chip inside most PCs), IBM, and Apple Computer. The pressure was intense.

This was the first-ever Multimedia Expo and the big players were out in force. Visionaries, treasure hunters, and practical business managers had started to see signs of a major transformation in the way we interact with computers, telephones, television. "Multimedia" was the catchword that described this mecca of information-age future David O. Selznicks. While the entire movie industry is only about $5 billion or so, the combined revenues of computers, communications, and entertainment would range in hundreds of billions of dollars. Multimedia was going to be *big.* Everyone could smell it.

Two minutes before my start time, a critical piece of equipment—a laser disc player—still hadn't arrived. I couldn't do the presentation without it. And the laser disc player—this last critical technical component of the presentation—was somewhere in San Francisco, in the unescorted hands of some taxi driver, winding its way from the Apple Multimedia Lab to Moscone Center.

I was on the keynote panel for the first Multimedia Expo. Apple had invited my tiny company to *take its place* and give the keynote address. It would have been heady stuff if it weren't for the fact that my company's life was on the line.

* * *

If, one month earlier, you had told me I'd be giving the keynote address at the hottest ticket in town, I'd have laughed in your face—and then sat down and cried. My company was in trouble. Our market had collapsed and we were out of cash. Our prospects were plainly bleak.

My company was then called Hyperpress. The name Hyperpress is no longer in active use. A number of years ago a few of its better products were folded into a new venture (my current company) called Component Software Corporation. You'll learn more about this in later chapters as we talk about positioning companies for particular audiences.

Hyperpress had based its business premise on selling add-on software for an Apple product called HyperCard. I'm not going to get overly technical, but it helps if you understand some of what this means.

HYPERCARD: HOW TO KILL A MARKET

HyperCard is a piece of software ordinary people (those who aren't programmers) use in building new pieces of software—sort of a "software erector set." Before HyperCard, the task of building new software fell primarily to experienced programmers and designers using tools of exceptional complexity. HyperCard was different. It made it much easier to build your own software.

Apple originally included HyperCard on every computer it shipped. In typical Apple fashion, the hype exceeded the reality. HyperCard was a great tool. It did (and still does) wondrous things. But it wasn't useful for or needed by everyone—as Apple had promised. Although HyperCard made software development much easier, most computer users have better things to do than write programs.

When after a year or so, HyperCard wasn't being used by everyone (only about 1 in 150 people with HyperCard on their disks actually tried to write programs), the folks at Apple began to think of HyperCard as a failure. They cut their investment, they completely eliminated their marketing, and they stopped shipping it with every new computer.

HyperCard's failure became a self-fulfilling prophecy. This "reality distortion effect" gone bad nearly cost my company its life.

You see, the problem wasn't that HyperCard wasn't any good. It was very good—for its purpose. When HyperCard was originally introduced, many of us saw real quality and potential in the product and formed companies that provided support products for HyperCard.

THE DANGER OF BEING AN AFTERMARKET SUPPLIER

My company provided tools to help those building software with HyperCard. We had a tool that helped write computer programs (the incantations linking the little pictures on the screen), another tool that helped create the pictures (called "icons"), and others to help organize the process of building new software. We didn't expect HyperCard to be a tool for all computer users, just a nice tool for crafting new software.

It was a sound business premise. It was also an accurate reading of the market. By targeting end-user developers and hobbyists rather than, at the high end, professional programmers or, at the low end, all users, we limited our total market size. But we had a coherent offering to a tangible, identifiable class of prospects.

Until Apple short-circuited HyperCard.

When Apple's management realized that HyperCard wasn't going to be used by every man, woman, and child on Earth, they lost interest, reduced funding, and moved HyperCard around between groups and subsidiaries like an unwanted stepchild. The trade press, of course, picked up on this and started calling HyperCard a failure, guessing that Apple might discontinue the product (eight years later, they still haven't). Many of those who actually had a use and need for HyperCard started to look elsewhere because basing computer software on a discontinued software environment is suicidal.

Those of us whose fortunes were tied to HyperCard felt the effects. Sales dried up overnight. Customer interest waned. Investors no longer were calling. Money stopped coming in. Yet there were still bills to pay and paychecks to sign.

Of the two hundred or so aftermarket companies that started after HyperCard's introduction, only about five (including mine) survived the first couple of months that followed HyperCard's bad press. Despite being survivors, all of us were in very bad shape—weeks or (at best) months from running out of cash.

So, a month before the Multimedia Expo, had you told me I'd be giving the keynote address (or at least be standing on the stage in a cold sweat hoping to be able to actually give the keynote address), I'd have either laughed, cried, or found a corner where I could park myself and suck my thumb. I certainly wouldn't have given it any credence. Hyperpress had no multimedia products. We had no funds to develop them, and we certainly couldn't have them ready in a month.

CHANGE HAPPENS

Ah, but the world is a very strange place. The least probable things can happen. And they do.

Here it was the middle of May. The Multimedia Expo would be in June (although that fact certainly didn't seem important at the time) and we were trying to make it through the fifth or sixth month of our near-death experience.

One of the survival tactics we had begun using was called "Anything for a Buck." We talked to every company we could find and tried to sell them any (legal) service we could perform just so that we could stay in business until we figured out how to recover from HyperCard's fall from grace.

We had managed to get a few contracts and, with extreme cost controls, were "hanging in." In desperation, I visited with Bill Atkinson, creator of HyperCard (now a cofounder of General Magic), and asked for some ideas.

Over a gourmet meal of melting soft vanilla ice cream and french fries, Bill graced me with his wisdom. He told me that if HyperCard products weren't selling, I should try doing something else. (Bill's nothing if not practical!) He mentioned another company that was, apparently, doing successful custom HyperCard work. He suggested we call on them and see if we could get some subcontracting work. (For the sake of its founders' feelings, I'll call the company Bill referred us to by other than its real name. Let's call it "Prosoft.")

A few days later, I went down to see Prosoft. They had really pretty offices compared with our more workmanlike digs. Everything was color coordinated. They appeared to have lots of industrious people working hard. Outwardly, they looked vastly more successful than we were. Hats in hand, my sales manager and I sat in their president's office, about ready to ask for any hand-me-down projects they could spare.

Boy were we about to be surprised!

Prosoft's president told us about a new technology they'd been working on. They were able to take a moving image from a video source (like a VCR or a laser disc player) and play it on the computer's screen—side by side or overlayed with computer-generated pictures. They could even control where on the screen the video image was placed. This was much more than just turning their computer screen into a glorified TV set. Since they could put both the video image and computer-generated information on the same screen and precisely and instantly control what video clip played when, they could create new and exciting kinds of software.

By using a laser disc player instead of a VCR, they could even control exactly what clip of video played—instantly selecting and playing a video clip appropriate in the current context. In this way, they could *interactively* control the video and computer images. The potential for training, entertainment, and education was astounding. This was real, honest-to-goodness multimedia like nothing anyone had ever seen before.

But, said Prosoft's president, they weren't able to bring it to market. They didn't perceive themselves as being able to do the marketing and generate customer interest. Would we, Hyperpress, be interested in acquiring the marketing rights to this technology?

Holy cow! Boy would we! This could be the break we were looking for. Except there were some problems:

1. We didn't have any money to acquire the marketing rights.
2. We didn't have any money to package or market the product.
3. We didn't even have the computer hardware to run it.

It was time for some fast thinking. I told him we'd be very excited about marketing his product, but we didn't usually pay anything in advance for the right. Instead, we'd pay a fair and aggressive royalty based on actual sales volume.

He actually bought into this reasoning. We met Prosoft's two other senior managers and within a few days put together an introduction plan and a finished, signed contract. The contract had us paying a larger than normal royalty, but it had Prosoft kicking in some marketing dollars for a launch at the Multimedia Expo. We decided to buy booth space to show off the as-yet-unnamed new product. The deal here was that they'd pay half the booth space cost and we'd pay the other half. Of course, we still didn't have the money for our half, but Prosoft didn't know that.

Then we found a book publisher and offered to let one of their authors do book signings in the booth if they'd help us pay the booth fee. Amazingly, the publisher signed up! They, too, paid half the booth fee (the other half). I felt a little like a latter-day Tom Sawyer.

This is a clear lesson in opportunism and the need for flexibility in business. Prior to stumbling onto this interactive video opportunity, we were in deep trouble because our market had collapsed. I didn't have the luxury of being stiff and inflexible. The opportunity came along and I grabbed it. I didn't have any choice.

Four weeks before the Multimedia Expo, we were broke and without prospects.

Three weeks before the Expo, we'd somehow managed to acquire the hottest new technology available for multimedia.

Two weeks before the Expo, we'd gotten two companies to pay for two halves of our booth.

One week before the Expo, we'd named the product BigTime TV (with full kudos and honors to the cult science fiction classic *Max Headroom*).

Three days before the Expo, I'd found the Apple product manager in charge of multimedia and arranged for a demonstration.

The next day, two days before the Expo, we drove down to Cupertino and put on our demonstration. That day, he offered us his slot as the keynote speaker for the Expo.

One day before the Expo, Prosoft's engineers were in my office (using much of their hardware), working around the clock to fine-tune and implement the software demonstration design I'd created for the Expo. I fed them lots of Chinese food, cajoled, harangued, and otherwise pushed them to completion. They were great engineers. I was thankful I didn't have to sign their paychecks.

The day of the Expo: We hadn't been able to afford to buy the laser disc player that provided the video images. So we were at the show without one of the most critical components—the source of the live video signal. My assistant had managed to convince the Apple Multimedia Lab (also in San Francisco) to loan us their player. By the time she'd accomplished this, there wasn't time for a round-trip drive across the city. Someone at the lab called a taxi, put the player in a cab all by itself, and sent the cabby to Moscone Center.

It was now two minutes before the keynote address was due to start. Still no player. If we didn't get the laser disc player, I wouldn't be able to do the keynote. Without a successful keynote, we wouldn't be able to create interest. And the house of mirrors we'd constructed in the past month for BigTime TV would collapse. If this presentation didn't go flawlessly, we were flat out of luck. And out of business.

THE MOMENT OF TRUTH

One minute before the keynote, Merrie Brown (at the time, my assistant and aide-de-camp—an extraordinarily capable young woman) came trotting up to the dais holding the videodisc player. It had arrived safely.

Five minutes after the published start time, I was still trying to wire the videodisc player into the computer. Sweat was now dripping onto electronics. I'd already been told three times that the other presenters were going to proceed without me, but I'd refused to physically move away from the computer. In front of the stage, a thousand people were watching this dance.

Finally, I got everything hooked up. There was no time for testing. Either it would work the first time out or fail spectacularly before the thousand most important people in the industry.

I sat in my appointed seat, perspired some more, and waited my turn.

First, Intel presented. They showed some graphics of Inca ruins. A click on one part of the picture (e.g., the entrance to a pyramid), would cause the computer to display a photo of the inside of the pyramid, while clicking on another part of the picture (e.g., the ball court) would display a different image. Pretty cool.

Next, IBM presented. Their presentation was done with color overheads written by hand. Clearly, IBM didn't yet "get" multimedia. (Now, years later, it sure does. IBM does indeed learn from its mistakes.)

Next in line was Apple. Instead of doing their own presentation, Apple's multimedia product manager introduced me and my company. I gave a 10-second intro and then told the audience I was going to present BigTime TV. Immediately, a fire bell blared across the auditorium. Thirty feet tall, on a huge projection screen, clips from the movie *Ghostbusters* were controlled with the computer.

First, I showed how we could assemble clips of the movie. A mouse click here and there, and it's done. Pretty neat stuff.

Next, I showed how video can be used in training. We annotated a scene in *Ghostbusters* where Bill Murray shows how ghosts are stored in a containment unit. A computer diagram lit up appropriately as the movie played. The audience was hooked.

Prosoft's engineers and I had constructed an MTV-like sequence that showed the Ghostbusters chasing after and grabbing a ghost. The visuals from the movie were spectacular; the music and explosions were loud and violent. BigTime TV moved images, made them jump and float and explode in time with the movie. The two-minute sequence was absolutely incredible.

When the roar of the video climaxed, I ended my presentation with the words, "Ladies and Gentlemen, Hyperpress Publishing introduces BigTime TV."

It was the first time I ever got a standing ovation.

Our small 10 by 10-foot booth at the Expo was the most crowded of any there. IBM, in the 1,600-square-foot booth next to us, complained to the show management that we were too loud and were taking their customers away (we were). We sold enough pre-release copies of BigTime TV at the show to turn the corner financially. We even made the front page of *MacWEEK*, the industry's weekly trade journal.

Taking hold of the BigTime TV opportunity saved the company and put us on the multimedia map.

*   *   *

For reasons soon to be described, we quietly returned BigTime TV to Prosoft 18 months later. It was no longer of any value to us. A year or so later, Prosoft closed its doors.

HIGH-TECH'S FIFTEEN MINUTES OF FAME

High-technology markets are in a constant state of flux. Companies come and go. Products appear with a big splash, only to fade into obscurity shortly afterward. Technology products make splashes for primarily the following reasons:

- *The promise of an as-yet-unheard-of capability.* Cellular phones were like this; now you can call anyone from anywhere.

- *The promise of a near order-of-magnitude gain in performance.* A common example of this was cable television—especially in the early 1980s. For a small fee, your dull antenna television with poor reception could be boosted from 13 channels to clear reception for 30 or 60 channels.

- *The promise of a near order-of-magnitude gain in price and performance.* A familiar example of this is the drop in cost of computers. Computers that a year earlier cost $6,000 and up were now selling for under $2,000.

- *The promise of a substantial increase in ease of use.* Both the Macintosh and Microsoft Windows promise the buyer that he or she won't need to use arcane and obtuse commands and codes to operate a computer.

- *The promise of substantially increased productivity on the part of the buyer.* A good high-technology example of this is desk-top publishing. We can now produce advertisements and brochures with an ease of modification that was unheard of before. The word processor is another example. I can't imagine trying to write a book like this one on a typewriter!

- *The promise of whole new worlds of entertainment value.* People pay to be amused and entertained. That's why there are always lines to see the hottest new movies. We've been seeing the beginnings of new ways to provide entertainment on CD-ROMs and in "electronic" Disneylands. A more tangible example is the success of three-dimensional, fully rendered video games.

Technology products often fade away for the related reasons:

- *There's a new performance benchmark.* Other products are faster and cheaper by an order of magnitude.

- *The reality wasn't as compelling as the vision.* It seemed as if everyone would rush to the new technology or product, but when the actual product reached market, it just wasn't that exciting.

- *There's some fatal flaw in the base technology of the product.* To really be useful, the product requires some critical functionality not provided by the technology.

- *The product isn't upgraded and features aren't added with regularity.* The user community either forgets about the product because there's nothing new to buy, or another product sounds sexier and takes away the buyers' limited attention span.

- *The product is too hard to explain clearly.* It is not obvious to potential users that they are, in fact, potential users. A corollary to this is that the product may be possible to explain, but the seller didn't do so in a clear manner.

- *There's some flaw or weakness in the business execution of the product.* The marketing isn't good enough, the price is too high, the channel isn't managed right, and so forth.

BigTime TV had its 15 minutes of fame. It was an exciting new technology and product that promised both unheard-of capabilities (live television controlled on a computer screen) and potent entertainment value. Its promise and reasonable execution drove product sales for about 18 months, giving Hyperpress the opportunity to turn the business around and prepare for the next technology cycle.

But in the long run, the fundamental architecture of BigTime TV was fatally flawed (again, I'm going to wax slightly technical, but I assure you its only for a short time). BigTime TV required the use of specialized hardware, and this became the product's Achilles' heel. To understand why, you need to know one small aspect of how the product worked.

BigTime TV relied on specialized hardware that took a video signal (like the one that comes out of your VCR and into your TV) and converted it to a digital form useful to the computer. This required special plug-in cards (called digitizing boards) for the computer. It was also necessary to have a random-access source for the video (usually a laser disc player).

As a result of these requirements, BigTime TV suffered from the following fatal flaws:

- Computers didn't come with the digitizing boards. Buyers of BigTime TV first had to go out and buy a board.
- The boards were expensive, in the $2,000 to $5,000 range. This eliminated any "just for fun" interest. The problem was, this cost also eliminated most final users of the video productions. How many high school classrooms or home video-game enthusiasts could afford a few thousand dollars on top of the computer's price just to run a program?
- The boards were made by many different manufacturers and were incompatible. Not only was the market limited because only a few people owned the boards, the boards they owned were different. We were constantly trying to come out with versions of BigTime TV that supported the favorite board of the week.

- Laser disc players were required to play the interactive video. These pieces of equipment cost $700 and up and also came in different flavors. More combinations and chances for incompatibility.
- It was easy to control a Hollywood movie like *Ghostbusters,* because it was already available on laser disc. But if you wanted to display your own video (which was the real reason for the product), you had to master your own laser disc. Costs ranged from $300 up *per physical disc.*
- Once you had all the hardware, discs, software, and so forth, you had to spend lots of time finding the right cables and hooking everything up.

Over time, it became clear that the cost to constantly build new versions of BigTime TV for each new digitizing board would become prohibitive and that our audience base of early adopters (folks who get a kick out of using a new technology before everyone else) was being used up. When BigTime TV had pretty much run its course, we returned it to Prosoft.

Even with all these disadvantages, we were able to attract enough early adopters to support Hyperpress for well over a year.

BigTime TV was not the final destination. Imagine you're on a long trip. You've been driving on a deserted highway for hours, en route to your next planned stop. But you're running out of gas. Big-Time TV was simply a filling station along the way that enabled us to keep driving on.

Tip: Always keep an eye out for filling stations. Think twice before you pass them by.

CROSSING THE CHASM

The key to going mainstream is what Geoffrey Moore calls "crossing the chasm" in his book of the same name. Moore contends that there isn't a smooth transition from the early adopters and innovators to the mainstream market. In fact, the very features that excite the early adopters about a product (newness, previously unknown capability, etc.) are the things that turn off the mainstream buyers. Mainstream buyers want multiple suppliers, they want a clear support system, they want lots of other buyers they can call and reference. Moore shows that there is a chasm between the stage where visionaries and innovators are excited and where mainstream buyers spend the big bucks. It is this chasm you must cross to reach the mainstream, and it is this chasm that kills many products.

One of the reasons that BigTime TV absolutely couldn't succeed in the mainstream market is that it wouldn't have been able to cross the chasm. The need for all that specialized hardware meant that Joe Average computer user couldn't play the interactive video on his computer.

Two years after we returned BigTime TV to "Prosoft," a video technology called QuickTime was introduced. Unlike BigTime TV, QuickTime *was* able to cross the chasm and go mainstream. Like BigTime TV, QuickTime provides interactive video capabilities. But rather than distributing video clips on a medium such as a laser disc and requiring specialized and expensive hardware to convert analog video signals to computer images, QuickTime "digital video" can be distributed easily on hard disks, floppy disks, CD-ROMs, and over the Internet—the same way the rest of mainstream software is distributed. Rather than requiring special custom video boards just to play back the video, any sufficiently advanced computer can easily play QuickTime video.

This meant that it was finally viable for software producers to include video in their products. Doing so added value to their customers but, since QuickTime video runs on most computers, use of it didn't limit the size of the potential customer base. With Quick-Time (and a clone from Microsoft called "Video for Windows"), we're now able to buy CD-ROM based encyclopedias that not only include descriptions of Apollo moonshots and John F. Kennedy's "We will go to the moon" speech, but the actual full-motion video and sound. This is world-shaking stuff.

The reason we didn't keep BigTime TV and engineer around the limitations was that our technology was too early and the engineering cost would have been prohibitive. It took the resources of an Apple (with many billions of dollars in yearly revenues) to make QuickTime. It made much more sense for us to squeeze all of the available dollars out of the early adopter market and return BigTime TV to the original authors than for us to pump huge engineering dollars into a market that wouldn't be mainstream for three to four years.

Today, my company sells products and services that live on both sides of the chasm. But we've been exceptionally careful not to attempt to jump the chasm without intense preparation.

One product we have is a database called FileFlex. FileFlex is able to store and retrieve lots of text-based information, but it can't work with pictures, sounds, graphics, or video. It's a relatively simple, basic database. The value of FileFlex is that it can be used inside another person's program—allowing that programmer to add database capability for a very small cost. Most often, FileFlex lives hidden in consumer multimedia CD-ROMs produced by our customers.

But databases are about as mainstream as software gets. Their providers are huge, powerful, and massively entrenched. Our strategy for FileFlex has been to intentionally limit both its market and its capabilities so it doesn't cross the chasm. Why? We know we can't compete with the entrenched guys in the mainstream (many have tried, all have failed), so we are limiting FileFlex to the smaller market. Yes, the product makes less total dollars. But we haven't had to pour into it the vast tidal wave of funds that would be required to leap the chasm. As a result, little FileFlex is happy, successful, and profitable—in its narrow, pre-mainstream market.

The key is to maximize the value of the product for its capabilities—not to try to force it into something it cam never be. If you combine that practice with providing real, tangible value to your customer while making sure your products are profitable for yourself, you can't help but be successful.

CHAPTER 2

Reinventing from the Inside Out

The current euphemism is "reengineering"—a
bloodless term for corporate bloodletting on an
unprecedented scale.

—BusinessWeek

We are awash in a sea of buzzwords: "RIF" (reduction in force), re-invention, downsizing, rightsizing, and reengineering. In many ways, these words are so similar that they are used interchange-ably—so much so that they have become both confusing and down-right dangerous. The intent is change, to "cause to be different." But what is our real goal? Is it really *just* change?

We are not concerned with making things different. We are con-cerned with making things work!

Every dedicated manager is committed to evolving and growing the enterprise so it is always at the best it can possibly be. But being the best requires more than making things different. Being the best involves being creative, disciplined, hard-edged, compas-sionate, aggressive, flexible, and smart.

I'm convinced that you and your organization must have many of these traits—just not necessarily all at one time. In fact, most large businesses have grown to be successful because their management and employees have demonstrated all these traits throughout the organization's history. However, once success is attained, the nat-ural desire is to preserve the status quo, a seductive and dangerous tendency for many businesses. As a result, the essential traits of flexibility and creativity are repressed.

Status quo and flexibility are natural enemies. Continuing successful practices is a valid and productive strategy. But when the continuation of practice leads to rigidity, responsiveness is lost. Without the ability to respond rapidly to market forces, new opportunities, and customer demands, you lose the capacity to change effectively.

The need for growth is another seductive and dangerous tendency. Taken on its own, there is nothing wrong with growth. But when growth becomes necessary just for the sake of growth, you lose the ability to manage change intelligently. Corporations become monolithic. Employee counts bulge beyond belief. And while revenues increase, so do the costs of carrying all these employees. The burning need for unchecked growth often can cause a company to lose focus, make bad decisions, and overburden already stretched resources.

THE DOWNSIDE OF DOWNSIZING

Here's a scenario that's now sadly common in many corporations (in this example, a defense contractor): A project is funded and is moderately successful. The company hires lots of employees to support the project. But eventually, the government decides to reduce spending on the project. Now employees are attached to a project with no future. The company long ago established a firm culture of inflexibility and bureaucracy designed to perpetuate its success. But that inflexibility now means that it's too rigid to know how to reallocate resources and personnel from the doomed project to something more promising.

How does it recover? It "downsizes" and lays off 30,000 employees. That's what Boeing did. IBM dumped 85,000; GTE 17,000; Hughes Aircraft 21,000; Martin Marietta 15,000; AT&T 83,000—all in the three years between 1991 and 1994. But, downsizing through gang layoffs doesn't take into account the ripple effects of the layoff, from devastated former employees to increased load on the government's unemployment system to the fear and reduced productivity of surviving employees.

No one is untouched by such drastic "change." I had friends working in each of these companies and the impact on them was terribly sad. Some who had been loyal employees for years now were in a panic fueled by concerns about mortgages, supporting their families, and reemployment. In all cases, their lives were torn apart. Fortunately, most of my friends have found new employment—and some have again been laid off in what has become a deranged game of musical chairs.

There is no question that many of these organizations were bloated and employees had to go. But just doing a layoff and a "reorg" will not solve anything. It will only assure the continuing need for more layoffs and reorgs in the years to come. This form of change results in terrified and confused employees, drastically reduced productivity, and plunging profits. Training and integrating employees into a company is a huge investment. Disposing of these valuable employees is, quite simply, poor asset management.

No good can come from desperate and mindless layoffs. The corporation is wasting its most valuable assets—its people.

There has to be a better way. There is. I call it "Reinventing from the Inside Out."

REINVENTING . . .

Reinventing your company is an incredibly powerful new method you can use to improve, awaken, or save your business. Reinvention allows you to keep all the good, working, effective parts of your company while you change your corporate mission (sometimes many times over) until you've got a working formula.

What do I mean by the term "reinvention"? And how does it differ from the other buzzwords *du jour?*

How we refer to change—literally the words we use—often colors how we react to and manage change. Using the wrong words (often words your board of directors wants to hear) may worry your suppliers, brighten the day of your competitors, put fear into the hearts of your employees, drop productivity, and doom the process to failure. Using the best, most appropriate words from the outset can positively charge the entire process. So use the right words.

The word "rightsizing" is wrong. Just because today a company should have only 17,234 employees, doesn't mean it wasn't rightsized at 16,000 or 20,000 employees at some other time. The term rightsizing is a condemnation. For a laid-off person to hear that his

company rightsized is a direct insult to all the work and all the loyalty he or she has contributed to the organization in the past. Don't
use the word.

Use of the word is "downsizing" is dangerous because it gives the
organization an excuse to sound strategic when downsizing is really
a short-term tactic to cut some costs. It doesn't take into account
the future actions, mission, or direction of the organization.

While I hold an engineering degree, I'm not a strong proponent of
the term "reengineering." There's nothing wrong with engineering;
remember, I'm a "techy" so I live constantly with the fruits of brilliant engineering. But companies aren't wires and electrons and pul-
leys and sprockets. Companies are people and processes and assets
and opportunities. Reengineering, in my opinion, is too practical.
Too cold. Too inhuman. Our companies are nothing if not human.
Reengineering seems at odds with that fact.

I like the term "reinvention" because I like the term "invention."
The American Heritage Dictionary defines the verb "invent": *To conceive or devise first; to originate.* Inventing is conceiving, devising; in
effect, creating whole new stuff from the sole fruits of intelligence,
experience, and intuition.

There's nothing practical (or impractical) here. There's nothing
"right" or judgmental in the term invent. Instead, it simply says,
"Let's figure it out."

The prefix "re-" implies doing something again. Change is continual in life and in companies. Therefore, you can't invent something once. You've got to do it over and over again, getting better as
you go and taking into account changes in your environment, constraints, assets, customers, and competitors.

You must go through the process of inventing over and over: You
must "reinvent" continually.

. . . FROM THE INSIDE OUT

Reinventing is clear, but what's this "inside out" stuff? The "inside
out" is the most important part. This is a fundamental business
strategy that will change your life. It did mine.

The time was right about when HyperCard's popularity did a swan
dive (as I described in harrowing detail in Chapter 1). My company's
sales had virtually crashed, and I was one unhappy CEO. I was also

caught in a very dangerous place—two and a half years into the company's life, right at that point where, statistically, many companies fail. But we couldn't afford to fail. I don't mean this from a spiritual or an honor-bound point of view. I mean this from a truly financial perspective. We couldn't *afford* to fail.

We had thousands of product units in retail distribution. Our agreements with distribution allowed them to return the products for a full cash refund in the event of bankruptcy or an assignment to benefit creditors. (I never signed an agreement like that again!) If we decided to go out of business, all of a sudden we'd not only be just broke, we'd suddenly have a liability to our distributors for hundreds of thousands of dollars. Not good.

It was with this depressing thought that I found myself having dinner with my long-time buddy, fellow alumni, sometime VP, usually perverse and regularly creative friend Jim Connor. So here we were, me being depressed and Jim tolerating my ramblings. I was telling him my troubles and how I was in this pickle where I was damned if I stayed in business and damned if I didn't.

Jim apparently was thinking about what I'd been telling him because he turned to me (about to change my life forever—I'm not sure whether I'll ever forgive him) and said, "Gee, why don't you just start another company?"

This had to be the *dumbest* idea I had ever heard. My current business was in the dumpster. There was no way I'd be able to go off and start another company. I told him this.

"No, Stupid," he said, "I don't mean start another separate company, I mean start another company *inside this one*. Do everything you'd do to start another company, but use this one as the shell. Just don't tell anybody you've deep-sixed the first one and you'll be fine."

It took me years to understand the incredible power of Jim's statement. When I did, my whole company (and the companies inside my company) were transformed forever.

The Benefit of Reinventing from the Inside Out

The benefit of reinvention *from the inside out* is that it allows you to work from your own established capabilities without being forced to rely on the magic of finding an outside "savior." At the most extreme, it allows you to, in effect, close down a nonworking business and start a new one, all without the damage usually caused when customers, creditors, press, and other constituents "smell blood."

Here are some benefits of reinventing your entire company inside out:

- Your "new" company is not an unproven entity.
- Although your new "company" is brand-new, the total time you've been in business is counted from the very beginning— your new business gets the seniority benefits of the older business. This is critical because it's often difficult for brand-new companies to get things, from merchant accounts to leases.
- You can keep all your merchant accounts.
- Your bank loans don't automatically get called in.
- Inventory doesn't get returned.
- You don't have to print new stationery.
- You don't have to find a new location and negotiate a new lease.
- You don't have to find new employees and train them.
- You can tell prospects that your business is expanding into a new area of opportunity and that's why you're calling on them.
- You can keep all your suppliers—and your credit terms.
- You can change your talent mix around and tamper with your organizational chart without causing panic among employees or outside constituents.
- You can keep shipping old products for incremental revenue; you just stop investment in all marketing, sales, and engineering for them.
- You don't have to invest in creating new brand- or company-name awareness; you can leverage off the awareness of the original name until you want to introduce a new one.

The concept is tremendous. I've used reinvention from the inside out at different times: once to effect a major turnaround (surviving the HyperCard crash) and other times to open new markets and take advantage of new opportunities.

THE TRUE ASSETS OF YOUR COMPANY

According to *BusinessWeek,* there were 615,186 layoffs from large corporations in 1993. In the first quarter of 1994, announced staff reductions totaled 192,572—that's more than 3,100 people losing jobs *each day!* This wholesale bloodbath must stop. We must stop throwing away our people, our trained resources, our assets.

Compassion for people is certainly important. But as a corporate manager, you must think in terms of what's best for the company. So think about this. When you "dehire" trained workers, you're wasting valuable corporate assets.

Our small companies must grow and change to take advantages of new opportunities. Our largest corporations, while they must stop unchecked hiring, have got to learn how to be both competitive *and* compassionate.

It *is* possible. Companies *can* be more effective, if only they give themselves credit for what they do well.

I believe, fundamentally, that your organization works and works well. Otherwise you wouldn't still be in business and wouldn't still have customers. Granted, you may have dissatisfied customers— but you probably also have some satisfied customers. Granted, you may not be making a large enough profit—but aren't you making some sales? Granted, you may not be manufacturing the best, the most reliable, or the most efficient products—but are customers still able to use them?

If you can answer any of these questions with "yes," then you have some strengths. They may be hidden or buried. They may be surrounded by tons of really bad garbage—your weaknesses. But you *do* have some strengths.

I part company from those who use terms like "radical" and "dramatic" as watchwords for reengineering. They believe that companies aren't going to change unless they commit to being radical about it.

I disagree.

I believe that every company has fundamental strengths. These are the true assets of the company, the "core competencies" that are holding the company together in even the toughest times.

I also believe that most companies have dangerous weaknesses. These are the true devils of the company, the factors that are trying to drag it down.

Do you want to know how to change your company so it is more successful? Do you want to know how to reinvent your company so that it can be a highly successful enterprise? The answer is actually incredibly simple. Here are the four steps:

1. Identify your strengths and use them to their absolute best advantage.
2. Identify your weaknesses and dump them as fast as you can; not in blind haste, but after making sure you're jettisoning a weakness and not a strength in disguise.
3. Make changes from the inside out so you don't alarm employees, vendors, creditors, or customers.
4. Learn to use change as a tool by developing the ability to change and evaluate again and again.

It's far easier to lay off employees than to subject yourself, your company, and your business practices to intense, objective self-analysis. It's easier, but it is also wrong. If you continue to arbitrarily downsize, then perhaps you don't belong in the big chair. Perhaps you should lead the next list of downsizing victims.

Exercise: Make me a promise. Right now, between you and me, I want you to promise that you won't lay off (or downsize or RIF or reorg) a single, solitary person until you finish reading this book.

Together, you and I can work together to turn your company into a solid, highly successful organization. Let's start right here and right now. Let's just do it.

CHAPTER 3

Change Drivers

The brutalities of progress are called revolutions.
When they are over we realize this: that the human
race has been roughly handled, but that it has
advanced.

—Victor Hugo, Les Misérables, 1862

I have a high-tech bias. If you've made it this far into the book, no doubt you've figured that out. But this is not a technical book. It's meant to be helpful for any business manager concerned with successfully implementing change. You will not be constantly assaulted by techy stuff throughout the book. Those of you have an aversion to or lack of experience with technology can breath a sigh of relief.

However, because technology changes so rapidly, my technology background has given me a wealth of experience with change—both reactive and proactive. Because I've lived most of my professional life in the company of wires and electrons, many of my examples and references will be related to technology. This does not mean that the lessons they teach are not applicable to you.

In Chapter 1, we talked about why technology products splash and fade so quickly. The same things (with slightly different words) could be said of any fad product. There are quick-flash products in nontechnical businesses (e.g., Cabbage Patch Kids, Pet Rock, and New Kids on the Block). Conversely, there are also long-standing, venerable products in technology. Examples include the Macintosh, 1-2-3, WordPerfect, and numerous others, each over 10 years old.

I'll be talking about technology throughout the book because that's what I know and love. Even so, you don't need to be technically inclined to understand and benefit from what's being discussed.

HIGH-TECH AND CHANGE ARE INEXTRICABLY LINKED

In 1984, I bought a nice new car. In 1984, I also bought a nice new computer. The car was a Mazda 626. The computer was an IBM PC XT—the top-of-the-line IBM machine at the time. I spent about $12,000 for the car and about $6,500 for the computer in 1984 dollars.

Today, an equivalent Mazda costs about $20,000, and the IBM PC XT is no longer made. Let's move from 1984 to 1994. In 1994, if I had bought one of the then top-of-the-line Intel Pentium-based PCs, I'd have spent about $3,000—half (less than half adjusting for inflation) the amount I spent in 1984. Table 3.1 shows the difference in what I would have gotten in these two computers.

The Pentium system profiled in Table 3.1 also included a floppy drive that stores 1,000% more information on each disk than the XT—in about two thirds the physical size and a CD-ROM drive that stores 650 megabytes for which there's no 1984 equivalent. The only thing that hasn't changed much since 1984 is the keyboard. Our fingers haven't gotten much smaller—although they've definitely gotten flatter!

Note: Since 1994, the price for equivalent systems has been dropping about $500 every six months—that's a 34 percent price/performance improvement every year.

If car manufacturers improved their offerings as much as the computer makers did in the same 10 years, I'd be able to buy a new car for $5,520 that would:

- Travel at about 1,350 miles per hour. At this rate, it would take me a little over two hours to drive to San Francisco from New

Table 3.1. An unprecedented increase in performance.

Feature	1984 IBM PC XT	1994 Dell Dimension	Difference in Capability
Processor (transistors roughly represent the calculation capacity of the machine)	Intel 8088 (has about 29,000 transistors)	Intel Pentium (has about 3.2 million transistors)	11,034% more computing and calculating capacity
Processor Speed	4 MHz	90 MHz	2,250% faster
RAM (the temporary memory used while programs are running)	64 kilobytes (KB)	8 megabytes (MB)	12,500% more program running capacity
Hard Disk (the permanent storage for files and data)	10 megabytes	450 megabytes	4,500% more file storage capacity in the same physical space
Video display	Green and white monitor capable of displaying 24 lines of 80 characters of text	24-bit (16.7 million colors) monitor capable of displaying 800 x 1,000 dots of true photographic quality images	835,000,000% more colors in 41,666% more display locations on screen
Price	About $6,500	$2,999 (with even more goodies than listed)	46% of the 1984 price (after adjusting for inflation it would be even less)

York (not counting traffic tickets and the regular backup entering the Holland Tunnel and crossing the Bay Bridge).

- Store my living room, my bedroom, my office, two boxes of Captain Crunch and Samantha's favorite kitty toy—all in the same trunk space of the car and still have room left to comfortably walk around.

There's no easy analogy for the 825 *million percent* improvement in video display capacity or the 12,000 percent improvement in RAM capacity. And while there's also no direct comparison in terms of what the car could do (as related to the increased number of transistors in the processors), suffice it to say my new car would also be able to compose a sonnet, do my laundry, walk the neighbor's dog, and talk the cops out of the traffic tickets—all at the same time and all without breaking into a sweat.

There has never been anything like this unprecedented level of change throughout human history. No technology or capability has shown this unbelievable level of improvement throughout all of time.

It's made life interesting for those of us forced to keep up.

YESTERDAY'S REVOLUTION IS TODAY'S OVERCROWDED MARKET

Understand that all this price/performance improvement in computers does not mean computer companies are experts at handling change. This stuff came as something of a surprise to everyone. The ability to place astronomically more transistors in the same millimeter of silicon every couple of years wasn't planned. But as soon as it became possible, chip manufacturers began scrambling to do more and more—because competitors were doing the same thing.

The PC price wars and the chip wars have been fueling the price/performance treadmill for more than 10 years. Consumers faced with more and more capacity at slightly lower prices each time have begun to expect this as the norm.

There's been shakeout after shakeout. Leading companies of their day—Osborne, Eagle, Processor Technology, Everex (and almost IBM and Dell)—have gone to that great silicon farm in the sky.

Software companies like Visicorp (makers of the seminal Visicalc spreadsheet) and resellers like BusinessLand have all gone poof.

Here's something to thing about. What has such an enormous increase in our information-processing capacity done to our way of doing business, and our expectations? Has that multi-thousandfold increase in capacity in some way shown us that the price/performance ratios of everything else are just abysmal by comparison? As the computer industry struggled to cut costs to keep improving on price and performance, the rest of our industries were forced to do so as well, although outwardly for different reasons. But once consumers were able to see—and understand on a visceral level—that price and performance *could improve drastically,* they became more selective and demanding in their spending habits. Businesses, and slowly but surely government agencies, have been forced to respond or wither and eventually die.

CHANGE DRIVERS

Change is driven by many factors, both human-made and natural. When the 1989 earthquake hit San Francisco, my business experienced considerable damage. It took us about three months to recover from 17 seconds of shaking, but thankfully no one was hurt. When the more recent Los Angeles quake hit, a large number of companies were hurt and some computer distributors were forced to close.

We're now located outside Princeton, New Jersey. While being closer to my family was the primary reason for relocating, the earthquakes certainly helped cinch the deal. Tidal waves, hurricanes, winter storms, floods, and earthquakes all force change on us. But so do more mundane business factors.

Changes in Manufacturing Methods

Physics, specifically the ability to put more transistors in the same physical space on a chip, didn't force the PC business to change. That didn't happen until the manufacturing processes allowed semiconductor manufacturers to have decent wafer yields (in English:

the chip makers could build the chips without lots of them going bad in the process).

Sometimes the *ability* to do something new (like chip making) drives change. Other times, change is driven by the *need* to do something new. For example, when the Japanese started making cars that were more reliable at a better cost than those made in the United States, the big three had to respond or lose market share.

History shows us that General Motors (GM), Chrysler, and Ford did, in fact, lose market share for many years. Huge market share. The resultant drops in profits caused the companies to cut costs, close factories, and lay off workers. Entire towns like Flint, Michigan, were all but mortally wounded by the closings. Eventually, it dawned on U.S. car makers that they had to make better products. That's when all sorts of interesting new initiatives took place. General Motors started the Saturn plant using processes initially developed in the United States, co-opted by the Japanese for what eventually came to be called the Japanese management method, and eventually remembered and readopted by American manufacturers. Chrysler built fabulous minivans and the Intrepid line of cars. Ford also came out with new, higher quality models.

All in all, while the Japanese became more American, building more and more of their "Japanese" cars in the United States, U.S. manufacturers were forced to change as well.

There was, however, a double whammy. U.S. car makers employ vast numbers of Americans. When the imports stole market share away from the domestics, the car makers laid off workers by the thousands to close the wounds of hemorrhaging profits. Then, as a competitive move to cut costs and improve productivity, yet more American car workers were laid off. The net result is that the United States now makes much nicer cars, but there are a lot fewer Americans who can afford them.

Changes in Customers

As our customers change and grow, so must we. In the past 10 years, we've seen substantial shifts in demographics. Women have more purchasing power. There are more senior citizens, and the baby boomers are hitting their 40s. The "me" generation of the 1980s has helped convince consumers that they should get what they, as individuals, want. And it's helped them know that their buying desires are different from others.

The more demanding requirements of consumers has resulted in a need for manufacturers to become more responsive.

Manufacturers are now building products that recognize the individual uniqueness of consumers. Not only are there family-size packages, but there are now single-service sizes for those who live alone. Not only is there dark beer and imported beer, there is now also "near" beer for those who like beer taste but don't need or want the alcohol. Not only are there luxury cars and sports cars, there are now luxury sports sedans for those who want to be in the fast lane but not feel the bumps in the road.

Changes in Selling Methods and Channels

As our customers have changed, so have the ways we get their attention. We've learned that customers are unique individuals, and we've learned to target what's being called the "market of one." As a result, we need to make sure costs are in line with results. One way of doing this is by being much more selective in marketing, doing our best to spend only on media that will reach potential prospects.

Targeted database marketing has mushroomed in the past 10 years. First off, almost any company can do it because (guess what?) they can afford to buy a PC with large capacity and the pre-built software to manage it. Second, it makes lots more sense to pay only for the ads that reach people who might possibly care.

But targeting gets much more sophisticated. Instead of producing the same ad for all consumers of a given product, smart advertisers are carefully crafting marketing messages for individual customer types, speaking of the features and benefits in terms that each customer profile (a body of persons with similar characteristics) would appreciate.

Direct mail works, but so do other focused methods like telemarketing. MCI's Friends and Family program is an ideal way to gather related groups of people together and is probably the world's largest database of extended families. MCI's telemarketing is so prevalent and so successful—and so annoying—that AT&T has been fighting back with a marketing approach that shows consumers experiencing potent social ostracism after giving out a name and number to MCI.

Consumers demand convenience, price, access, and selection. Superstores nationwide have been cleaning the collective clocks of smaller retailers. Home Depot has caused smaller chains like Rickels serious damage. The effect of a new Wal-Mart can be felt by retailers up to 45 miles away. And computer superstores like CompUSA combined with effective mail-order suppliers like MacWarehouse have all but driven the small mom-and-pop computer store out of business.

Changes in a Product's Life Cycle

As customers, channels, and manufacturing methods change, so must our products. And vice versa.

When PCs first came out, they were adopted primarily by hobbyists and the technical elite. You needed to hand-assemble your own machine, know all about how it worked, and have the time, energy, and motivation to build the darn thing.

Later, while PCs were not used by everyone and still required technical expertise to configure, they were beginning to find their way into small and large businesses.

Today, PCs are everywhere, and it's easier to find a computer or software store than it is to find a stereo or music store. Customers are not the early adopters who are the "experts." Instead, they're kids who want to play games and whose parents want them to use CD-ROM encyclopedias and write reports. PC users and buyers get thousands of percent more power for much less cash—and can walk into a store in just about any town and buy a bigger hard drive or a CD-ROM drive, video card, cable, or more RAM.

I remember, not that long ago, having to call airport security days in advance to arrange for an escort because I was carrying a huge, weird electronic box onto the airplane and couldn't afford to wait hours while they found a security expert to determine if it was safe. (For PC purists, I was carrying an S100-bus computer.)

Now, I can easily show them my PowerBook laptop and every gate inspector knows what to look for when you power it on. They should. Ten other people on the plane will be also be carrying them.

PCs have gone from a market where customers were early adopters, visionaries, and experts to a market where customers are everyone. PCs have gone mainstream, which is where the bulk of the money is and where the competition and customer demands are the fiercest.

Here are some other examples of products that have gone from early adopters to mainstream:

- Cellular phones (the phones, once costing over $1,000 for a big boxy unit) can be bought for $59.95 or less, as long as you sign up for a year of phone service.
- Pagers are used by everyone from repair people to school kids. They even come in designer colors and screaming neon. You can't get much more mainstream than that.
- Microwave ovens went from absolutely nowhere to mainstream with very little stop in between.
- Videotape has been around for 30 years. Yet it's only been in the past 10 years that nearly everyone has owned a low-cost VCR and can rent tapes at two or three places around town.

SITUATIONAL AWARENESS

A successful fighter pilot has exceptional *situational awareness*. When flying a jet above Mach 1 and engaging enemies traveling at the same speed, the pilot must be constantly aware of all that is around him.

He must deal with a steady stream of information: the speed of his craft, his operational orders, conditions of hundreds of variables on the plane itself, the locations of his wingmen and those in his strike force, atmospheric conditions, potential threats from triple-A (anti-aircraft artillery), airborne threats, distance to next check-point, rules of engagement, and lots more.

At any given time, his primary attention must be on one or two highly focused aspects of his mission. But at all times, he must maintain a constantly updated general awareness of everything in his theater of operation. It is this ability to maintain situational awareness that ultimately will determine whether the pilot, his weapon's systems officer ("wizzo"), and his squadron will live or die.

When threatened (like when a missile has heat-signature lock and is about to fly up his tailpipe), the pilot must be able to take immediate, instantaneous action. There isn't time for him to scan the skies, check all his instruments, look out the window, check in with an orbiting E3-C AWACS radar plane, or any of the thousand other things he might do if he had more than three seconds (literally) to take action.

He must be constantly aware of his surroundings, his situation, so that when attacked, he can drop a chaff flare and perform a braking maneuver or make a hard turn—and not bump into another plane or run into a stream of bullets.

Like the combat pilot, corporate management must maintain constant situational awareness to assure the survival of their organization.

What must you keep track of? That will differ from company to company. Here are some of the items I'm always, constantly, aware of in my organization:

- Employee count, problem employees, and employees I can trust in an emergency.
- Approximate cash balances in each of our bank accounts.
- Current clients, key customers and projects, and potential problems pertaining to each.
- Next items due for each project, their due dates, and the fall-back strategy if a due date is missed.
- Relative priorities for each project so I know which projects I can stall and which I can't.
- Any supplier who might be slow in shipping critical supplies and backup plans for getting materials when needed.
- Threats from potential creditors and which companies we're late paying.
- Problems with any receivables due us and the backup plans for making sure we get paid.
- Status of sales efforts with critical prospects and a good idea whom we should call on if we run into snags.
- Backup plans for a whole host of potential emergencies.

I don't spend an enormous number of hours on any of the preceding, but I'm always generally aware of what's happening. In this way, if urgent, immediate action becomes unavoidable, I have enough situational awareness to be able to make the best possible decisions under the circumstances. While I try to avoid unplanned change, being aware of key elements of my business helps me manage our reaction in a clear and well-informed manner.

You should do the same. Avoid reacting when possible, but be properly prepared and situationally aware when necessary. This will help you reduce the probability of being forced into sudden, unplanned change.

AVOID EXCESSIVE PLANNING

While I recommend you avoid reacting suddenly to the need for change (unless it's unavoidable), I also recommend you don't paralyze your organization with excessive planning. I've seen this problem a hundred times. A manager wants to get a certain end result. Before that end result can be attained, something else must be done. And before that can be done, yet something else must be done. And so on until the manager and his company are paralyzed, with absolutely nothing being accomplished.

We know it is good to think through every change and to plan our actions. But we must be careful to keep in mind reaching the end goal.

That's the key to overcoming analysis paralysis: *Just do something.* What you choose to do, and what you actually accomplish will not necessarily be the best, or even the most appropriate for the moment, but you'll be doing *something.* And doing something's much more important than doing nothing at all.

RECAP

- Keep in mind that you're striving for the *effects of change,* not change for the mere sake of change.
- Develop regular *situational awareness* so you can act when necessary with reasonable judgment.
- *Plan and think* through the steps of change, but don't get caught in analysis paralysis.
- When all else fails, *do something.* If you have good situational awareness, your actions should be reasonably successful and will get you going.

CHAPTER 4

The Reinvention Lifecycle

There is a certain relief in change, even though it be from bad to worse; as I have found in travelling in a stage-coach, that it is often a comfort to shift one's position and be bruised in a new place.

—Washington Irving, 1824

As a discipline, reengineering is process oriented. Reengineering attempts to make the inner workings of a company more efficient, allowing it to be more competitive in its chosen target markets. The idea is that a company has laid claim to certain tangible markets and opportunities. To better service those existing markets, companies can reengineer themselves to become more efficient and cost-effective.

By contrast, strength-based reinvention, the new methodology I introduce in this book, is most often oriented around changes in market dynamics. Compared with reengineering, strength-based reinvention is more reactive to external forces. Table 4.1 illustrates these contrasting methodologies.

To operate a business as though the world is standing still is ludicrous. Many companies are terrified of change and are desperately trying to hold onto their existing markets. They do everything they can to make themselves more effective, to communicate better, to satisfy their customers better. Yet, in many cases, they don't seem to understand that the best intended internal changes won't do a lick of good if their market is changing or collapsing.

Table 4.1. The choice of a business dynamic.

	Relatively Constant	Dynamic and Changing
Process Reengineering	Target markets and customer base	Internal processes
Strength-Based Reinvention	Organization's inherent strengths and capabilities	Markets, customers, and opportunities

The tremendous economic upheavals of the past few years have virtually guaranteed dynamic market changes in every industry. Strength-based reinvention can give your company a clearly defined set of tools and methods that will enable you to change rapidly as your world changes.

THE STRENGTH OF STRENGTH-BASED REINVENTION

In virtually every organization, it is fair to assume that something works, that there are some advantages, some abilities, some resources. While the degree of such abilities and resources will vary widely among organizations, it's reasonable to assume that each organization does some things right.

These abilities and resources are the company's strengths.

OK, you're thinking that some organizations are so bad, they can't do anything right. I'll admit I feel the same way sometimes, especially when facing robotic and bureaucratic employees. We'll get to the problems of organizations when we get to the section on weaknesses. For now, let's focus on the good stuff and accept as truth that somewhere, perhaps buried, hidden, reviled, or ignored, there are certain gems—things your organization can do with regular and consistent success.

The key to strength-based reinvention (the heart and soul of *The Flexible Enterprise*) is to leverage everything off your strengths. *It's easier to continue to do something you excel at than it is to learn to excel at something new.* It's also often easier to find new, viable opportunities than it is to sweat the last remaining pennies out of old, tired ventures.

Strength-based reinvention lets you use your existing tools, abilities, and resources to search out and take advantage of new opportunities. The world does not stand still. Markets change. Customer requirements change. Business climates change. It's important to be able to change with the times.

It's far, far easier (and much less costly) to locate new opportunities than it is to develop entirely new abilities. Sometimes, in the most troubled companies, it's impossible to develop new abilities or locate additional resources. For them, being able to tap their inner strength is the only chance for survival.

By definition, a strength-based business is an opportunistic business. More importantly, a strength-based business *has the ability* to be opportunistic.

THE CONTINUAL CYCLE OF REINVENTION

Changing your company is not something that can happen overnight. Rather, it requires lots of little steps. After each step, it's necessary to evaluate the results of your actions and decide whether to retrench, retreat, continue, or change course.

Reinvention doesn't just occur once. It's not something you write in your corporate calendar or schedule like a tradeshow. Reinvention should exist throughout the lifetime of your organization, helping you to respond intelligently to changes in your markets and external conditions.

In Chapter 2, you learned that successful reinvention from the inside out always follows these fundamental steps: Identify your strengths, eliminate your weaknesses, reposition appropriately, evaluate, and repeat (see Figure 4.1). To be most effective, the evaluate and repeat components are critical. It's here you determine the results, recognize if you've added any new strengths or weaknesses, and do it again—always striving for constant, incremental stepwise improvement.

STRENGTHS, LACKS, AND WEAKNESSES

When reinventing an organization, you need to know where you're starting from, and, at least generally, where you want to wind up.

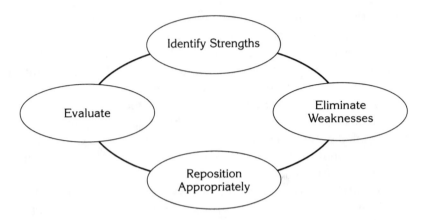

Figure 4.1.   The reinvention lifecycle.

You start from your strengths. A *strength* is something you lean on. A *lack* is something you fix. A *weakness* is something you jettison or avoid. The sum total of your strengths make up that which is good about your company. Your weaknesses are those things dragging your company down. And lacks are those things that are missing in the process of creating and leveraging off of strengths.

This triad of strengths, weaknesses, and lacks (S-W-L) defines your organization. Changing them *is* reinvention. In the next few pages, we'll visit two fictional organizations and identify their S-W-L triads. Then we will look at a real organization that reinvented itself.

Example 1: Music Club

The vivid neon sign over the Culture Force door has changed more times than Hillary Clinton's hair style. Opened in the late 1960s, the music club has experienced regular and radical changes in audience and trends.

When the club first opened in 1967, the Beatles were in their experimental stage, introducing new textures, forms, rhythms, melodic designs, and lyric conceptions. The Rolling Stones presented a darker view of rock: anger, alienation, and sensuality. Groups like the Supremes and the Temptations merged rhythm and blues with black gospel, creating the Motown sound.

The problem was, each of these styles attracted a different audience. Those who liked one sound were apt to be violently opposed to another.

The club was centrally located in a college town. The owners chose to play groups with the same angry style as the Stones. While the management was religiously careful about serving alcohol to minors and extremely vigilant about chasing drugs off the premises, hallucinogenic drugs (particularly LSD, or "acid") were very popular. To keep the club "hot," the owners soon found themselves forced to play the "Acid Rock" of groups like Jefferson Airplane and the Grateful Dead.

In 1972, the club was sold, and the new owners changed the name, the decor, and the musical style. Rock had divided into the extremely loud, electronically amplified hard rock and the mellow, more acoustic soft rock. The mellow sounds of soft rock didn't interest Watergate-disenchanted students, and so the new owners found themselves forced to invest in amplifiers and other electronics. The investment proved wise. Students and locals flocked to hear the repetitive, loud, and electronically distorted heavy metal music by bands like Iron Butterfly and Led Zeppelin.

In 1976, the Bee Gees rocketed onto the stage with their *Children of the World* album. In 1977, *Saturday Night Fever* brought disco to the nation's attention. While most period rock wasn't suitable for dancing, disco was intended for nothing but. It was intensely popular among the college crowd, and the owners broke ground on a major extension with a new dance floor and electronic stage lighting. They even added a spinning light ball. Within months, disco dominated the club. For next few years, Club Nightlife was the hottest ticket around.

Things changed in 1983. Disco died hard. Not only had it become unpopular overnight, it became terribly "out" among the "in" set. In the space of just a few months, Club Nightlife went from a packed dance floor to an empty parking lot. Feverishly, the owners changed the name, even built a new facade on the front of the building. New music and DJs were brought in. But the local community still thought of the place as a "disco dive" and treated the club as though it had leprosy.

The club's owner had just gotten the then-new cable TV service. One of the channels was something called "MTV," which played music accompanied by videos. Here was something new and excit-ing—and a possible opportunity to save the club.

Over the next five months, he desperately pitched his idea to various investors and finally got a small group of local investors to fund a complete retrofit of the club. In late 1984, Culture Force opened its doors. Rather than being removed, the dance floor had been extended across the entire club. Throughout the club were walls of television screens playing videos of the then most popular artists—Michael Jackson, Prince, and the Talking Heads. Computers controlled lighting and fed the appropriate video signal to each of the more than 100 video screens located throughout the club.

Enough time had passed to remove the disco stigma from the club. Culture Force opened with a bang and has been packed ever since.

While Culture Force has had its ups and downs, it has remained essentially successful for three decades in a decidedly fickle market. The club has regularly reinvented itself while generally leveraging off its native strengths.

Let's look at how the S-W-L triad is constructed for Culture Force:

Strengths

- *Location.* Near a number of local colleges.
- *Facility.* A building with a manageable mortgage, regularly maintained and upgraded.
- *Operations.* Good control over liquid (literally!) inventory and light (appetizers, snacks, etc.) food service.
- *Cash Management.* Solid management of lots of loose cash.
- *Relations.* Comfortable relationship with local schools and with local police department; problems always handled in a low-key and low-threat manner.
- *Licensing.* Good relations with local law enforcement and the community have guaranteed continual renewal of liquor license.
- *Promotions.* Over the years, the club has learned to mix radio advertising with posted handbills and flyers distributed in student mailboxes.

- *Investment Capital.* Because of their good reputation, owners have been able to regularly raise the capital they need for improvements and growth opportunities.
- *Intelligent Management Team.* Owners and board members think and communicate and have been able to work out problems in a constructive manner.

Weaknesses

- *Fickle Customers.* This is a key weakness; if it's not "in," the students aren't interested.
- *Changing Musical Climate.* The popular musical climate is constantly changing; sometimes the club stays ahead, sometimes it doesn't.
- *Abilities and Resources.* Abilities and resources don't easily translate into new ventures.

Lacks

- *Poor Trend Awareness.* More than once, club owners have been caught by surprise.

After nearly 30 years in business, it's not surprising the club has many strengths and relatively few weaknesses. Unfortunately, the weaknesses evidenced by Culture Force aren't going away any time soon; they're the natural outgrowth of being in that particular business area.

Even so, the owners have choices. For example, they could transform their lack of trend awareness into a strength. By subscribing to trade publications, establishing stronger relationships with radio disc jockeys and music publishers, and staying in better touch with their audience, they'd have a much better chance of anticipating trends and changing to meet them.

This process of fixing a lack and upgrading it into a strength is called *strengthening.*

Even the weaknesses can be overcome *if they must.* The building contains beverage and food service capabilities; it's located near colleges on a central road; its management understands

food-service operations. If they absolutely had to, they could reinvent their club and turn it into a restaurant.

Note: Here's where the S-W-L process cycles. As a restaurant, they'd have new weaknesses and lacks. The biggest lack
would be a menu and a chef. By hiring a qualified chef and
designing a popular menu, they'd *strengthen* the business.

Example 2: Defense Contractor

Not all defense contractors make bullets, tanks, or airplanes. Some,
like Busby Corporation (fictional, yet so like many struggling post
cold-war firms), make products used by the military that are not
strictly military in function. Located just outside Columbia, South
Carolina, Busby manufactures camouflage jackets. There's nothing
particularly special or technically different about these jackets.
They're made in varying sizes, and they have the specified military
camouflage pattern.

Busby is another company that's been around for years. It has a
loyal workforce and has been turning out essentially the same product since the Vietnam War. The firm saw orders surge with Desert
Storm (they got a new silk-screen design for desert combat).

After the war, contracts dried up. Defense spending dropped
tremendously. The subcontractor really had only one customer.
Profits became losses, payroll couldn't be met, and a large percentage of the workforce got its walking papers. Busby is about to go
bankrupt—unless they can figure out how to make money doing
something different.

Strengths

- *Facility.* The mortgage on this factory has been paid.
- *Clothing Production.* They know how to make clothes and
  they've got the equipment to do it; whether it's cost-effective,
  popular, or saleable is another matter.

- *Credit Rating.* For the moment, the company's credit rating is good; they can borrow against the facility to get new equipment.
- *Machinists.* They've built much of their own custom machinery and they have two master machinists who can construct almost anything for fabric.

Weaknesses

- *Management Team.* This team is in trouble; they've never done anything different and they're so bureaucratic and political it's amazing anything gets done.
- *Available Workforce.* Workers only know how to do their current task and are poorly educated.
- *Machinery.* Much of it is old and special purpose.
- *Reliance on Government Contracts.* This is another major weakness; they've been living off government contracts for so long, they have no clue how to conduct business in any other way.

Lacks

- *Marketing and Sales.* The closest these guys have ever been to a marketing strategy or a sales plan is buying season tickets for their customer's buyer.
- *Suppliers.* They've been buying the same cloth from the same company for years; if they need different materials, they're out of luck.
- *Designers.* They've never designed their own clothes; it's been specified down to the stitch by the government.
- *Experience.* Other than their one narrow niche, they're totally inexperienced in the world of fashion.
- *Trained Workforce.* South Carolina's per-pupil expenditures are among the nation's bottom 20 percent; not all workers are even able to read or write.

On the surface, Busby seems destined for extinction. But more careful examination of the high-level S-W-L triad shows us that Busby's lacks and weaknesses are both relatively easily repaired—

if the board of directors makes the decision to do so and can stick with it. Let's look at weaknesses first.

Busby's killer weaknesses are its back-stabbing management team, unskilled labor force, and its reliance on government contracts. Courtesy of defense downsizing, Busby's already been forced to shed reliance on the government. Whether they find something to take its place remains to be seen.

The management team, however, is a real problem. If managers can resolve (or subordinate) their differences with the purpose of moving ahead, there's a chance. If not, the corporation's board is going to have some tough decisions—who stays and who goes. While I rarely advocate dumping a management team in favor of new hires, in this case the managers are a big part of the problem. Either they play fair or they walk. It's as simple as that.

So much for the weaknesses. The company is still not functioning, but the forces dragging it down will have been removed.

The promising part of this picture is Busby's lacks. Just about everything on the list can be remedied by a visit to an effective executive recruiter. Hiring marketing, sales, and design personnel won't completely turn the company around, but it will orient it in the right direction. Salable clothing *can* be designed. It *is* possible to sell uniforms or other styles of clothing to lots of potential customers. Sales and marketing personnel *can* locate prospects. It *is* possible to call on these prospects and learn what products are needed. It *is* possible to hire a designer to create patterns that are functional if not spectacular. And it is possible to train workers to cut on a different set of dashed lines.

Even without outside investment, the company's credit rating will give it short-term fuel to make the transition. Whether it can successfully reinvent is entirely in the hands of management. If they really want it, it can happen.

Example 3: Long-Distance Phone Company

When I make a long-distance call, I'm using a long-distance telephone service. There's nothing unusual about that. What is unusual is a little-known fact: my long-distance carrier was once part of a railroad.

The Southern Pacific Railroad (SPRR) was a company with many far-flung field offices. Rather than relying on the Bell System to provide communication between offices, they ran their own communications cabling along their right-of-way (trackside)—creating their own internal nationwide communications network. When Judge Green broke up AT&T, the door was opened for other companies to add long-distance service. SPRR's, trackside communications system was transformed into a long-distance service provider with revenues far exceeding those of its parent.

Today, Sprint is an independent public company and one of the top three long-distance providers.

Sprint's story is an ideal case of strength-based reinvention. Here was a company with a strength: the railside right-of-way. It took advantage of that strength by running fiber-optic cabling, connecting its far-flung offices. This created a second strength: a high-quality, nationwide communications system.

Once the long-distance monopoly was broken, an opportunity became apparent: selling long-distance service to everyone. Of course, no one was going to associate long-distance phone service with a railroad. So the part of the company that was the phone network got itself a new name (Sprint) and repositioned itself as a phone company. After some creative merger and acquisition action, Sprint was in fact a phone company. It left the low-profit, low-growth railroad business far behind.

REPOSITIONING TO REACH CUSTOMERS

Repositioning is the *hunter-gatherer* part of reinventing from the inside out. It is here that you take a long hard look at your strengths and try to identify any and all opportunities that you can gather using your strengths.

Note: Opportunism is often hard to sell to other managers and investors. But just imagine how hard it was to tell those railroad barons, "Hey, congrats! We're now a phone company. Surprise!"

Opportunity hunting is an incredibly empowering process. You know all the things you can do well. Now you're able to take a look at all the opportunities your strengths buy you. Even the smallest organization can find many available categories of opportunity based on their strength set.

Filtering Opportunities

At any given time, business conditions may require you to look for (or plan for) new opportunities. If you've been hunting and gathering opportunities based on your strengths, you should have lots of exciting choices. At this point, you should filter those choices based on various criteria (time to implement, cost to implement, training, etc.) and choose the ones you want to explore next.

Repositioning

So, you've discovered a gold-mine opportunity that you're uniquely suited to take advantage of. Unfortunately, there's no connection between what you're currently doing and that opportunity. They're as dissimilar as moving freight on railroad tracks and providing long-distance telephone service.

At some point, you've got to reach customers. This requires you to tailor your message to those customers. In many cases, this involves giving the opportunity/product/service a new name, just as SPRR gave its phone company the name Sprint. In other cases, it involves using different marketing channels, different packaging, different advertising vehicles, different customer lists, and so forth.

Note: For the purpose of this chapter, I've oversimplified the repositioning process. We'll go into it in much greater detail in its own chapter later on.

Repositioning requires targeting specific messages to reach certain customer segments. In Southern Pacific's case, they needed to continue to sell rail transport services to corporations through their normal sales channels. But Sprint had to be promoted using vastly different methods.

TEST, EVALUATE, AND REPEAT

If you get only one thing from this book, let it be this: *Reinvention is a way of life, not an event.*

Reinvention doesn't occur once. It is continuous. As you look for changes, hunt and gather opportunities, reposition and remarket, and do all the things necessary to transform your organization, you must constantly evaluate the results. Keep what works and discard or avoid that which does not.

Even the so-called steps of reinvention aren't really tangible steps. You should always be seeking and cataloging your strengths, always looking for new weaknesses, always turning lacks into strengths, and always seeking out new opportunities and new customers. The only constant is change. And with constant change must come constant reinvention and evaluation.

*   *   *

We've looked at the reinvention lifecycle from a generalist's view. In the next few chapters, we'll explore specific techniques for identifying and managing strengths, weaknesses, and opportunities.

First, let's find your strengths.

CHAPTER 5

How to Identify and Leverage Your Strengths

Being forced to work, and forced to do your best, will breed in you temperance and self-control, diligence and strength of will, cheerfulness and content, and a hundred virtues which the idle never know.

—Charles Kingsley, 1861

In this chapter, you'll discard all your doubts, fears, and negative impulses and seek only the positive. In this chapter, you'll learn to map your strengths.

Understanding your strengths can be incredibly empowering. On a day-to-day basis, we all see the nitty-gritty details of our work environment. We see the results of our actions, the deals that fall through, the mounds of phone messages on our desk or in our in-box, the complaints of customers, and the pressures of creditors. But we don't often allow ourselves to see the simple magic that ties it all together.

Any functioning organization is 96 percent magic. That any organization functions at all is often nothing short of miraculous. Think of all the variables that must come together for even the simplest sale—the products that must be designed, the marketing campaign that must be done, the raw materials that must be purchased, the customer that must be located, the order that must be processed, the package that must be shipped, the money that must be raised. Frankly, I find it all somewhat amazing.

The systems that we set up to run our businesses are, in many ways, nothing short of wonderful. Let me give you a simple example: mail order. When we sell a product through direct mail, the process of finding customers is fascinating. We'll mail a letter to 100,000 people; this means that *one hundred thousand* individuals are each delivered letters. When we mail across the country, this often means that close to a hundred thousand different letter carriers are taking the time to make the delivery. Out of these thousands of hands—this human haystack of 32-cent stamps—2,500 or so individuals will eventually emerge. With the power of great copy, they're compelled to reach for their phones and dial ten numbers in unique combination. Shortly after, a product designed to appeal only to those individuals is winging its way across thousands of miles while our bank account is enriched slightly by the event.

In our workaday world, we don't often take the time to see this magic. We worry about the cost of postage, the likelihood that the post office will lose another mailing, the question of having the right price, the need to get products complete on schedule, the risks of returns, and so forth. These are all legitimate concerns. But we won't have a chance to spark our creativity if we don't let ourselves see the magic.

I understand that you have concerns about your business. I understand that some (or much of it) may need to work better. But for the next little while, I want you to forget all that. I want you to look at, dig for, prospect for those gold nuggets that are your strengths. We're panning for gold in them thar hills!

KNOW YOUR STRENGTHS

Simply stated, a strength is anything your organization does well or is of benefit to your organization. Here are some examples of "public" strengths:

- You're the producer of a situation comedy that immediately follows *Roseanne*. For whatever reasons, *Roseanne* is one of the hottest shows on TV. So regardless of how good (or how bad) your program is, if it follows *Roseanne* it has a good chance of making it. Your time slot is your strength.

- There's a company called 800-Flowers. It takes orders from customers by telephone and transmits them to local florists in the recipient's geographic area, taking a cut of the order value in the process. While it is essential that the company's operations are good, that its prices are reasonable, that it has sufficient capital to advertise, its primary strength is the telephone number. It's just incredibly easy to remember 800-Flowers when you want to send a bouquet.

- Similarly, both MCI and AT&T have collect calling services that are ostensibly cheaper than going through a local operator. MCI's is called 800-COLLECT, AT&T's was called 800-OPERA-TOR. Again, while quality of service and price are of an advantage, it can't be any easier when wanting to make a collect call than dialing 1-800-COLLECT. By contrast, AT&T's number was actually a weakness. They advertised against calling a local operator and then used the phone number 1-800-OPERATOR. They found themselves contradicting their own message. Oops!

Note: This was eventually figured out by AT&T. Between the time of writing and editing this section AT&T stopped marketing 1-800-OPERATOR and now advertise their service as 1-800-CALLATT.

Public Strengths

Both the phone number 1-800-COLLECT and the time slot following *Roseanne* are *public strengths*. A public strength is one that an observant outsider (typically a customer, investor, or—often—a competitor) can discern without being inside your organization.

Public strengths are important because they typically determine how your constituencies perceive your organization. When customers are asked about the strengths of 1-800-COLLECT, they can often be counted on to reply, "The number is easy to remember and the service is less expensive than using an operator." Whether this is in fact true is left as an exercise to the caller.

You must use considerable caution when considering and relying on your public strengths. Very often, a good marketing person can put a "spin" on a problem and make it appear to be a strength. Don't get caught up believing your own marketing!

Private Strengths

Private strengths are the cornerstones of strength-based reinvention. These strengths are your real advantages. It's important to understand that private strengths are rarely immediately apparent. They're the things your company does so well that they're taken for granted.

Every business, from the most successful to the most troubled, does some things *very right.* The most important part of the reinvention process is identifying these things you do so well—from the simplest office procedure to the massive, companywide operation. Often, your business strengths will be small, isolated islands of effectiveness. The key is finding these strengths and using them as foundation cornerstones that will support your entire reinvention strategy.

CRITERIA FOR IDENTIFYING STRENGTHS

For the purposes of strength-based reinvention, a strength is something you do well. Here are the three criteria for identifying strengths:

Three Criteria for Identifying Strengths

1. Anything you consistently, regularly do well.
2. Anything that consistently, regularly generates a positive result.
3. Anything that consistently, regularly results in or provides an advantage over others.

The key to identifying a strength is the *consistent, regular* component of the ability, attribute, resource, or skill. If it's not consistent and regular, it cannot be reproduced on demand and it's not a strength; it's a quirk or a fluke—and quite possibly a weakness.

The preceding criteria for identifying strengths are highly generalized. You can use broad license when attempting to relate a strength to a business attribute. For example, you might say that anything that generates a profit is a strength. As such, it would fall under Criterion 2: *Anything that consistently, regularly generates a positive result.* But to truly determine if it is a strength, you'd need to understand the individual attributes that make up a strength.

DISSECTING A STRENGTH

One of Component Software's most clearly defined strengths is its ability to produce specialized computer software in low volume (not mass-market) at a profit. This has become one of the cornerstone abilities with which we've weathered recessions. This strength has kept us profitable while much larger competitors were going belly up.

The original founding premise of the company was to build computer software tools for programmers (also called developers). This is an area where I have strong experience and where we felt there were unexplored frontiers. But there are also a number of factors that make selling developer tools a difficult business:

- There are many different "platforms"—the systems your tools must run on (Macintosh, Windows, DOS, UNIX, etc.); choose the wrong platform and your tool won't sell.
- The platforms you must support can change as often as each year.
- While many developers are in larger corporations, many others are independent consultants; as a rule, these independent consultants are very, very frugal and very demanding of a tool-provider's time.
- While most computer users use only three or four programs, developers may have 50 or 60 development tools sitting in their toolbox.

- Compared with the overall computer user market, the developer market is quite small—less than 1 percent.

- Even the most successful development tools will sell only a fraction of the number of units of a commercial product (e.g., a word processor).

- Developers often need supporting tools for their primary tools (the analogy might be custom socket sizes for a socket wrench). These supporting tools sell in even smaller volume but must be available to sell the primary tools.

- Developers like to buy from companies with a number of different tools; they like to feel you really have a technical understanding of their needs.

Marketing to developers is often difficult for a host of reasons. But a principal problem has always been volume: It just costs too much to create and support a new developer tool for the volume it sells. To understand this, you'll need to understand that most software is mass produced in quantities of one thousand to ten thousand units. Getting a manual printed on a traditional press requires achieving an *economic sweet spot,* that point where it actually makes sense to print. In other words, because of the time it takes to set up a printer (or, for that matter, a disk duplicator), it might cost $2,400 to print 500 copies of a manual and $2,450 to print 1,000 copies.

In my market, a typical development tool bill-of-materials consists of a package, one or more manuals, a manual cover (front and back), one or more disks, a disk label, a registration card, and a variety of supporting goodies. When produced in typical production volumes, a new development tool would often cost over $50,000 to manufacture the very first unit (this does not count the huge cost to develop the product in the first place).

For our higher volume products, a $50,000 manufacturing investment was more than justified. It would be repaid in a very short time. Unfortunately, it wasn't always possible to predict which product would be a high-flyer and which would land a dud. Launching a few unexpected duds a year could zap the entire organization's profit picture in a big way. As you might imagine, this scenario makes many small software companies risk adverse.

The problem is, our customers want a steady stream of new products. Without new releases, they tend to forget about us. So here we are, caught in a Catch-22: We need regular new releases but if the release fails, which it may, we lose profitability.

It is this problem that we turned into a major strength. *You can often identify a strength by the damage of its inverse.* In other words, if you didn't have this particular strength, how big would the problem be? In our case, we figured out the solution to the manufacturing Catch-22. This became our strength. But if we hadn't figured out the solution, the curse of being forced to roll the dice regularly on a stream of low-volume products would have been a major weakness.

There are many benefits to our low-volume manufacturing strength:

- We can introduce new products at a tenth the cost of our competitors.
- We can produce a new product in a third the time of our competitors.
- Because all work is done in low volume, we maintain no inventory.
- Because we maintain no inventory, we generate little waste.
- Little waste generates little environmental damage and less money is thrown out with the old versions.

Those are just a few of the benefits of having our strength. It's also possible to split apart a strength into components, many of which are strengths in their own right:

Strength

- Component Software Corporation can profitably produce software in low volume.

Components

- Disk duplication is done in-house; there's no waiting time, no production minimum, and masters can be changed instantly.
- Our low-tech system of bins allows rapid sorting of duplicated disks without the worry that one disk will be confused with another.

- Document binding is done in-house; we're able to provide a high-volume "look and feel" without production minimums, added cost, or wasted time.
- Our vendor relationship with our print vendor is strong; they're able to produce only those manuals and packages we need for that week.

Look closely at the preceding strength. Earlier, I outlined the benefits of the strength. This is also important: *Every strength must have at least one identifiable benefit attached to it.* Now look at the components. Often strengths are composed of individual components or attributes that make up the strength. *Often these components are strengths in their own right.* Compare each subordinate component with the criteria for identifying strengths and you'll see that each meets the criteria and most have benefits attached.

Remember that strengths do not have to be—often they are definitely not—big, highly visible attributes of your business. Often the smallest, apparently unimportant elements of your business provide the foundation for your greatest strengths.

In Component's case, a set of about 40 small, plastic, laundry bins are the key to one of our most relied-on strengths. The bins cost about one dollar each from the local Home Depot. Yet, until we had an easy way to keep one indistinguishable pile of disks from getting mixed up with the next, our entire production process was unreliable. While I can't say that the reason we succeeded and our competitors failed was that we use plastic laundry bins, it's clear that without being able to build on reliable production as a cornerstone strength, we might not have done as well.

One strength isn't going to make or break your company. But by using strengths as cornerstones, and building one on the other, you'll eventually have a solid foundation to conduct, change, and grow your business.

WHERE TO LOOK

By now, I hope you'll accept that your organization has strengths. I also hope you understand what I mean by a strength. Now it's time to find them.

By this time, you probably have some questions:

Q: "Where do I look?"

A: Good question. Everywhere.

Q: "Do I have to do this alone?"

A: Of course not. Everyone should be involved. In fact, you'll miss what could be very important strengths if you try to find all of them on your own.

Q: "I don't have time. Why can't I just use those strengths I already know about?"

A: I guess you could. But you could be missing a powerful strategic or tactical weapon. Imagine you're in a war. You're being shot at. You're about to run out of ammunition. You'd like to reload, but if you stop to reload, you'll be shot at. So, what do you do? Eventually, you run out of ammunition. There's no downside to taking time to reload. You'll be shot at anyway.

Searching for strengths follows the same pattern. You could avoid looking for strengths because you're too busy. Or you could look for them now, and maybe prevent some future crisis and be prepared to leverage a future opportunity. It is completely up to you. It's your business—literally.

I cannot tell you exactly where to look for your strengths. If they've been hidden from you—and you know your business far better than I—they're certainly going to be hidden from me. You have to look everywhere and involve everyone.

I've told you what to look for. You've seen criteria for identifying strengths and their benefits. Just remember that no strength is too small or too obscure. You may choose to do nothing with a teensy little strength that you find today. That's fine. It will, however, be in your tool bag of strengths the next time you need to tap some internal advantage.

In fact, you probably shouldn't use a newly discovered strength as soon as you find it. Finding strengths and using them are two very different processes. Finding a strength is an analytic process akin to gathering data. Later, when you're hunting for opportunities, you'll be able to connect various strengths together into a new competitive advantage. One lone strength won't cut it.

For example, if I told a fellow software publisher that he'd be more successful if he bought a bunch of laundry bins, and if he listened, he'd deserve what he'd get—absolutely nothing. One strength, which is of high value when used in context with others, may be valueless in the wrong context.

TRACKING STRENGTHS

The process of reinventing from the inside out requires both analysis and action. Identifying strengths is a form of data gathering. Like any form of data gathering, there are lots of ways to organize what you find.

Here's a minimum list of what you should record for each strength:

- *Short Name of Strength.* This will give you an easy handle to refer to when talking and communicating about this strength with others.
- *Detailed Description.* Your understanding of the strength will be freshest when you identify it. Write a detailed description. Amend it over time as you learn more uses and benefits of the strength.
- *Who Identified It.* Often, someone intimately associated with the strength will identify it; you'll need to know who that is for further information.
- *Strength Criteria.* Which of the three criteria does it meet? What are the advantages of meeting each criterion?
- *Benefits of the Strength.* How can you take advantage of the strength? This is an area that will also (hopefully) grow over time.

There is no "right" way to organize strength-based data. Here are some ways you could do it:

- Write down each strength on an index card; write benefits on the back.
- List strengths in a word processor.
- Enter them into your pocket organizer or Wizard.

- Keep them in your head.
- Scribble them on scraps of paper around the office.
- Organize them in a database.

This is your business. You can organize your information as you see fit—and in your own style. However, I often advocate using computer technology when it is available. Gathering and storing strength data is an ideal task for a database system.

Tracking Strengths in a Database

A database is ideal for strength tracking; it's also ideal for tracking weaknesses, lacks, and opportunities. Using a multiuser database, anyone with the appropriate access security could add, update, and search for strengths.

Even in a small company, there are often hundreds of strengths. Your understanding of them will change over time. Rather than appointing one person as the "keeper of the strengths," it is far easier for everyone involved to enter and look up strengths on their own.

Searching is a big win with databases. Let's assume you've found an opportunity and want to find out whether your organization can take advantage of it. Using the database, you can search for various keywords and recall appropriate information records about areas you might use to advantage.

Just the very act of keeping track of strengths is a great advantage. When you print or display a tangible list of all your strengths, it becomes much more difficult to have all that much self-doubt. Here's tangible, undeniable proof that, yes, you can do something—lots of somethings—right.

The strength database is also helpful when you are communicating to privileged outsiders (bankers, investors, spouses) about what you do well. You'll have tangible evidence of much of what the organization actually does successfully.

Access Control

While tracking strengths, weaknesses, and lacks is critically important as a foundation for turnaround, growth, and success, you *must* use extreme care with who has access to the information. While you can pretty well let anyone add information, read access must be jealously guarded.

Your strength database is your crown jewel.

Your weaknesses/lacks database is your Achilles heal.

Both of these are resources your competitors would love to know about. Most modern database systems have vast levels of access control—it's often easier to secure an online database than a written document in your desk drawer.

Use a database, but use care about who can read it.

Example: StrengthBuilder Database

One of my company's strengths is database technology and computing resources. We've got a high-speed network connecting our computers both in the office and remotely. We also have programming, development, and database design skills. So it's no wonder that we built our own Flexible Enterprise database system for tracking strengths. We call it StrengthBuilder.

StrengthBuilder is a multiuser database system that runs on Macintosh and Windows computers. This was very important because we wanted everyone to be able to add new strengths. The actual data for StrengthBuilder resides on a server computer. Network connections (inside the office) and phone lines provide access to computers throughout the organization. Figure 5.1 (on page 64) shows a sample screen.

A system like this allows us to track any number of strengths. We do a wide variety of searches. For example, we could search for everything with "Competitive Advantage" checked. Or we could search for the word "disk" in the benefits field.

Through searching, we can collect benefits together and then print out a detailed report describing a set of strengths pertaining to problems we're trying to solve. In this way, we never lose track of our core foundation advantages.

While we have unique strengths in database development, almost anyone with a personal computer can build some form of

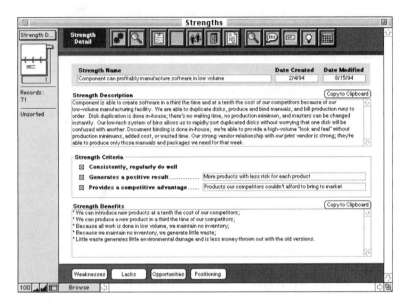

Figure 5.1. Strengths database from StrengthBuilder 2000.

strength-tracking database. The scope of the database often depends on the size of your organization. A small organization might have a few users connected. A much larger organization might have thousands of contributors, all connected through an enterprisewide Lotus Notes installation.

The simple rule is this: Keep track of your strengths. Use whatever works best for you.

RECAP

Your strengths are the core of your business advantage. There are three primary criteria for identifying strengths: Is it something you do well? Is it something that has a positive result? Is it something that results in a competitive advantage? For something to be a strength and not a fluke, you must consistently and regularly generate the same positive results. All strengths must have identifiable benefits.

Identifying strengths is a gathering process, not an action process. Strengths you identify now probably shouldn't be used immediately. Rather, they should be stored up for the day they have a beneficial use. No strength is too small, but it may not be something you're able to immediately identify. Enlist your entire organization in the process of searching out and recording strengths.

Strengths should be written down. Then they'll be useful in the future. Database technology makes an ideal tool for recording and searching strengths.

*   *   *

Identifying strengths is not a phase in a step-by-step plan. You should always, constantly be seeking your strengths. New strengths always turn up. Keep your eyes open and you'll see yourself and your company in a whole new, much more positive, light.

Your organization has value, abilities, skills, and advantages. Now you know they exist *and* how to find them. When you see all your strengths displayed in a simple list, you can take great pride in your abilities. Often, you'll find there's a lot more to your organization than you might have originally thought.

In the next chapter, you'll go through a similar process to identify and eliminate impediments to your success. Good hunting!

CHAPTER 6

Eliminate Your Obstacles to Success

It still holds true that man is most uniquely human when he turns obstacles into opportunities.

—Eric Hoffer, 1973

As every business has strengths, every business also has weaknesses. The goal, of course, is to eliminate weaknesses and maximize strengths. To accomplish this, you'll need to first identify the trouble spots (the poor performers, the "come back and haunt you" creatures, those products and services with clear fatal flaws, the products customers are always dissatisfied with, and those things that are high cost with little return). Sometimes if you're lucky, you can just stop doing what doesn't work. But often, you'll have to replace a poor performing strategy, program, product, or service with another that's more effective.

Because knowing what will be more effective isn't always possible (unless you have your own crystal ball), it's often necessary to try and discard multiple replacements until something works. When you find something that works, it becomes a strength and is another aspect of your business that helps leverage reinvention.

Obviously though, your weaknesses aren't your only obstacles to success. Weaknesses are lacks within your organization, whereas your business problems may come from external sources as well;

aggressive thrusts from competitors, changes in market dynamics, new regulations, and so forth.

Weaknesses, problems, lacks, competition—these are all obstacles standing in the way of your goals. In this chapter, we'll explore how to handle your obstacles: eliminating them, transforming them to more benign forms, turning them into new opportunities, shelving them for a better time, or confronting them when all else fails.

Once you understand your organization's ever-improving strengths and you know how to eliminate and reduce obstacles, you'll be ready to run your business like a rabid opportunist. Only then will you be prepared for our new, radically different business climate.

You're here. You want to get there. Anything that stands in the way of getting from here to there is an obstacle.

TIME VALUE OF OBSTACLES

This getting from here to there, of course, presupposes you know where "there" is. It also assumes that your "there" of record is a practical "there" to be going to.

Pretty vague, huh? Not really. We're always going from "here" to "there." Let's make it more concrete. We're always at a certain point in an organization's life, and at a certain condition (healthy, growing, weak, dying—and all the millions of degrees of variation in between). And we're always trying to get somewhere. In the most general terms that somewhere, that "there," is more profits, more growth, more sales, more success.

These are the organization's goals. And they're admirable. They're just useless from a day-to-day tactical perspective. Of course you want your business to be more successful. But what do you do to get there?

Take one company I know, a small, well-run casual restaurant with revenues of about $750,000 per year. After four years in operation, they have a happy, steady customer base and good products (great food, good service, good value). By all accounts, they're successful. But the founder's business plan calls for hundreds of these restaurants all over the country. His "there," his goal, is to open lots of stores.

Q: "What are the obstacles to opening a restaurant in every community?"

A: None.

I can hear you screaming in disagreement.

"What about capitalization?"

"What about finding the right locations?"

"What about deciding between ownership and franchise?"

Whatabout . . . whatabout . . . whatabout.

The real answer is that there are absolutely no obstacles he faces today between his small, successful single restaurant and a chain of hundreds across the country. The goal is too large for tactical consideration. He can try to define smaller, more practical goals. But the goal of a restaurant in every community isn't an immediate issue. Therefore, there are no immediate (or even near-term) obstacles—because "there" isn't a restaurant in every community.

For this restaurant, a valid "there" would be opening a second store. For this practical, near-term goal, the valid immediate obstacles would be:

- Deciding whether to open a second restaurant.
- Determining the location strategy.
- Raising the money and/or deciding to take profits out of store number one.
- Figuring out how to split management time between keeping the first restaurant running at peak performance and starting a second store.
- And on, and on, and on.

Too many organizations waste far too much time dealing with obstacles that won't be real for years—if ever. Deal with near-term obstacles. An awful lot will change by the time you get to the point where you thought the obstacles would be.

This doesn't mean don't operate with an eye toward the future! Not at all. But obstacles and weaknesses are creatures of the here and now. Worrying about far-future obstacles is like worrying about the monster that lives under your bed. Both will keep you up at night but neither will impact you in the morning.

IS IT IN YOUR WAY?

An obstacle is something in your way. Not sometime years from now, but in your way *right now*. Obstacles can take any of the following forms:

- Weakness
- Lack
- Problem
- Objection
- Barrier

The common factor of them all is *they are in your way*. Your job will be to get the obstacle out of your way (or—often better—to get out of the way of the obstacle).

OBSTACLE OR EXCUSE?

This is a tough question. We often use our obstacles as excuses. "I can't do this because of that."

For years, Apple has made exceptional computers. But until recently, they were very expensive. Even though they were easier to use and arguably better machines than their DOS and Windows counterparts, Apple was unable to gain market share due to the higher price. Apple claimed it couldn't cut prices because the company would lose margin and lose money. But cutting prices has no direct connection to losing margin and losing money. Yes, given no other changes in the company's strategy, cutting prices would cause profits to dip. The real issue, though, was, could Apple reduce its manufacturing costs? It might be true that lower margins are an obstacle to greater profits—but not if the volume of sales increases and the cost to build goes down. As history has shown, Apple's cutting prices was *not* an obstacle to profitability.

Here are some lessons we can learn from Apple's fixation with margin:

- Make sure you connect the obstacle with the correct goal. "We can't cut prices because we'd lose margin and lose money" wrongly reduces prices with a drop in profits. Saying, "It's hard to be profitable with these manufacturing costs" or "We need to get manufacturing costs down so we can cut prices" is more accurate because these statements accurately connect the cost of manufacturing to profits.

- Make sure the obstacle isn't manufactured. Apple has always enjoyed the "premium" positioning of their products. While it's been good for the ego, the substantial (unrecoverable) loss in market share was not good for the company's mission.

- If the obstacle is an excuse, find out what you're hiding. In Apple's case, perhaps it was the realization that changing manufacturing costs and going from a profit strategy to a market strategy would require substantial changes in the overall company philosophy and culture.

- If your obstacle is an excuse, perhaps there's a strength buried underneath. In Apple's case, there was an amazing strength buried within. Apple is now selling more computers with more profits than ever before—at a competitive price. But the fear and inbred doctrine prevented Apple from taking advantage of its unique strengths.

- An excuse may indicate that within an obstacle to one endeavor is the sign of a strength in another.

Lots of organizational excuses wind up described as obstacles. They often hold you back. These are some of my favorites:

- *"That's against our policy."* The obstacle is really an excuse for telling the customer that you're inflexible and unwilling to meet his or her needs; or that you don't have the authority to do the job; or that you're not sure what to do.

- *"We're freezing hiring because the quarterly results are down."* This obstacle is an excuse for poor hiring review practices. In virtually every company with a hiring freeze, some "strategic" hires take place during the freeze. Why? Because they're clearly important. The hiring freeze is a convenient excuse when you don't have the procedures in place to separate a good hire from a bad.

- *"It costs too much to sell at a competitive price."* Apple suffered from this "obstacle" for years. They tried to protect their margins and lost enormous market share. They've since redesigned their products for lower manufacturing cost—the workaround for this excuse—and now their products are flying off shelves.

- *"We've been doing it that way for years."* So what? So you've been doing it the same way for years. That's no excuse—or at least now you've been caught with your excuse red-handed!

- *"Advertising costs too much."* This is one I've been guilty of— *mea culpa, mea culpa.* So, an ad in one publication is too expensive. What about more targeted publications? What about different marketing vehicles? What about tagging along with other products? There are lots of ways to make products profitable if you stop turning excuses into obstacles.

Daily life presents us with plenty of real obstacles. Don't manufacture your own. If you do, you could become your own worst enemy.

Exercise:

1. Make a list of your obstacles.
2. How many of them are disguised excuses?
3. Cross off all the disguised excuses from your list of obstacles.
4. Notice how much smaller your list of *real* obstacles has gotten.

STRENGTH MAKES IT HARD TO BE A VICTIM

Fred Marshall, CEO of Quantum Learning, conducts sales training and customer satisfaction seminars. He's always in front of salespeople,

Table 6.1.   Psychological effects of strength versus weakness.

	Psychological Effect	Impact on Success
Strength	Empowering (these are all the things you can do)	Motivates you forward
	Obligating (these are all things you should be doing)	Pressures you to move forward
Weakness	Depressing (these are all the things you can't do)	Holds you back
	Comforting (look, you don't have to do this because you can't)	Justifies the status quo

helping them to maximize their selling power while partnering with customers. Fred tells me that often salespeople are more comfortable facing their weaknesses and obstacles than their strengths.

Now this is really counterintuitive. You would think it would be much easier to handle your strengths than your weaknesses. After all, strengths are generally good news, while weaknesses are pretty much bad news.

That isn't necessarily so. To many people, weaknesses can be comforting. They're safety nets. Strengths are obligating. You are expected to take advantage of your assets. It's a pretty ghastly paradox. Table 6.1 shows how strength obligates you to be challenged, whereas weaknesses give you the excuse to be safe.

Here's a scary thought: Are you cherishing your weaknesses because they're comforting?

Exercise:

1. Which is more important: survival or comfort?
2. Which is more important: comfort or success?

There is nothing wrong with playing to your weaknesses (using them as a safety net) if:

- The corporation's survival is not in question.
- You can live with a less-than-stellar business.

But if your business survival is an issue or if you are absolutely dedicated to building a successful, profitable, growing, responsible, and valuable enterprise, make sure you aren't allowing your company the excuse of being a victim. If you are determined to succeed:

- Cherish your strengths.
- Grab on to the obligations of your abilities.
- Push forward.

BLOCKADE OR PROJECTILE OBSTACLE?

Not all obstacles are the warm, friendly, wag-their-tails, wait-till-you-dispatch-them, puppy dog type of obstacles. No way. Some are the dive-from-the-sky, heat-seeker-locked-on, fly-up-your-tailpipe projectile type of obstacles.

Projectile obstacles (also called *attacks*) require immediate prioritization and immediate action.

Most obstacles will be of the benign, block-your-path form—like a river that would block your path to the other side. They give you the time to think through and explore various options: Do I build a bridge? Do I swim across? Or do I take a flying leap over it? Do I go downriver and hope there's already a bridge? These obstacles are not particularly *time sensitive*. Their primary impact is to block your path, which prevents you from reaching your goals.

Projectile obstacles are *extremely time sensitive*. Their primary intended effect is to damage your business in some way.

A barrier of entry to an industry is a *blockade obstacle*. If you choose not to pass over, through, or around it, you won't incur any direct damage. The early-adopter-to-mainstream gap described by Geoff Moore is a blockade obstacle.

A competitor dumping deliberately underpriced product into your market is a *projectile obstacle*. Like a blockade obstacle, if you choose to ignore it, it will usually not go away. Unlike a blockade obstacle, if you choose to ignore it, you will probably lose market share and customers and thereby be damaged.

Most often, blockade obstacles are creatures of your own creation or of nature. In other words, they're not launched as an intent to attack *you*. On the other hand, projectile obstacles are *aimed at you* by the tactical or strategic decision of a thinking entity.

When dealing with projectile obstacles, you don't really have the time for the planning and analysis functions that we've been describing. Reinvention is a somewhat measured operation and is mostly *proactive*. Defense against attack requires immediate response and is *reactive*.

Your situational awareness will be your primary (and first used) weapon when defending against an attack. If you're clearly aware of your environment, you'll know—figuratively—when to duck or when to jump aside.

Let's look at an example of a projectile attack: the tobacco industry versus just about everyone else. (Up front, let me say I'm a nonsmoker. It's an interesting exercise for me to take the strategic side of the tobacco companies.)

While smoking has always been a contentious issue, tobacco companies have pretty well held their own against government regulation. This is now changing. The recent and largest projectile obstacle hurled at the tobacco industry has been the intent to declare nicotine an addictive drug.

Let's analyze the situation:

Projectile Obstacle (attack)

- Declaring nicotine a drug.

Situation (situational awareness)

- Smokers as a percentage of the population have been declining for 30 years (42.4% in 1965, 25% in 1994 according to *BusinessWeek*).
- The rate of decline has radically slowed in the past four years versus the previous five years (15.2% from 1985 to 1990, 1.2% from 1990 to 1994).
- Those who smoke are avid supporters of a number of issues including the belief that smoking is not addictive and it's their right to smoke anywhere they want.

Defense Strategy

- *Litigation.* Use armies of lawyers to challenge smoking bans in court. Phillip Morris sued ABC for $10 billion (that's *billion* with a "B"!) in a defamation case.
- *Intense Lobbying.* In the state, local, and federal halls of government, tobacco lobbyists are working hard to influence the opinions of every government official they can corner, cajole, and coerce.
- *Public Relations.* Like government lobbying, tobacco lobbyists have been pushing on the press for favorable (or at least unbiased) reportage. The tobacco lobby has attempted to link freedom-of-puffing with everything from smokers' rights to freedom of choice.
- *Powerful Advertising to the Converted.* In addition to their normally heavy brand marketing, tobacco concerns have been designing ads that will appeal to and mobilize their millions of followers. Ads show smokers being forced to sit on the outside of office buildings or on the wings of airplanes.

Although tobacco has been losing population share for three decades, the latest attacks have been the most threatening. Were nicotine declared an addictive drug, it is actually possible that smokers would need a prescription to buy tobacco in any form. And were it to be proven that the tobacco companies knew about the addictiveness of nicotine all along, there would be damage suits of unprecedented and mind-boggling proportions.

In this literal fight to the death, both sides are lighting off some pretty destructive projectile weapons and putting up massive defenses.

Know Thy Enemy: Finding Realistic Obstacles

When determining your strengths, you must be on a constant quest. You must constantly seek out every possible strength you have. When it comes to obstacles and weaknesses, you're not on a quest. Rather, you're going to need to train yourself and your employees in the fine arts of identification and qualification.

Guideline 1: We Can't Do That Because . . .

Any time you can't travel down your path because of something in the way, that something is the obstacle. You can tell when you've found an obstacle when you hear yourself or anyone in your organization say, "We can't do that because . . ."

Guideline 2: Would You Care in a Crisis?

Recall our discussion of immediate-term "valid" obstacles and those so far down the road that you might never have to deal with them. There's an easy way to tell if an obstacle is a valid, now obstacle. Imagine your business is in a crisis. Would the obstacle be something *you must take into account* or would it suddenly become irrelevant.

Let's look at another example. Malloy's (a fictitious name for a real place) is another restaurant I frequent. Malloy's is located in a small shopping center in an off-the-beaten-track corner of Princeton. At the heart of Princeton is a one-square-block shopping mecca—the central square. Many of the best and fanciest stores are located in this square. Recently, the owners of Malloy's opened a new store on the square: a bagel shop.

These restaurant entrepreneurs might have learned that one of the stores was going to close, making very high quality space available. There were many problems, though: The space available was too small to duplicate the format of Malloy's; they had to come up with the money and credit to make the lease happen; they also had to come up with the money to fund the launch of a new store. These were all immediate-term obstacles that needed to be handled *now*. They're valid.

Exercise:

1. What would be some other valid immediate-term obstacles?
2. What obstacles would *seem* to be near-term, but could be shelved until the new store was opened?

Guideline 3: Will You Be Damaged If You Do Nothing?

This is an immediate clue to a projectile obstacle. If you see the obstacle and decide to take the whole summer off, will there be a business to come back to? If so, it's not a projectile obstacle. Breathe easy.

Guideline 4: Will You Grow and Succeed If You Do Nothing?

You've encountered something that might be a valid obstacle. You ignore it. Will you still grow and succeed? Or does the obstacle sufficiently block you that your business will stagnate if the obstacle is not overcome?

Guideline 5: Is the Gain from Overcoming the Obstacle Worth the Effort?

Sometimes the cure is worse than the disease. I tend to believe this about trade shows in the Macintosh industry. I used to subscribe to the general wisdom that if you didn't exhibit at Macworld Expo, you wouldn't succeed. Macworld became the obstacle that had to be overcome for Macintosh industry success. We went to lots of these shows. They were expensive (in the tens of thousands of dollars each, what with all the exhibit, travel, and union expenses). They also wiped out the whole company for about six weeks: three weeks preparing for the show, the week of the show, and two weeks after where we'd all walk around like zombies because of total exhaustion.

One summer, I just couldn't face the thought of going to the show. I didn't want to blow all that money and worse, I didn't want to put in another week of standing on concrete floors and being nice to everyone. I looked at the cost of the show versus our sales. Each show made something of a profit—but not a lot. Then I looked at the cost of effectively shutting down my business for six weeks and discovered that going to the show cost way, way more than staying home.

Now, instead of going to the show and spending tens of thousands of dollars, I spend a few thousand on magazine ads. Our feet hurt less. And we have 12 more productive growth weeks per year (two shows per year, six weeks lost per show); *we gain an entire quarter's productivity* by avoiding the industry convocation.

Do we lose contacts? Sure. By contrast, think about what you'd do if you suddenly discovered a free quarter of productivity. In Macworld's case, we really didn't gain more from going than staying home. Overcoming the obstacle cost more than just letting it alone.

Someday we may go back to Macworld. Deep down, we are masochists. But we'll go because we want to—not because it's "the way things are done."

MAPPING YOUR OBSTACLE COURSE

As you *identify* and *qualify* your obstacles, you should start making decisions about them. Any obstacle you identify needs to be placed into one of the following categories:

- *Those That Are Projectiles.* As discussed earlier, these require immediate attention and action.
- *Those You Confront.* Sometimes, an obstacle needs to be dealt with head-on. Those obstacles that you choose to confront will require a large amount of your available effort to deal with and dispatch. Choose these wisely. *Hint:* Confront only one or two obstacles at a time.
- *Those You Accept.* These are obstacles that you're not able to get rid of with ease. One obstacle faced by many small businesses is a lack of cash. Accept it. It's a fact. Rather than fighting against this lack, it's going to be much easier to accept this as one of the physical laws of running your business.
- *Those You Avoid.* These are obstacles you choose neither to confront nor to accept. These are obstacles you duck under, skirt around, or climb over. Sometimes its just easier to move the path than to move the obstacle.

At any given time, your business will have its personal collection of weaknesses, lacks, problems, and troubles. Constantly prioritize them, making sure you deal with the attacks first. Then determine whether *at this point in time* you're going to confront, accept, or avoid.

I've used this mapping function in my own business for years. Whenever I feel overwhelmed with obstacles, I first list them on a piece of paper. Then I determine whether I want to confront them, accept them, or avoid them by moving the path. When I'm done, I've often taken a list of 40 or 50 totally debilitating obstacles and reduced it down to three or four I need to deal with over the next 30 days. What looked like a totally unmanageable disaster became easily controllable.

YOUR TOOLKIT FOR WRANGLING OBSTACLES

Don't think of obstacles as creatures you fight, confront, or do battle with. That'll put you into the wrong frame of mind. Instead, think of your collection of obstacles as being like wild horses who need to be herded in a particular direction. This analogy is important. Forget about your business problems and think about all those cowboy movies. There were three or four guys on horseback and they usually had some dogs running around, working together to get the cattle going in the right direction. While the untaimed animals didn't present a direct threat, they were certainly recalcitrant. The cowboys, with the help of their barking dogs, cajoled and pushed the cattle from all sides until they managed to get the herd going in the right direction.

Over the years, I've developed my own toolkit for wrangling obstacles. Like the cowboys of old, I use whatever technique works best at the time for obstacles of different personalities. Some guide easily. Some require direct confrontation. And every so often, one or two decide to branch off in a totally unexpected direction. Hey, business wouldn't be so much fun if there wasn't any challenge!

And now for the techniques.

Technique 1: Discard

Often you'll strengthen your business by simply dumping the losing parts. Sometimes, the elements of your business that aren't the top performers are also the biggest obstacles. They take time, they take energy, they take cash.

I'll illustrate this with a story from my own past: PictureLink. PictureLink was an image-editing module for a database. It was great for those applications where you needed to store pictures as well as text (like magazine artwork, engineering diagrams, assembly photographs, and the like). We acquired PictureLink from some Singapore nationals living in the United States and sold it successfully for about two years.

But it had problems. As the host database technology (which we didn't control) evolved, PictureLink had to be updated. The more the database changed, the worse PictureLink performed. Had we controlled the source code (the internal writings that make up the product) as we normally did, we could have made the changes ourselves. Experience teaches much, however, and apparently I hadn't had enough experience by then. We didn't have the source code. We didn't employ the programmers (this was a publishing arrangement), so what did we need with the source code?

One day we tried calling the developers. The phone was disconnected. We drove over to their offices and were told they had gone back to Singapore—without giving us the courtesy of a forwarding address or phone number or even letting us know! This discourtesy aside, we had a real problem. PictureLink was falling apart and we had no way to fix it. Yet it was contributing a considerable amount to our bottom line.

For almost an additional year, we sold PictureLink. Yes, the revenues came in. But so did a steady and constant stream of unhappy customers. Customers for whom PictureLink didn't work right. Customers who had bought it years earlier and expected an upgrade. Call after call and we couldn't do anything—except watch our reputation decline and our stress increase.

Exercise:

1. Eliminate unhappy customer calls.
2. Start to get happy customer calls.
3. How does that make you feel?
4. What does it do for your employees? Your revenues?

Finally (it sure took me long enough!), I made the decision to just dump the product. We stopped selling it. We also started being honest with our customers and told them that the developers had skipped town. We were sorry, but PictureLink was dead.

This was a case where I simply dumped an obstacle. It wasn't cheap and it took six months to recover the revenue. But we stopped getting unhappy customer calls. And we regained our self-respect.

There are tangible benefits to cutting your losses and dumping problems:

- *Focus Is Improved.* By freeing up all the time and effort required to manage the problem, you're now able to focus on more important issues.

- *Money Is Saved.* While revenue may decline over the short term, you're no longer risking real dollars on poor performers.

- *Money Is Raised.* We didn't raise money with PictureLink. It was obsolete and unsupportable. But some properties that are poor performers for you may have value for others. Selling them off can raise money.

- *Time Is Saved.* Problems are time-sinks. They just suck down hours with no tangible return, like the three months per year we lost by going to two one-week trade shows. Problems often take far more time than they're worth.

- *Hassle Is Reduced.* Not only do you save time, but the general level of annoyance goes down. Don't get macho and say "Stress is good." It's not. Anything you can do to productively increase the quality of work life for everyone—including yourself—will help your business.

Dumping your problems (whenever possible) is the most valuable weapon in your obstacle wrangling arsenal. I use it as often as I can. You should as well.

Note: This isn't just another excuse for downsizing. Make sure you're dumping real problems and not something of value. Think before you dump.

Technique 2: Avoid (i.e., Nichemanship, Changing the Rules, Cheating)

One of the most effective ways of eliminating obstacles is simply avoiding them. Get out of their way, do an end run, dig underneath, jump over, walk around—all of these result in your company never coming into conflict with the obstacle.

I've shown you this strategy twice: with FileFlex and with Macworld. Recall that FileFlex is a database product in a market unbelievably overcrowded with database tools and dominated by some of the largest software companies including behemoths Microsoft and Oracle. These are not competitors you want to meet even in broad daylight in a deserted alley!

Yet FileFlex is amazingly successful. Why? Is it because it's a better product than those produced by the big boys? Is it because our marketing is vastly superior? Is it because we're entrenched in some industry-critical installations?

If you answered "No" to all of these, you'd be correct. In fact, the "Yes" answer applies to our competitors. Had we attempted to compete with them on their terms, we would have been squashed like a bug. And justifiably so. FileFlex has neither the engineering technology nor the marketing muscle to compete in the major leagues. But it is a highly successful farm league player.

The big products (names like FoxPro, dBASE, Oracle, Ingres, Informix, Access, 4th Dimension, FileMaker Pro) are general-purpose database products. They contain all the features you need to build whatever you want. Not only do they manage the data, but they have tools for building the interface (how the computer interacts with you), generating reports, and controlling operation (usually a built-in programming language). FileFlex has none of that. FileFlex just manages data. Figure 6.1 shows how much more of the database "solution" our competitors provide.

So, how *do* we compete? We have different customers. The big market in databases is in full solutions (accounting systems, order processing, banking). But there's also a market (much smaller) that just needs to get at and retrieve data. The buyers in this market are programmers and developers themselves and their desire is to embed data access technology inside their own products and solutions (without becoming beholden to some large monolithic technology provider).

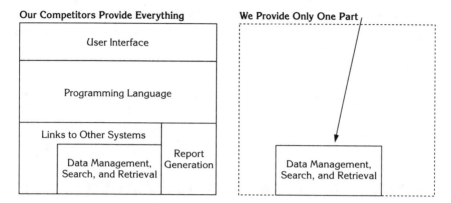

Figure 6.1. Nichemanship by doing less.

The overall database market is in the billions. The total market for embedded databases is way under $50 million. Very few players are in the embedded market, so we're able to make money. Many of the big database systems, while most effective in the hands of programmers, can still be used by almost anyone. But to use FileFlex, you must be a bona fide, card-carrying propeller-head. No non-nerds need apply.

If you haven't guessed already, *nichemanship* (playing to market niches) is an obstacle avoidance strategy that works. When it comes to databases, our competitors were on the high road, so we took the low road.

My decision to forgo Macworld was a use of the avoidance technique for a different purpose. Nonattendance was an obstacle to market growth, yet I weighed the pros and cons and decided that the market growth provided by going wasn't worth the cost (more time and sweat than money) of attendance. So we avoided the obstacle.

Followers of the United Federation of Planets will be familiar with a particularly famous use of obstacle avoidance. Jim Kirk, once and future captain of the starship *Enterprise* is said to have passed the impossible test. In the mythical Starfleet Academy, every cadet was subjected to *Kobiyashi Maru,* the test with no solution. Rather than teaching cadets to win, it taught them that some challenges just couldn't be won. Except that James Tiberius Kirk, contrarian that he was, managed to win.

How did Jim Kirk win the unwinnable? He cheated. He reprogrammed the computer administering the test and changed the rules.

Changing the rules is a perfectly valid form of obstacle avoidance. So, for that matter, is cheating (within appropriate legal and ethical bounds, of course).

Here's a recap of some valid obstacle avoidance techniques:

- Nichemanship
- Changing the rules
- Cheating

Technique 3: Ignore (Problem? What Problem?)

Ignoring obstacles is not my favorite solution. Yet for many business owners, just blowing off the problem can help. If you're going to use the Ignore Technique, make sure you follow these guidelines:

- If you're not overflowing with obstacles, don't use the ignore technique. You'll have enough time to dispatch the problem, which is better than forgetting it's there.
- If you are overflowing with obstacles, ignoring the least troublesome will work for a limited time.
- Always think carefully before zoning out on an obstacle. Make sure it doesn't have the potential to become a threat. Threats that are surprises are particularly nasty.
- Ignored obstacles have an unpleasant propensity to return as projectile obstacles.

Some people use the Ignore Technique as their primary means of obstacle avoidance. This "I know nothing!" method of management can lead to lots of disasters. Over the years, I've ignored my share of obstacles and most have come back to haunt me. In fact, I now do everything possible to make sure I ignore as few obstacles as possible. There were some tough times, though, when I had so many obstacles (most of them projectiles on afterburner!) that I simply couldn't handle them all. Some got ignored out of necessity, freeing me up to deal with the more immediate threats. When most of the ignored obstacles finally exploded, I was less occupied with other threats and was able to dispatch them one by one. Not fun. But it did work.

Technique 4: Shelve

Shelving is the much more healthy variant of the Ignore method. Both recognize that you can't handle every obstacle at once; in fact, attempting to do so is stupid! The difference between shelving an obstacle and ignoring it is the threat factor. An ignored obstacle will almost always explode. A shelved obstacle should never be a time bomb in hiding. You'll almost always need to use your situational awareness and survival skills to deal with an ignored obstacle turned time bomb. You should always have the luxury of deciding when to deal with a shelved obstacle.

When you ignore an obstacle, you take no proactive action. When you shelve an obstacle, you take some specific steps that become the shelving process:

- Determine whether the obstacle *is* a threat, *can become* a threat, or *has any chance* (no matter how remote) of becoming a threat at any time. If so, don't shelve it. Handle it in some other way.

- Understand what roads cannot be traveled while the obstacle is active. Think through all your other plans and tactics to make sure you're not going to need to travel this road anytime soon.

- Understand clearly what conditions would need to exist for you to take the obstacle off the shelf.

- If you are ever lucky enough to have the spare resources available, consider taking the obstacle off the shelf and dispatching it—even if it's not an immediate issue.

- Regularly check the obstacle to determine (a) whether it's still an obstacle or has become a moot issue, and (b) whether there's any near-term possibility for it to become a threat.

Shelved obstacles are *never* ignored. They are regularly inspected and cared for. However, that regular examination will often take far fewer resources than handling the obstacle in another way.

The ubiquitous FileFlex provides us with a good example of shelving an obstacle. Most customers for FileFlex were originally Macintosh developers. A version of FileFlex works with a Mac animation product from Macromedia called Director. Director's great for producing multimedia presentations and CD-ROMs but has a serious lack: no way to store database information. FileFlex solves this problem neatly by giving multimedia developers the ability to embed a database as though it were already part of Director.

So far, so good.

Except that Director now works on both Mac and Windows platforms. Previously landlocked developers stuck on the Macintosh are now able to deliver their work into the much larger Windows market using Director for Windows.

FileFlex originally didn't work under Windows. Director users on the Mac who chose to rely on FileFlex were on their own when they ported to the other environment. And we lost all the additional sales of Windows versions to our Macintosh customers.

Not having a Windows version was an obstacle to FileFlex. Although we do lots of Windows work, porting FileFlex from Macintosh to Windows was not to be an easy undertaking. Even though there were sales to be had to our Director customers, porting FileFlex to Windows was not our top priority. There were still lots of sales to be gained on the Mac side, and substantial development was needed to meet the bulk of our customers' desires. So, I consciously decided to shelve the FileFlex Windows port. This did not mean I forgot its need. To the contrary. I was reminded every day when talking to customers and users. I kept thinking about the issue and kept my mind open to ways to minimize the porting effort. Whenever we had some free time, I reexamined whether the port should be done.

We've since pulled this obstacle off the shelf, actively moved FileFlex to Windows, and are happily taking orders and shipping product. We used the intervening time to become prepared. Such is the advantage of shelving a product after proper preparation.

Technique 5: Transform (Poof! You're a Benefit)

Not all obstacles are what they appear to be. Sometimes, when you're at your most creative, you can turn problems into opportunities.

I've run a business for many years. Some of those years were pretty tough. I made lots of mistakes and put myself, my employees, my contractors, and my family through lots of pain. But I also learned an incredible amount. When I was 20, I didn't believe in the value of experience and seasoning. I sure do now!

At the most fundamental level, the problems and adversity I experienced creating a sustainable enterprise were transformed into the opportunity to gain experience, expertise, and occasionally—wisdom.

You can also turn problems into opportunities.

Imagine you run a consulting company. Obviously, the best way to reach service customers is through referrals. Another highly effective way is through direct mail.

Direct mail can be very costly.

Obstacle alert! Dead ahead!

Here then is the problem: How can you do ongoing direct promotion of your services and still steer clear of the costs of postage, printing, collating, and mailing?

Let's turn it into an opportunity. Find the strength buried in the problem statement. Try this:

Problem: How can you avoid direct mail expense?

Strength: You're doing a targeted mailing to 10,000 people.

Great. Now you've got a strength. What could you do with that strength?

- Sell off the mailing list to another company to offset the expense.
- Instead of mailing a brochure promoting your services, mail a newsletter or "journalzine" (a cross between a journal and a magazine) educating in the area of your services.
- Sell advertising space in said "journalzine."
- Include your own ads or soft-sell articles to promote your services.
- Actually make a profit—not only off the services but also off the journalzine itself.

You've solved the original problem of paying for the mailing. Plus, you've added a whole new profit center playing off your strength. Here's a tangible example of a problem transformed into a serious opportunity.

Technique 6: Divide (and Conquer)

The Divide Technique suggests you take any given obstacle (or set of obstacles) and break it into two parts—one easy to knock off and one harder. Knock off the easy part. While you've still got the other part of the obstacle, it will be (a) smaller than the original obstacle, (b) easier to identify and manage, and (c) much more at the core or root of the problem.

You can use the Divide Technique with particular effectiveness during contract negotiations. Taken as a whole, the process of negotiating a contract can seem overwhelming. But if you actually itemize most of the contract issues, you'll soon realize that a good 75 percent are things that become fair and easy to agree on.

Take a software publishing agreement. These are some of the terms that are almost always of mutual agreement:

- *Acts of God.* If something nasty happens, the contract's put on hold until a suitable recovery time.
- *Maintenance.* If the program breaks, the programmer will fix it (although the time to fix is almost always disputed).
- *The Product Being Licensed.* Although the feature set is sometimes in dispute and versions for alternate platforms like Windows or UNIX are almost always disputed.
- *Definitions.* Meanings of words like "program," "source code," "user."
- *Payment.* Yep! There's almost always no dispute about *when* the payments are made. Only about *how much.*
- *Auditing Rights.* When and where accounting records can be checked by an impartial outsider.
- *Termination.* Nearly everyone can agree that the contract can be terminated if one of the parties reneges in performance.
- *Term.* It's pretty easy to decide whether you're doing it for one year, three years, or automatic renewal.
- *Marketing Freedom.* Software authors are often seeking marketing help. So they rarely put up a fuss when publishers say they need to have freedom to design ads and packaging.
- *Confidentiality.* Who's going to argue about blabbing to outsiders?

- *Warranties.* The author's got to guarantee that what the publisher is buying is the author's to sell. Not an issue of dispute.
- *General Lawyerly Boilerplate.* Stuff like the rest of the contract stays valid if one clause isn't, that the contract can't be assigned, and arbitration rules.

Our contracts are usually about 20 pages. I paged through one of them as I wrote the preceding list. The dozen items listed here account for almost 17 of the 20 pages in the contract. Usually, we can barrel through these 12 items (85%) in less than an hour.

By dividing the easy from the hard, we're left with the important 15 percent that will require serious negotiation. Another important benefit is that by dividing the negotiation into the easy and hard, we're no longer disagreeing on everything. Instead, both parties have discovered that the other is pretty easy to get along with. After all, we agree on 85 percent of the deal straight off!

Technique 7: Chip Away

Another technique you should use every day is the secret weapon I call "chipping away." It works thusly: Take a big problem. Find a tiny part you can chop off and solve. Chop it off. Big problem just got a wee bit smaller. Repeat for the rest of your life. Eventually, the big problem becomes manageable.

This tactic works well with:

- *Creditors.* Paying a bit at a time will eventually reduce your liability.
- *Book Writing.* Writing a chapter at a time, regularly, will eventually get the book written.
- *Business Reinvention.* Find one problem and solve it. Then solve another. Don't try to solve the whole thing.

While you shouldn't ignore the fundamentals of your product, you can still improve your customer service—one chip at a time.

It used to take us about two weeks to ship an order. We would get the order, sit on it for a while, then enter it into the computer. Then we'd build the product. Then, eventually, we'd ship it to the customer. God help the customer who needed software the next day! How could we possibly ship the product if it wasn't in the computer, wasn't built, a label wasn't printed, and the customer wasn't charged!

We were losing business in a big way. Not only could customers go to our competitors, they could go to our distribution channels. So a sale that we might have gotten at full value, we would (at best) lose to a reseller at 50 percent to 60 percent off and payment 30 to 60 days out.

Enough was enough! Finally, I said I didn't care. Just ship the products. The results were shocking.

The next time we got a rush order, Denise Amrich, my newly promoted Director of Operations, came into my office. She wanted to "borrow" my manual. What I only discovered later was that she'd taken the following actions:

1. Told the customer we were out of finished stock.
2. Asked the customer if he'd mind terribly if we sent him a copy that wasn't shrink-wrapped.
3. Stolen (outright swiped!) the manual off my desk.
4. Found a spare disk and duplicated it.
5. Found a blank label, fed it into a typewriter, and hand-typed a label.
6. Asked the customer for *his* Federal Express ID so she wouldn't have to call in a pickup and wait.
7. Packed the whole thing into a reused padded envelope and drove it to the drop box.
8. A day or so later, checked and charged his credit card (she correctly decided that a bad credit card was not nearly as bad as a frustrated customer).

Denise didn't solve the entire order entry problem in one shot. She chipped away at the problem by simply *doing it!* and getting one product to one customer at a time. Granted, all the extra effort made it a lot more expensive to ship to this guy, but he later went on to order more stuff.

Eventually, we subjected each stage of our order processing and production process to chipping and we're now down to about two to three days from order in to product out (including the time it takes to manufacture the product from scratch). We also maintain a (very small) finished goods inventory so we can handle emergency orders.

Note: We've chipped away at this again. Our full products are available 24-hours a day on our Internet Web site. A phone call and a credit card gets the customer a password and immediately thereafter, the software.

Technique 8: Confront

Sometimes you'll come face to face with an obstacle and you'll try everything. You'll discover you can't discard it. You'll try to apply nichemanship, changing the rules, and even cheating—all to no avail. Ignoring it wouldn't be safe. Shelving it isn't feasible because it might explode. There's no apparent opportunity the obstacle can be transformed into. And if you were to try, it wouldn't respond to the divide and conquer or chipping away techniques. Face it. You're staring into the deep dark black eyes of a genuine obstacle. You're just going to have to deal with it—somehow.

The first thing you should do is get creative and see if you can invent a new technique that fits the situation. If you do, use it. If it works, write a letter and tell me all about it.

If all else fails, you'll need to prepare for war. Sun Tzu, the ancient Chinese general, describes offensive strategy this way:

> . . . It is of supreme importance in war to attack the enemy's strategy. "He who excels at resolving difficulties does so before they arise. He who excels in conquering his enemies triumphs before threats materialize";
>
> Next best is to disrupt his alliances. "Look into the matter of his alliances and cause them to be severed and dissolved";
>
> The next best is to attack his army. "If you cannot nip his plans in the bud, or disrupt his alliances when they are about to be consummated, sharpen your weapons to gain the victory";
>
> The worst policy is to attack cities. Attack cities only when there is no alternative.

We've seen the "destroy alliances" strategy in action in the health care debates. Bill and Hillary have proposed sweeping health care reforms. Bob Dole and his army of Republicans eventually made the Clintons' plan go away by—in apparent concert with health insurance providers—attacking the Clintons' alliances.

Larger constituents have even "persuaded" some Democratic members of Congress that such features as employer mandate would be so expensive that if enacted, enormous damage would be done to their businesses. As retaliation, they'd have to place their support with other candidates.

The Republicans eventually eroded support sufficiently to cause the President to lose the war before it even reached a vote (which failed).

Sun Tzu and I agree: Go on the offensive only as a last resort.

As you prepare to do battle with the obstacle of your choice, remember this further piece of 2,400 year old wisdom:

> *If weaker, be capable of withdrawing;*
> *And if all respects unequal, be capable of eluding him.*

Technique 9: Live with It (Accept)

I'll end this exploration of obstacle elimination techniques with the technique of last resort: Just live with it. Some obstacles just aren't going to go away. You won't be able to finesse them away, you won't be able to attack them away, you won't even be able to run away. They're there.

How you deal with impenetrable obstacles is a real window into your character. Do you continue to beat your head against the figurative (or literal) brick wall? Or do you learn to accept defeat with grace and find other battles to fight?

I've seen some (most) small companies start with too little cash. Some conquer the obstacle by raising funds. Others find ways to work within their means. But I've seen a few unfortunates go down in flames because either (a) they acted as if they had resources they didn't and depleted cash with incredible speed, or (b) they spent so much time trying to raise money that they never did get started.

For these entrepreneurs, it's a matter of priority. If you really, truly, *viscerally* want to start a company, you'll change your business plan to fit your reality. If, instead, you want to live your business plan, you may spend months or years in a futile effort to mold the world to your needs. Only masochists need apply.

To accept reality and not live in a fantasy world is essential for a successful enterprise. Understanding both your strengths and your limitations is critical. There is no shame in not being able to do everything—and this applies not only to your business, but to you as well!

Tom Peters has a strangely wonderful perspective: "The predictable price is not just a few failures, but also occasional fiascoes, a wee price to pay compared to the payoff: almost unparalleled craziness and zest from a monster institution."

I've committed some real whoppers in my business (OK, and personal) life. I hope you will, too.

RECAP

Obstacles are a big part of business life. The more ways you have to diffuse them before they become serious threats, the more effective you'll be at less cost. Here are some things you should remember:

- All businesses have strengths, all have weaknesses, lacks, problems, and obstacles.
- Worry and manage obstacles that are valid *now*. Don't obsess on future problems that may never materialize.
- If it's not in your way, it's not an obstacle.
- Sometimes it's not an obstacle, it's an excuse.
- Strength makes it hard to be a victim.
- Some of us avoid our strengths because being a victim is more *comfortable*.
- Prioritize problems and obstacles. Immediately handle those that are threats.
- Make sure an obstacle is real and current.

- Map your obstacle course. Divide obstacles into projectiles (threats), those you confront, and those you accept.
- Techniques for eliminating obstacles: Discard, Avoid, Ignore, Shelve, Transform, Divide, Chip Away, Confront, and Accept.

In Part III, you'll learn how to transform your strengths, weaknesses, lacks, and obstacles into a wide variety of new and exciting opportunities.

PART III

Strategies and Tactics for Change

CHAPTER 7

Becoming a Strength-Driven Company

If a man has a talent and cannot use it, he has failed. If he has a talent and uses only half of it, he has partly failed. If he has a talent and learns somehow to use the whole of it, he has gloriously succeeded, and won a satisfaction and a triumph few men ever know.

—Thomas Wolfe, 1939

Let me tell you something: No matter how strong your company is, no matter how many obstacles you're capable of overcoming, nothing is going to happen unless *you make it happen.*

So let's start making things happen.

Every enterprise—whether it consists of a guy sitting at home trying to sell insurance on the phone, a large corporation, or even a government agency—has two things in common:

1. The need to sell something.
2. The need for someone to buy it.

Our home-based salesperson selling insurance needs people who need insurance. IBM sells computers. They need customers who buy. Even our government needs to sell and for people to buy: Politicians

97

need votes and campaign contributions, agencies need funding and the semblance of results to keep said funding flowing, and even each and every police officer needs citizens who need protection and criminals who need incarceration.

Need.

Need drives enterprise.

So if you *need* profits for your profitable business, you *need* to find a consistent, repeatable source of revenue. You *need* people who *need* you.

WHO NEEDS YOUR STRENGTHS?

If the very essence of your ability to profit is to find people who need what you've got, then you've got to have something people want.

What do you have that people want? What are your most valuable assets (from their perspective)? The answer is your strengths.

For your enterprise to profit, you must do these four things as long as your business shall live:

1. Find people who need your strengths.
2. Find ways to turn your strengths into things people need.
3. Find people who need your transformed strengths.
4. Grow new strengths that give you the ability to meet people's needs and then find those new people.

I don't care if you run General Motors, if you're the owner of a pet shop, if you're the head of the FDA, or if you're the President of these glorious United States. If you don't have something people need and if you can't find the people who need it, well, then, *who needs it?*

If your strength is an unnatural ability to build a better mousetrap, then you need to find people who are desperate to catch mice. And you either need a mousetrap that's better than everyone else's (in lots of subjective ways including, but not limited to mouse-catching ability and/or price) and/or you need to find a better way to reach those mouse-killing desperadoes who need to terminate some elusive rodents.

FROM PROSPECT BASE TO PROFIT

If you find a target prospect base that needs what you've got *and* if you can figure out how to reach them, you will generate sales. If you can reach them and produce what you've got in such a way that it costs less than your prospects are willing to pay, then you've got profit.

In *Midnight Engineering* (a great publication that every active change artist should subscribe to), William E. Gates presents a wonderful way to look at making all this work. He asks the question: "If I want to build 10,000 model airplanes a month, I can't and don't *want* to put all the wings on—it's tedious, boring, and I have better uses for my time." He lists some possible solutions when faced with this problem:

- Hire some workers to assemble the wings to the body of the plane for you.
- Contract out the wing attachments to the body.
- Conceive a fast and fun way to do 500 wing attachments per business day yourself and take some joy from that productivity gain and the savings you pocket by not paying anybody.
- Redesign the subassembly molds so that the wings are integrated with the body of the plane during the molding of the parts.

There are lots of creative ways to solve problems. Gates's goal, though, is not to teach you how to make better model airplanes, but rather to help you see that a similar goal (building airplanes) can have different approaches. He calls the last approach "inherent assembly" and asks the question (paraphrased) "Why can't everything be designed to have 'inherent assembly'?"

It's a good question. If you keep your (and mine, and every other enterprise manager's) mission statement in mind, you'll see that looking for different approaches is necessary. Everyone must find the most creative, most effective, and often not the most traditional path to solution.

Oh, you want to know the universal mission statement that applies to all enterprises? Here it is:

> **Universal Enterprise Mission Statement**
>
> *We will find needs that we are able to fill and we shall find customers with those needs. We will fill those needs and we will do so in a such a creative and effective manner as to provide quality service to our customers at good value to them and at a profit to us.*

Whether you're the resourceful publisher of *Midnight Engineering* or a government bureaucrat or a Fortune 500 chairman, if your enterprise follows this mission statement, you'll win.

RECONCILING YOUR MISSION WITH YOUR MARKET

To say that your mission is "Making items that others want, and to do so at a cost lower than potential customers are willing to pay" would be a drastic oversimplification of the realities of business. Even so, some important ideas are contained therein. As we discussed earlier, there are three primordial elements to the formula:

1. Making things (products, services, whatever . . .).
2. Making things people want.
3. Making things at a cost that's lower than people wish to pay.

Q: What can you make?
A: Whatever you're good at making.

At first blush, these statements seem to be oversimplifications. But they're not. In fact, a mistake in choosing what you provide to customers can kill your company. To wit: The conventional wisdom has always been "listen to your customers." On the surface it makes sense. If your customers tell you they want a left-handed wind-shifter, it stands to reason that if you build wind-shifters containing the left-hand control option, customers will seek you out, cash and credit cards in hand.

But because customers aren't product experts, their requests aren't fully considered specifications; numerous implied features are never spoken aloud or written in request letters.

For example, a customer may request just such a wind-shifter. Here's the complete specification as provided by the customer:

- Make it shift wind.
- Make it left-handed.

But, as is *always the case,* the customer did not provide a complete specification. Here are many (not all, definitely not all) the attributes the customer *implied* (which you can think of only as questions):

- How much wind, going at what speed?
- Controlled or operated by a left hand? Moving the wind to the left? Or accepting wind coming in from the left?
- How large a hand? How strong?
- Does your company, in fact, have the expertise in-house to understand wind dynamics?
- Does your company have the manufacturing ability to build wind-shifters.
- How many people need these things? How big is the market?
- What kind of maintenance do wind-shifters require?
- How much are customers willing to pay?
- And on, and on, and on . . .

The problem with many companies is that they listen to the customer without listening to themselves. This isn't a customer- or market-driven world, contrary to all you've been told. It's a world driven by customer demand *and* your ability to meet that demand. So if you constantly let your customers lead you around by your nose, you're going to lose.

MAKING WHAT YOU'RE GOOD AT

Think instead of leveraging off your strengths. You know what you can do well. If you know you can design highly reliable auto parts but aren't a sales firm, focus on building great parts and find another company that's a great sales firm. Team up. They need great parts as much as you need sales representation.

There are numerous customer-*oriented* (not customer-*driven*) benefits to leveraging off your strengths:

- In the areas you're strongest, you'll know more about the features, functions, competition, needs, weaknesses, and opportunities than your customers possibly can.
- Leveraging off strengths-related knowledge provides substantial added benefits to the customer.
- In areas where you're strong, you can often produce above-average products and services for reasonable prices.
- In areas where you lack expertise, you often wind up producing below-average products and services. Worse, your cost to produce something you're not expert at may be substantially above average. At best, you can only charge an average price. Both you and your customers lose.
- In areas where you're strong, you'll often have most of the systems, facilities, and staff in place to produce your products.
- In areas where you're weak, you may have to invest heavily just to reach parity with those competitors who are already strong in this area.
- In areas where you're strong, you've most likely climbed over the barrier of entry (whether it be in skills, distribution, capitalization, or other areas).
- In areas where you're weak, you've got a huge barrier of entry, again sapping your ability to provide great products.
- Fundamentally, if you provide customers with products and services by leveraging your strengths, they'll often get *great* products and services. Otherwise, they'll wind up with products and services of questionable value—and you'll be exhausted, unprofitable, and cranky.

The Value Limit

It's the rare customer who again and again will spend more on items than the value limit perceived by that customer. When I go out and buy a desk lamp for my office, I expect to spend somewhere between $25 and $200. For a fake brass, rolled tin lamp, I'd probably only be willing to spend up to about 30 bucks. For a solid brass antique that perfectly fits my decor, I might actually be willing to go the full $200. Let's say I'm walking through Home Depot and I see a great little fake brass lamp for $35. I might buy it.

Some time after I hand over my credit card to the store, the store sends out a check for somewhere around $17 to the manufacturer (let's leave the potential of a middleman distributor out of this example). Out of this sum has to come cost of sales, marketing, material cost, overhead, and the like. If the manufacturer's lucky, has sold a sufficient number of lamps, and hasn't gotten too many returns, a profit of a dollar or two may be left over. Pretty tight margin, but typical.

Just to break even, the manufacturer has to sell enough units and have a fully successful manufacturing process. This, as I'm sure you know, is not easy. Yet, those companies who are experts at lamp manufacturing have been making a profit for years. And every year they turn out new lamps, design in better features, and often cost-reduce in the process. You can't do that if you don't know your business.

You can't do that if *you* don't know *your business!*

INTRODUCING THE MICROBUSINESS

Reinventing from the inside out means that rather than being a product-, market-, sales-, or engineering-driven company, your company becomes "strength-driven." Because these strengths may exist in different parts of your business, it's very hard to present customers a view of "what you do" based on your list of strengths. This becomes most evident if different strengths have a perceived value to widely different groups of customers. From the point of view of those within your company, you define "what you do" based on your strengths. But from the external point of view of your customers, you may define "what you do" (your positioning) totally differently from customer group to customer group.

In some cases, the positioning based on being strength driven is so different from customer group to customer group that the customers of one group wouldn't recognize your company based on the products or services you provide to another group. In these instances, the "microbusiness" model may be very valuable. A *microbusiness* is defined as a group of business lines where all leverage a common set of capabilities and resources (strengths) but have diverging target prospects. These "companies within a company" are designed so that when the market changes or a strategic opportunity becomes visible, flexible reinvention of the company from the inside out can occur instantly.

DIFFERENCES BY CUSTOMER CLASS

You may find that your customer base determines how you position a product or a service. There's an interesting paradox here: an ideally named product or service for one customer base may be wrongly named for another.

Corollary: The more targeted and well defined the name for one customer class, the more inappropriate for another.

Hyperpress and MediaLab are a case in point.

Case Study: Hyperpress and MediaLab

When I originally founded Hyperpress to provide development tools for HyperCard developers (propeller-head hobbyist programmers), its name was perfect. Here was a company that published products for HyperCard. From HyperCard, we took "hyper" and from publishing, we added "press." Hence, "Hyperpress."

Over time, we discovered that in addition to providing tools for building programs, we also, mostly, provided prebuilt modules that could be used by programmers to enhance their programs. We had modules that solved complex expert systems problems, added telecommunications, added user interface features, added live video, and more. We became absolutely standout expert in creating modules that were designed to plug into and extend programming languages like HyperCard.

A few years into the company, we were approached by a group of engineers from Singapore. They had developed an imaging plug-in for a high-end relational database called 4th Dimension. In many ways, 4th Dimension is like HyperCard: It allows developers to build powerful applications in a reasonably short period of time; it has its own programming language; it manages data; it provides a way for the programmer to specify the user interface; and it allows itself to be extended via plug-in modules.

It seemed to us that an imaging plug-in for 4th Dimension would be an ideal product line extension. After all, we were plug-in experts.

The product eventually became PictureLink. We introduced the product to the 4th Dimension user community. While the product itself was reasonably well accepted, we found it virtually impossible to get through most doors. Calls were not returned (even from ACIUS, the manufacturers of 4th Dimension). We were reviled at the trade show we attended to launch the product. It was, overall, a shocking experience.

But we didn't have a bad product. Instead, our company name, so well positioned for sales to HyperCard developers, was an affront to 4th Dimension developers. You see, at that time, 4th Dimension developers considered their language a "serious professional tool" and HyperCard a "toy." Part of this was due to marketing efforts by ACIUS; they were concerned that Apple's HyperCard would take away some of their market share. But more of the animosity was the perception that HyperCard was used by hobbyists and entry-level programmers, whereas 4th Dimension was used by the corporate set.

Note: Five or so years later, the profiles of the HyperCard developer and 4th Dimension developer are surprisingly similar. Most are developers in corporations or consultants doing development on contract. Even so, HyperCard still carries the stigma of being a toy among 4th Dimension community.

There was no doubt about it. If Hyperpress continued to try to market PictureLink, it would fail. The issue was religious. The user community *would not buy* from a company with that name. Period.

So, in concert with the folks from Singapore, we started "Media-Lab." Housed within the same offices as Hyperpress, employing the same workers, using the same production facilities, MediaLab was (at least according to the 4th Dimension community) an entirely new company with no ties to Hyperpress.

When MediaLab relaunched PictureLink, it sold well. It was accepted immediately into the 4th Dimension user community—and was supported by ACIUS (where it had been shunned before). In fact, PictureLink wound up capturing a full 20 percent of the 4th Dimension market—a total success (until two years later when the authors vanished back to Singapore as described earlier). What a difference a name makes!

When you manage your company based on its strengths, you may find that your products appeal to customer communities that *perceive* themselves as unique—even though the actual profiles of the customer communities are very similar. The HyperCard community and the 4th Dimension community share many characteristics:

- Both develop software and hence are programmers.
- Both develop software for Macintosh computers.
- Both are concerned with managing *and* presenting data.
- Both develop for internal or external customers.
- Both develop products requiring debugging, revisions, and maintenance.
- Independent contractors and salaried programmers in both communities have similar hourly pay rates.
- Both support an aftermarket of development tools, training, and plug-ins that extend the base product's functionality.

Differentiating by customer class works because:

- You use similar strengths, resources, and facilities across all customer classes.
- The actual profiles of the customer classes are highly similar.
- Even so, the perception of difference by those within the customer classes is enormous.

If you look around you carefully, you can find many instances of differentiation by customer class. One of the most common class difference is product price. Two examples (well, really 11):

1. *Acura and Honda, Lexus and Toyota, Infiniti and Nissan, Ford and Lincoln and Mercury.* These are similar cars, with similar features, that are positioned for customers based on whether they're buying luxury or performance or economy.

2. *IBM and Ambra.* Ambra is part of IBM. Yet IBM has launched a low-cost product line ostensibly from another company. Why? To protect the high-value image of IBM. Is this wise? In IBM's case, it would probably be better to market it all under the IBM name since IBM is fighting the battle of value all the way through its product line.

DIFFERENCES BY FUNCTIONAL AREA

Customer perceptions are inherent in successful sales. In the same way that it would be difficult for my mom to accept buying her phone service from a railroad (as she would have when Sprint was just coming into being), it's difficult for many customers to accept that they're buying what they perceive as widely different products or services from one company. This is particularly the case when the disciplines used to provide the products or services seem diametrically opposed to one another, as they are with engineering and advertising.

Case Study: Component Software and Product Power

In 1992, I moved my company from California to New Jersey. I did this primarily for personal reasons: to be closer to my family. But along with the substantial personal relocation, the company was to undergo dramatic change.

I bought out the other participants in both Hyperpress and Media-Lab, laid off all the employees from Foster City, California, and moved East. While the layoffs meant that I lost the clerical support, sales, and manufacturing staff, I didn't lose either product distribution or engineering. That's because all the engineering was external to the company, as was distribution. And by the magic of direct mail and an unchanging 800-number, the combined customer base of Hyperpress and MediaLab were easily retargeted to New Jersey and similar staffing rehired here (although with many less bodies).

Note: It came as a major shock that we were *more profitable* and more productive with less than a fourth the headcount of the California operation. To get things up and running quickly here in New Jersey, we subcontracted many aspects of our work. Lo and behold, we were getting much more done with less.

I used the move as an opportunity to reposition the companies as well. HyperCard's influence was in decline, my HyperCard-based products were starting to work within other development systems, and we were attracting clients for custom development projects (usually based on doing work around our own technology).

One of our most significant strengths is our understanding and mastery of embedded or "plug-in" technology. Since the late 1980s, more and more programming systems have been supporting plug-ins, many of them of the same format. Further, many of the delivered systems (databases, multimedia productions, corporate information systems, etc.) were developed by combining lightly modified off-the-shelf applications. It seemed clear (and it still does) that the future of economical software development was with reusable components.

And so, without much ado (but with much paperwork) Hyperpress and MediaLab's products were acquired by the newly formed Component Software Corporation.

Component Software is unquestionably a technology firm. We design and develop reusable components (plug-in systems like the FileFlex relational database); we prepublish products that other companies take to market; we integrate off-the-shelf components and applications; we develop multimedia productions, and we support numerous clients with development services.

On the surface, we're unquestionably propeller-heads (engineering types).

Ah, but we have other, significant strengths. For example, we market our products through often-complex redistribution deals. We also do an amazing amount of direct marketing. In fact, our direct marketing and advertising efforts are so substantial, it's as if we have our own in-house ad agency.

Segue to the Product Power Group . . .

To provide the marketing required by Component's products and services, we had built up a fully equipped product-marketing, communications, and business strategy operation within Component Software. Thankfully, we already had the advertising and marketing strengths in strong measure; we also already had many of the necessary resources. Most ad agencies and marketing firms have been moving to desktop publishing and buying computers. We go through computers and software like cookies. One of the big buzzes in marketing circles is "database marketing," which uses high-powered specialized databases to reach target audiences. Not only do we do database marketing, we wrote the database technology that thousands of others use!

Over time, a number of other companies had approached Component about marketing. They'd seen our marketing (particularly the direct mail) work and wanted a referral to our ad agency. When we told them our ad agency was ourselves, most were initially surprised. A few of the more adventurous asked if we'd be willing to produce marketing materials for them.

Our hard-earned experience with Hyperpress and the 4th Dimension community helped us decide to create a second business name. It turned out that we were using the very same skills and computer equipment to do outside marketing as we used to do our own. And the outside marketing was proving as profitable as our custom development business. We wanted to grow that profit center.

I knew that as "Component Software" or even "Component Client Services" we might be able to attract some brave software developers to our marketing services, but there'd be no way we'd convince architects, phone companies, sales training organizations, and other companies (each are now Product Power clients!) outside the computer industry.

This side business turned real when we opened The Product Power Group, dedicated to help businesses reinvent themselves from the inside out; identify, acquire, and introduce winning products; and make tough decisions to guarantee long term survival and growth.

As was the case with customer-base differentiation, there are often substantial cross-overs in functional areas. While the prospect community looking for one service (e.g., direct marketing) would often not look for another (e.g., software development), there are many aspects in common:

- Use of database technology.
- Use of desktop publishing to create marketing materials.
- Available computing resources for both.
- Graphics skills to create attractive screen designs, marketing brochures, and direct-mail pieces.
- Copywriting skills to explain it all.
- Order processing, purchasing, phone answering, and other "overhead" internal functions.
- Networking and telecommunications.

Although we've had a presence on CompuServe, America Online, and Internet (the "Net") since the earliest days, we've recently begun doing formal marketing on the networks. We estimate that a full 80 percent of 1996 revenue will be directly attributable to customers found through the network. And we've launched a Web site, where customers all across the world 24 hours a day can view technical information and product literature instantly.

"In 5 to 10 years, the entire marketing process will be digital," says Martin Nisenholtz, director of content strategy at Ameritech. "The front end of the relationship with the customer is media. It's very important that ad agencies understand the application of technology at the front end." The potential prize is "the most affluent consumer group in the world," according to the CEO of ProductView Interactive: 25-to-45-year-old, college-educated, upwardly mobile users of online services (*Information Week*, 10/3/94, p. 24).

Here's a strong case where strengths can be convergent. Historically, advertising and technology have been separate beasts. But over time, those two markets are converging, and we'll be able to apply strengths at both ends of the problem.

The potential for Internet-based marketing is beyond belief. On August 16, 1994 at 3:42 P.M., we released a new product to our in-house manufacturing. At 3:48 P.M., we sent an e-mail message to those customers and prospects for whom we had e-mail addresses, telling them of the availability of the product. At 3:52 P.M. (that's right, four minutes later) we received the first e-mail messages back from customers containing credit card orders. At 4:06 P.M., we delivered those first orders to the post office. We went from prepro-duction through mass marketing to first orders to actual customer shipments in 24 minutes! We're now also able to bypass the ship-ping process and deliver instantly across the Net.

If you look around you carefully, you can find many instances of differentiation by functional area. Many companies that have appar-ently vastly different services, offer them under substantially differ-ent customer names:

- Pizza Hut and Taco Bell are both part of PepsiCo.
- Minute Maid is part of Coca Cola.
- GE (for the moment) also has NBC.

Of course, these are all huge corporations and these alternate-position subcompanies are major enterprises in their own right. So be it. That doesn't mean your smaller business can't create new businesses within your own business, each tasked with fitting an ideally targeted market, customer base, and functional area. As large corporations have subsidiaries and divisions, smaller com-panies can have their own stable of microbusinesses.

CHAPTER 8

Reinvention Planning

*In preparing for battle I have always found that
plans are useless, but planning is indispensable.*
                                    —Dwight D. Eisenhower

By definition, reinvention involves trial and error. Even so, planning plays an integral role in your reinvention efforts since you always need some sort of road map to guide your efforts. The difference is, reinvention planning can't take the form of grandiose long-term plans. Rather, reinvention requires planning with the understanding that uncertainty, change, and unknown factors will impact your business decisions. Further, reinvention planning dictates you prepare for multiple contingencies (including the contingency of not having a contingency plan) and that you plan to plan again.

THE REINVENTION ROAD MAP

Change can be an amorphous thing. Hard to pin down. Of indeterminate form. One day you're in the railroad business. Sometime later, you're a phone company. When did the change happen? At what point on the time line of transformation, did you leave the clickety-clack of wheel on rail for the almost-silent pin drop of the telephone line?

With hindsight, everything's easy. Even so, it's often difficult to trace the root point where a change occurred. Frankly, it's also often unnecessary. If a change has happened, it's only of academic historical interest when and why. The important time is not after the change has occurred, after a transformation has mutated a once-familiar enterprise into something new (and hopefully) exciting. The important time is before the change has occurred.

Of course, you can embark on a voyage of change by simply getting started. And you can bounce around like a ball in a pinball arcade hoping you will rack up points and not fall into the black hole at the bottom of the table. While I'm all for getting started and *doing something,* it's often (nearly always) wise to plan ahead, to map out your general course of action.

ANALYSIS PARALYSIS

Planning is a wonderful thing. It helps you think through all the issues in advance. It gives you an opportunity to work with your coworkers, employees, investors, and family and to make use of all their ideas, resources, and perspectives. And it sometimes, when you're very lucky, helps you discover hidden traps that you might otherwise have stumbled into had you not had the foresight to plan ahead.

But planning itself can be a trap of nearly fatal effect. Many people (and companies) spend so much time planning, so much time getting ready, so much time finding things that have to be done, have to be discovered, decided—that they never actually do anything. One company I know of had a wonderful market window for a new product. But they spent so much time planning and budgeting that by the time they decided to produce the product, it was already too late. There were competitors, and their new, wonderful, precisely planned feature set and product introduction were too little, too late. The amount they had spent on planning, considering, staff meetings, and worrying was more than they would have spent to launch the product and see how the market would respond. A major opportunity lost to analysis paralysis.

When you decide to undertake reinvention, you're going to have to be very, very honest with yourself. The planning process is the place to start. And making sure you're not planning yourself or your company into oblivion is a great place to begin honest self-assessment.

The key is to not get paralyzed in the planning process. Try to avoid making everything dependent on one or two deductions. Try to move planning from that-which-must-come-before-all to that-which-occurs-at-all-times.

Here are some other ideas on how to combat analysis paralysis:

- *Break Plans into Phases.* Rather doing one sweeping plan, do lots of little plans. Determine a general direction, then sit down and plan in tiny chunks. Then, when you've finished a small chunk-plan, begin executing it. There's no reason you can't execute one miniplan while planning the next phase.

- *Set a Time Limit.* If you're an obsessive planner, you may find that the only way to get beyond the planning stage is to set a deadline. For example, give yourself one full month to do planning. Then, when that month is over, regardless of how finished the plan is, get started on making things happen. You can always refine your plan as you go.

- *Set Regular Planning Sessions.* If you go through planning withdrawal, allow yourself small, regimented time periods for planning. A good way to do this is to schedule a day off-site for senior managers once every quarter. Communication among the parties will improve, you'll all get a change of scenery, those of you who obsess on planning can get a regular fix, and short, regular planning sessions allow you to change, duck, bob, and weave according to market conditions.

- *Hire a Consultant.* Not that consultants can do the job any better than you can. But if you're spending all your time planning, you're not operating your business. Give the job to a consultant, let him or her plan until you run out of patience paying for planning services, and you go on with the task of operating your company. Whether you plan or a consultant plans, you're paying for it either way. But if you're writing a real, honest-to-goodness-cash-money check to a consultant, you're more likely to realize how much it costs.

- *Recognize Unknowns.* Many plans would be completed much earlier except the planners wanted to make sure every issue was examined and every possibility accounted for. If my years of experience in this game have taught me anything, it's that plans are never valid for more than a few minutes after they're completed. So instead of trying to resolve all unknowns in the plan, just make a list of what you don't know, consider that list to be a part of the plan, and move on.

I rarely, if ever, consider finished plans themselves worth all that much. But the *process* of planning is invaluable. That's where you're forced to look at issues from a variety of angles, think through various possibilities, discuss options, and get the point of view of others on your team. The process of planning is essential. The pretty plan, printed and bound so nicely, often isn't worth the paper it's printed on.

TOXIC-CHANGE SYNDROME

At some point, you and your team will come to the conclusion that, quote, "Something's gotta change around here." The very moment you reach such a conclusion is the moment that reinvention begins. I call this the *launch point*. Sometime after the launch point, the first actual change will occur. I call this the *ground zero of change*. Usually, there's some period of time (as little as a few days, as much as a few months) between the launch point and ground zero. During this time, all hell can break loose.

Employees have amazingly powerful noses. While they never notice the odor of the old sandwich rotting in the back of a file drawer, their sniffers are incredibly powerful when it comes to figuring out that something's up. Sometime, very shortly after the launch point, your employees are going to know that change is in the air. In fact, they may know it before you've fully internalized it yourself. I've never quite figured out just what magic allows them to have this incredible degree of perception (other than humanity's powerful self-preservation instinct), but it happens.

Fact is, as soon as you've passed the change launch point, the rumors are going to start flying. The degree of office politics will rise by a significant percentage. Your employees' fear for their jobs will impact productivity. Communication between individuals and departments will become strained. Profitability will begin to decline. All of this, and you haven't even decided on your first act of change. You may still be weeks or months away from actually doing something, weeks before ground zero.

This is *Toxic-Change Syndrome* and it can severely damage your company. It is during this period that your employees go from being a happy (such as it is) workforce to a pack of wolves cornered and running scared. It's not pretty.

The first thing you need to know about Toxic-Change Syndrome is that no matter what you do, some employees will be scared. The second thing you need to know is that you can do a whole lot to help employees deal with change—and to get them to help you deal with change at the same time.

NEGOTIATING BUY-IN

The most effective antidote to Toxic-Change Syndrome is honesty—plain, simple, honesty: "Yes, we're considering changes. No, we haven't decided what they are. Yes, we'll keep you informed. Yes, we'll listen to your ideas."

"Yes, We're Considering Changes"

It's critically important to let your employees know that what they're sensing is real, that change is in the air. By simply acknowledging their initial suspicions, you'll take a big step toward helping them believe there won't be surprises. By admitting that some changes are coming, you're also making yourself credible—you're not hiding something. This will definitely help reduce the "us" versus "them" feelings among the rank and file.

Another benefit to admitting the intent to change is to provide some encouragement. If your company is having problems, employees are often much more aware of them than you are. By acknowledging the intent to change, you help give hope where before there was only worry.

"No, We Haven't Decided What They Are"

By admitting you haven't completely planned out the changes up front (remember, we're between the launch point and ground zero), you have the option of involving your staff in the decision-making process. Also, by telling them that you haven't yet figured out what's going to change, you can sideline the inevitable feelings that you're hiding something. Further, you're giving employees breathing room—if you haven't decided on the changes, they're not going to happen tomorrow morning.

"Yes, We'll Keep You Informed"

Again, you're making an up front commitment to be honest with your team. You're telling them that you'll keep them in the loop. You're giving them (as best as you can) your word that you'll try to avoid surprises. This sort of thing can go a long way to combating the inevitable fears that are churned up out of change.

"Yes, We'll Listen to Your Ideas"

You cannot overestimate the importance of this statement. First, listening to your employees is valuable—they know stuff you don't. That's why you pay them. Listen to their ideas, integrate those new ideas with your own, discuss the questions and issues openly, and together generate a buy-in. As management, the final decision is yours, but by involving employees, you get much better buy-in. By listening to opinions, there's a much better chance that you won't go off and do something—from the perspective of the employee— that's downright stupid or uncaring. Overall, listen to and talk with your team.

GOAL SETTING

Mapping out all the changes that will be necessary to complete the reinvention process is often impossible, especially since reinvention needs to go on every day, for the rest of the life of your company. But, it is possible to outline goals and guidelines governing reinvention.

You should be careful about how you set out goals and guidelines. Some goals are highly subjective, almost ethereal, and certainly long term. Others are tangible, tomorrow-oriented goals. During its start-up phase, my primary business goal was simple: consistent solvency (being able to pay the bills, the payroll, and do business as usual). It was a simple goal, but it allowed us to understand that our mission, initially, was to get the company running and keep it running. There were no fancier goals for many years.

Note: Try not to do what one founder did: His stated corporate goal was to make himself rich. Obviously, his employees, who were not included in that goal, didn't buy in. He had zero employee loyalty beyond the regular paycheck.

Example: The MediaLab Manifesto

In 1990, we'd pretty much completed integration of the MediaLab-brand imaging products into our product line. The partial collapse of the HyperCard market, combined with the potential of the imaging products had us positioned in the eye of a storm of change. To make sure our employees understood *exactly* where we were coming from, I wrote *The MediaLab Manifesto.* This document outlined both goals and measurement criteria for the next year's reinvention process. With a few names changed to protect the innocent, here's the complete Manifesto (I've annotated the original statement with comments within bracketed italics):

The MediaLab Manifesto

1. On October 1, 1990, we are transforming our company.

2. We are encountering market and economic issues impacting our growth: (a) Apple has effectively neutralized the HyperCard market *[it has since recovered, but its never managed to rebound to it's former glory]*, and (b) we're heading into a what we believe will be a widespread recession. *[Boy, did this turn out to be true!]*

3. At MediaLab, we are planning to weather the recession with two key strategies: product line expansion and geographic expansion. *[We'll learn more about these growth strategies in later chapters.]*

New products and wider distribution will become a high priority to stabilizing our revenues between now and January.

4. We are expanding our product line by *shipping* one product by September 20 (PictureLink) and two more by October 31 (PictureAccess and GlobalTalk). We are planning at least five other high-priority products that we intend to ship as soon as possible. *[Those products, names irrelevant to this discussion, were listed here. This is another way to be tangible about goals—actually listing what's going to be done makes it more real.]*

5. We are expanding distribution through broader channels and wider geographic coverage from national to international. Our goal is to generate 20 percent to 30 percent additional sales over what could be achieved in the US alone. This will help us get more revenue from each product. *[This is another expansion route we'll look at in depth. With the exception of a few glitches, this has worked wonderfully.]*

6. For the first time since the company was started, we believe we have the key ingredients for creating a stable growth company: (a) products that have a direct, usable benefit, and (b) products that have identifiable markets and customers of reasonable size, and (c) services that are clear, understandable, and competitive *[This clear, tangible, understandable mission statement is one that all employees, not just the founders, can buy into.]*

7. We will be ruthless about cash management. All expenditures must be justified and "smart." All large purchases must include some measure of bargaining or looking for the best deal. *[And so it has been, forever more.]*

8. We will always evaluate whether a purchase is important now or later. We will look at "opportunity cost"; that is, the cash cost of making a purchase now versus the pain and suffering incurred by making a purchase later. Stationery and business cards will suffer this ruthlessness: We'll get them when we can no longer put it off. *[Cash was tight; our customers were slow in paying; we held off on all but the most critical purchases. And we showcased it to all employees so they knew it was part of the plan, not part of the problem.]*

9. We will always evaluate a purchase based on the "silver bullet" theory. The theory is, You only have so many silver bullets (meaning if you don't buy one thing, you can get something else). For example, we consider a powerful computer for James to be more important than fancy chairs in the lobby. And once

we're able to get a working demo system for our products, we'll consider conference room chairs important. *[We were a start-up. Our top engineer needed computing power, but for meetings, just dragging in our own chairs worked fine.]*

10. We will no longer have departments *[this was a big problem that I'll discuss in detail later in the book]* or "supervisors". This company has two bosses: David and Jim. Your "rank" in the company is not determined by whether you work for the CEO or VP; it's simply a matter of the span of management attention either of us can give. Your "influence" and growth in the company are determined by your experience, expertise, and contributions. And whether you can work and play with others.

11. Job titles are for people outside the company. They're marketing tools so outsiders can get a specifically intended message about what we want them to *think* you do. "Influence" and "power" are not determined by the title "manager" or "supervisor," nor are they determined by the number of people your business card says you can boss around.

12. We will be adamant about team support. Everyone is on call to help meet the needs of our customers and other employees. Activities such as customer visits, personal meetings, helping other employees, and covering phones are part of the job for everyone.

13. We will be ruthless about sales personnel. The rules are simple: If you regularly meet your quota (which essentially means you pay for yourself plus some contribution to company overhead), your future is assured. If not, it's not. *[Here's how to keep your job: Produce.]*

14. We will be ruthless about hiring sales personnel. They (a) must have sales experience, and (b) must have computer experience, and (c) should have Macintosh experience. *[We let people know our hiring standards up front, across the company.]*

15. We will be boundless about rewarding sales personnel. Many companies have commission programs that let you earn commission as a percentage of salary. We have a no-cap commission program. Your commissions can be 50, 100, even 1,000 percent of your salary. It's up to you. *[If you produce, you will be well rewarded.]*

16. Given the rapid change in our core markets and in the general economy, we will be flexible about selling just about anything related to our business. This can include standard products, software development, production, etc. The keys to success are

(a) understanding our strengths and rapidly adding new products and services to take advantage of those strengths, and (b) constantly experimenting (or test-marketing) new product and service ideas. So, if you see an opportunity, we're open to giving it a try. *[Ah, the core of our reinvention policy begins . . . we have strengths, let's use them.]*

17. We will be ruthless about nonsales personnel. If you make direct contributions to producing new products or servicing custom customers, your future is assured. If you make a direct contribution to producing products efficiently and effectively, your future is assured. If you make a direct contribution to the day-to-day operations and management of the company, your future is assured. If we (or you) can't figure out what you do to benefit the company and your coworkers, your future is not assured. *[In changing environments, people are always concerned about jobs. This item and the next let people know that we'll never be secretive about this most important of concerns.]*

18. We will be clear at all times about your status. If you're not sure whether you're making a contribution, ask. We'll tell you. If we can't figure out *whether* you're making a contribution, we'll work with you to identify *how* you can make a contribution. We are willing to continually adjust to ensure that you are always making a contribution and your future is assured. *[In other words, we wanted our employees to know that we'd support them . . . but at the same time they needed to know that they'd be asked to be useful.]*

19. We will be active about making sure your job provides you with at least three benefits besides a paycheck: (a) You will learn skills that you can apply in future jobs; (b) we hope, far-in-the-future time if you leave for another job, you'll be at least one or two "ranks" higher than when you joined us; and (c) whenever possible, we (as managers) won't be stuffed shirts and you'll have fun. *[This has always been my philosophy as a manager. If employees get more out of a job than just a paycheck, they'll put more in than just hours. Besides, it makes my job more fun.]*

20. We will be aggressive about employee training. We are purchasing a computer for use in the conference room for training and customer demonstrations. We will hold a product or business training session on company time for all employees at least twice a month. *[You can't reinvent a company without continually growing and reinventing the people.]*

21. We will be aggressive about free flow of information. We will post our total sales and expense numbers monthly so you can see how we, as a company stand. *[This is exactly what I've been talking about. Employees may worry when there's bad news. That's natural. But when they don't know how bad the news is, when there's a blackout of information—as is so common in many companies—the worry turns to speculation, rumor, innuendo, and often panic. Your employees are adults. Treat them as such.]*

22. We will be aggressive about our goals for ourselves. We intend to grow revenues and bookings by (at least) 200 percent per year, recession or not. *[OK, well, it was a bit optimistic. This was a case where, as Mom would say, our eyes were bigger than our stomachs. While the previous year, we'd actually grown 350 percent, we found that we couldn't comfortably integrate more than about 20 percent growth per annum (and often as little as 5 percent) without screwing up someplace big. As a result, we changed our strategy being a company concerned with market share to one concerned with profit margin. This fundamental change rippled throughout the company and affected everything from employee count to product line to customer base to corporate mission. This is why flexibility is so important. We found something that flat-out didn't work and we changed. We're a lot more successful today than we were then. P.S. This year we grew revenues 60% over last year!]*

23. We'll be proud of ourselves and our accomplishments. We have lasted three years as a company where 60 percent of "start-ups" fail at the end of the first year and another 96 percent fail at the end of the second. We have built a viable company with over 22,000 customers and, with our custom projects, soon to be over 50,000 users. *[Change can either be depressing or exciting. In either case, it's certainly not boring. But the important thing, as you deal with the day-by-day hurdles natural to your business, is not to lose your respect for yourself, your company, and your accomplishments. It's good to say, "Hey, we did good." Oh yeah, we've now got over one million users of products and services created by the company.]*

From time to time, it's necessary to look around and see what's really what. We should simultaneously pat ourselves on our collective backs for a job well done and kick ourselves in our collective butts for the accomplishments we've yet to prove we can do.

RECAP

When you set out to transform your organization, you'll need to do some planning and thinking. But don't get carried away or the hours you spend doing the planning will become time lost. Here are other important planning considerations:

- Change is a constant. You can't just make one plan for one reinventing effort and assume all will be perfect.
- Assume that change is a constant and plan to change constantly.
- Remember to revise your plans within the planning cycle.
- Rather than planning specific actions—which will not remain valid for long—determine your short-, mid- and long-term goals.
- Remember that even your goals are malleable. If you fall into the trap of constantly banging your head against the wall to meet an unrealistic (or unsafe) goal (my company's original 200 percent per year growth plan may have been possible, but it was also very dangerous!) you'll hurt your business more than help it.
- Be open with your employees about change.
- Get their buy-in. It is good and natural for them to buy in after a period of negotiation and discussion.
- It's natural to worry about change. But if your employees have real details instead of rumors, they'll worry and panic less and contribute more.
- Consider developing a written manifesto or game plan that everyone can see, feel, and read.
- Don't forget that even written plans can be changed if something in them isn't wise, valid, or working.
- Don't be afraid to admit you've screwed up. It's a lot easier to admit that one part of your plan isn't working or needs to be changed than it is to appear in bankruptcy court.
- Consider creating a bunch of very clearly defined contingency plans, including a general action plan for situations that don't have plans. Our emergency action plan is simple: We swear a

lot (sometimes we cry—same idea); we sit around a table at the local restaurant, eat burgers, and brainstorm; we go off and call our influencers, advisors, and champions for advice; and then we take action.

The bottom line: Planning is good. Action is good. Balancing them is critical.

Next Up

Up through this chapter, I've discussed change, reinvention, and transformation in relatively strategic terms. In the upcoming chapters, we're going to get tactical and discuss tangible, immediate, and flexible tactics you can use for everything from product acquisition to creditor management. Buckle up.

CHAPTER 9

Revitalizing Your Product Line

A new gadget that lasts only five minutes is worth more than an immortal work that bores everyone.
                                    —Francis Picabia, 1922

Your products and services define your company to your customers. To them, your company doesn't have manufacturing processes, a sales compensation program, an advertising agency, a positioning strategy, or even a 401(k) plan. To customers, your company is your products and your services. Sell high-quality, reliable, interesting products at a good price and you've got a good company. Provide valuable services with knowledge, compassion, professionalism without overcharging and you've got a good company.

To your customers, you're only as good as your current offerings.

PRODUCTS AND SERVICES

We typically characterize what we sell as either a product or a service. A product tends to come in a box, has a tangible, physical existence, and a somewhat fixed price. A service is provided by one human to another, is typically intangible in that you can't take what you buy and put it into a car trunk, and has a time-based price structure. In short, a product is something you build, a service is a set of tasks you perform for another.

As we dive further into this chapter on product and service tactics, here are some good things to remember:

- What you sell to customers can be products, services, both, or hybrid combinations of both.
- Services often seem more tangible and real (and therefore more valuable) when packaged as a product (e.g., given a name, a price, a descriptive brochure).
- Product purchases often seem "safer" when backed up by high-quality service. Of course, you can't just claim high quality. You've got to build a base of loyal, happy customers who refer others to you.

Note: To prevent us all from going quietly insane, I'm generally going to refer to both products and services simply as "products." So, when I refer to "Evaluating Products and Product Lines" in the next section, the discussion will apply to any enterprise that provides goods and services in any combination.

EVALUATING PRODUCTS AND PRODUCT LINES

Since it is your products that customers trade money for, your products must come under initial and intense scrutiny when considering corporate change. If your products aren't good, customers will lose interest and sales will plummet.

Poor products are often leading indicators of failings in the rest of your organization. For example, in the 1970s and early 1980s, Detroit's reputation for quality automobile manufacturing was virtually nonexistent. The poorly built cars were indicators of more diabolical problems within the automakers: poor competitive awareness, poor quality control, poor vehicle design (bad engineering), and a disregard for the power of the consumer. Eventually, severe loss of market share convinced them to make improvements. It was almost too late.

Products require considerable investment even after they've been designed and placed into manufacturing. Any given product requires:

- Technical and customer support personnel.
- Documentation.
- Regularly revised marketing literature and advertisements.
- Manufacturing share of factory.
- Warehouse floor space.
- Upgrade and revision by engineering staff.
- Slotting fees or other costs of sales directly related to the products.
- Purchasing, receiving, and materials control staff.
- Computing resources.
- Opportunity cost (resources used on one product that might be better used on another).
- Ongoing, repeated, continual investment.

With all these cost generators, it is absolutely essential that you invest only in the right properties.

There are only three good reasons for a product to exist:

1. It's making a considerable profit.
2. It has a clear, viable, not-fantasy-world potential of making a profit in the future.
3. It fills a critical hole in a product line that would cause customer defection from higher-profit products to your competitors.

You can't believe all the rationalizations I've heard (uh, and occasionally used myself) for keeping products in a product line. Table 9.1 lists some of my favorites (and my responses). Can you see where I'm going with the examples in this table? Products must exist for a specific reason. *Inertia is not a good justification for product retention.*

Table 9.1.   Rationalizations for preserving a product line.

Rationalization	Response
"But it's the only product we have."	So what? It's losing money. Get another product (preferably a few) or consider polishing your resume.
"It's a popular product. We've sold a lot."	But is it making money? If not, it doesn't matter if it's popular. You're throwing money away. Stop it.
"It's got a great reputation."	Again, is it making money? Is it selling well? If not, then clearly, reputation isn't helping. Fix it or dump it.
"It's a sacred cow" (Variation: *"Oh, we never muck with this product."*)	So?
"It's holding an important market segment open for us."	For how long? Why should you invest for years in a product that's just bleeding capital?
"But it's preserving shelf space until we get product X (under development) ready to ship."	If—and only if—product X is going to be ready in a predictable, measurable, and credible period of time, this rationalization occasionally is valid. But make sure you get the new product out and you compare investment costs in keeping the old dinosaur alive vs. forcing a new product back onto the shelf.
"At least it's paying for its costs (breaking even)."	Are you sure? Have you factored in all the costs? And do you really need a hobby—because we're in business to generate a profit, not just break even.

Exercise:

1. Make a list of all your products and product lines.
2. Check off those you *know* are making money.
3. Cross off those you *know* are losing money.
4. Investigate those products that aren't checked or crossed off. Eliminate those products you've crossed off. Be deeply thankful for each and every product with a check mark.
5. Repeat in a year.

THE GROWTH-SHARE MATRIX

Here's another, more strategic way to look at product viability. Draw a chart like the one shown in Figure 9.1.

Market share tells us how strong a player the product is in its market segment. *Market growth* tells us how fast the market segment itself is growing.

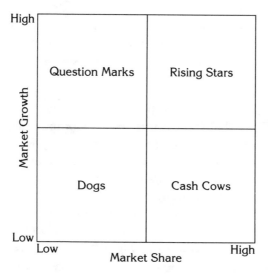

Figure 9.1. Growth-share matrix.

"Dogs" are products that live in a market environment that isn't growing and that offers minimal market share. These products should be jettisoned as quickly as possible. They're not doing all that well now and there's limited hope for them in the future.

"Cash cows" are products that have a large share of a slow-growing market. Because the market shows little growth, the overall opportunity isn't going to get much larger. But if your cash cows hold their high share in their relatively low-growth market, you should be able to extract dollars from them for a good long time. Consider them to be an annuity. Invest only enough to make sure you sustain your market share.

"Rising stars" are products that have a large share of a rapidly growing market. These are where you're most likely to make the biggest bucks and where your biggest investments should be. But be forewarned: being a winner in this quadrant makes you a target. Be careful of your competitors.

"Question marks" are products that have a smaller share of a high-growth market. Is the segment big enough to support multiple players? How strong is the competition? Is it worth the investment to fight for market share? Will you get a return on your investment? Products in this segment raise many questions; they have the potential for being winners, but they could also be a serious money sink. Watch them carefully.

Let's, for fun, take a couple of well-known products and place them on the growth-share matrix as shown in Figure 9.2. Starting with the question marks and moving clockwise, let's see what we can learn from this rather eclectic chart:

- *NeXT.* The market growth for desktop workstations slowed somewhat in the early 1990s. NeXT Computers (run by Apple cofounder Steve Jobs and funded in part by Ross Perot) never achieved anything resembling measurable market share. Based on just the growth/share matrix, the product was questionable. But an examination of the position on the matrix would indicate concern. In fact, the computers were taken off the market and the company is only a shell of its former self.

- *Macintosh (the desktop models).* The market is growing at a moderate pace, and Apple consistently has between 12 and 15 percent of the PC market (when measured PC-clone vs. Mac).

Figure 9.2.   Products in a growth-share matrix.

But they've been able to sustain that share forever and in unit volumes, they always bounce between first, second, and third place. The company is healthy, but a few missteps could push it back into the question-mark limbo.

- *Newton.* We'll talk more about this little hand-held computer in a later chapter. The market growth is *potentially* enormous and Newton's share is reasonable. Unfortunately, the market today is small, the growth is only potential, and for many people, the Newton doesn't actually work. I'd rate this product a "worth watching, but be cautious."

- *Motorola Cellular Phones.* The cell phone business is booming and Motorola has the lion's share of the market. What a wonderful place to be.

- *Macintosh PowerBooks.* In the laptop segment of the PC market, the PowerBook has a commanding lead. The market is growing strongly. This is also a happy place.

- *FileFlex.* I've talked before about purposely limiting FileFlex's market niche. In its admittedly small niche, it has a commanding share of market and there's some moderate growth; it's a healthy product. But were I to aim FileFlex at the big boys in the larger, general database market, it would drop straight into the dog category. Here's a good example of how the growth/share matrix can help you determine the right market for your product.

- *Big Mac.* This is McDonald's constant winner; the fast food chain owns the majority of the market. But growth is relatively slow. Therefore, investment must be made to hold share, rather than in growth-related investments.

- *Dogs.* Notice that no dogs are listed. Dogs disappear too quickly to be well-known enough for a listing like this. Beware the dogs of your product line. They can eat up your profits!

EXPANDING YOUR PRODUCT LINE

If your organization is like most, you'll have crossed off a couple of obvious dog products. Remind you of anything? How about our quest to remove our obstacles? *By definition, a money-losing product is a weakness.*

After going through this voluntary self-amputation, you might feel somewhat diminished. This is natural. But you should also feel a great deal of satisfaction because you've gotten rid of corporate cancer cells. And you should have more resources to devote to your winning products which should help make them even more successful.

Yet eliminating poor products isn't the only action you should take. You should also regularly consider adding new products to your product line. Consider these tips:

- If you're in viable market segments, add products to your current product lines.
- If you're in questionable or declining market segments, consider starting new product lines or opening new markets.

ACQUISITION TECHNIQUES

Generally, you add products in one of two ways: Create them yourself or get them from someone else. Adding products by creating them entirely in-house often requires considerable investment and, frankly, skill. In technology-intensive businesses like software, it means funding engineering staff, and often art and design staff, as well as having the technical creativity and engineering ability to create something new and exciting.

Yet, the paradox is often that just when you need new products:

- You can't afford to fund internal staff.
- You can't figure out how to design a new piece of technology.
- You realize you must complete the entire development cycle (often a year or more) before a product will be ready to ship.

Often, the best choice is to look outside the organization for products. There are some tangible benefits to avoiding NIH (not-in-house) disease and looking outside your walls for products:

- You can get products that are ready or nearly ready to ship *now*.
- You don't have to pay salaries to product developers for that oh-so-long period of time before you can ship that first unit.
- You can get access to products outside your current markets or area of design expertise.
- You can get products that have a different style or approach than your own—adding new blood, new perspectives, and often appealing to different audiences.
- You can get products that are either already proven in terms of sales, or at least already proven in terms of "will it work?"
- And, often, you can get products for absolutely, totally FREE!

That's right. It's amazing but true. Sometimes, instead of paying salaries for lots of designers, you can get products for absolutely no up-front money.

THE ART OF THE FREE PRODUCT

Most of the products my company has produced have been acquired from outsiders. And virtually all of them have been acquired at no cost to us. Back when I first started the company, I had no real choice: (a) I needed new products (*any* products) to have something (*anything*) to sell, and (b) I couldn't afford to pay anything for the rights to the products. It wasn't an option. If the selling person or company insisted on an up-front purchase, I had to move on to the next opportunity. And I did. But eventually, I started to develop a process by which I acquired some great products. For free.

To be successful at product acquisition (across my various jobs, I've acquired well over 200 products—most at no cost) you need to know the three secrets: three amazingly simple, all-powerful secrets to opening the doors to product riches beyond belief. All right. Here they are:

The Three Secrets to Acquiring Great Products for Free

1. The people with products want to find you as badly as (or even more than) you want to find them.
2. They're as desperate (often more so) to find a marketer as you are to find the product.
3. There's a heck of a lot of people with great, unsold products out there just waiting for you to call.

Let's look at each secret in turn.

Secret 1. The people with products want to find you as badly as (or even more than) you want to find them.

Different people and different companies have different talents. Some companies may have great sales and marketing abilities. On the other hand, there may be spectacular engineers without even a clue how to bring a product to market. Often, they're looking as hard for a way to sell their product as various companies are looking for new products.

Secret 2. They're as desperate (often more so) to find a marketer as you are to find the product.

The reality is that many, many organizations are looking for marketing help. There are even more individuals. These folks may have the ability to create a product, but they don't have the ability, resources, or desire to market and sell the product, once created.

I found that software developers fit this pattern perfectly. While almost anyone can buy a powerful PC and anyone with talent can build a small, sellable software program, very few software developers have the operational skills (sales, marketing, direct mail, fulfillment, licensing, production, packaging, support) to bring a product to market.

Here are some other obvious (and less than obvious) categories where there are lots of product creators just dying for a marketer:

- Writers (magazine, novel, nonfiction book, technical, etc.).
- Musicians (many are just dying to get signed to produce an album).
- Inventors (of all sorts of product ideas).
- Contract manufacturers (companies that have products that "just happened" as the result of a job-shop manufacturing contract).
- Offshore manufacturers (lots of Malaysian, Taiwanese, Chinese, and even former Communist bloc manufacturers are seeking distribution).
- Architects (there are tons of reusable building plans out there).
- Integrated circuit chip designers (with the advent of PC-based CAD systems, almost any good engineer can design a chip).
- And lots, lots more . . .

Secret 3. A heck of a lot of people with great, unsold products are out there just waiting for you to call.

A pyramid effect occurs because there are fewer positions at the top than there are at the bottom. Likewise, in an organization, there's usually room for only one CEO, a few VPs, a lot of managers, and a very large number of individual contributors. Figure 9.3 illustrates this pyramid effect.

Likewise, there are a lot more individual product creators out there than there are companies to bring the products to market, as shown in Figure 9.4. Unquestionably, there are tons of products out there. You just have to look for them.

Figure 9.3.   The pyramid effect in organizations.

How to Find Product Creators

By now, you've learned that there are lots of products out there. But how do you find them? If you want to find a product creator, you've got to think like a product creator. Get your message to them where they'd see it. Here's some ideas:

- Sell your current products. I've gotten many of my best products because a developer saw one product on the market and asked if we'd be interested at looking at other products.
- Tell everyone you meet who's even remotely connected to product creators that you're looking.

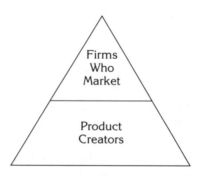

Figure 9.4.   The pyramid effect in marketing products.

- Put notices in your company newsletters and in your product documentation.
- Network by attending user-group or professional society meetings.
- Buy an ad in a trade publication.
- Post a note on a BBS or on the Net (or on-line services such as CompuServe and America Online).

How to Structure the Deal

When I talk about free products, I do not mean that you pay nothing, ever to the product creator. This wouldn't be fair. Rather, you don't have to pay anything up-front. But you will need to fairly compensate the creator.

I always structure these as royalty deals. I prefer a simple percentage of gross sales (say 5% to 15% of the amount received). I then generally subtract from this the real costs of marketing (advertising, packaging, etc.) plus manufacturing before computing a royalty.

Example

> Let's assume we have a product with a suggested retail price (SRP) of $100. We sell it to a dealer for $50. The cost of goods is $15, and we've figured out that marketing costs attributable to the individual sale are another $10. This leaves the adjusted gross revenue as $25 ($50 − $15 − $10). If we pay a 10% royalty on the adjusted gross, we'd pay $2.50 to the product creator.

Note: For hints on additional contract terms and conditions, see Chapter 6, the section "Technique 6. Divide (and Conquer)."

Free Product Pitfalls

While acquiring products for free is a great way to grow a company and be flexible, there are some pitfalls to be aware of:

- *Loss of Control.* You don't own the developers, so new versions, fixes, upgrades, and so forth are dependent on the developer. Don't assume that just because you've got a contract, you'll get upgrades on time. Remember the lesson of PictureLink.
- *Limited Share of Mind.* If you're only paying a small royalty that doesn't fully support the developer's time, you must be aware that the product creator's highest priority will not always be your product.
- *Choice of Second- or Third-Tier Products Only.* You're never really going to be able to get the very best products for free. The best products are rare commodities and other companies are often willing to pay for the privilege of marketing these products.
- *Cost of Time.* You will rarely find that a product you acquire from a creator is ready to go to market immediately. You'll need to provide feature input, packaging, positioning, marketing, and an occasional kick in the pants.
- *Inconsistent Product Presentation.* Because your products come from different sources, they may not be completely consistent in terms of look, feel, and usage. The result is that your product line may look a bit fragmented.
- *Increased Cost of Goods.* Granted, you're not paying for development (which could be amortized in budget across the life of the product). But you will be paying a royalty, which definitely will increase your COGS by some percentage.

REMARKETING OTHERS' PRODUCTS

A variation on the theme of product acquisition is the remarketing of preexisting products from other companies. Some enterprises make remarketing their entire business: stores, dealers, distributors, mail-order catalog suppliers, and the like. But even if you're primarily a product manufacturer or primary service provider, you can flesh out your product line with other people's products.

Generally, remarketed products differ from traditional acquired products in being truly ready-for-market. They're packaged, finished, and already shipping to customers. This isn't to say remarketed products are without flaws. Nothing could be further from the truth. But remarketed products are available for you to sell "as-is" or by adding value.

I've used remarketed products successfully to flesh out a product catalog and to solve occasional nasty customer problems. For example; back in its heyday, HyperCard was being provided to anyone who bought a Macintosh. While you and I know that HyperCard is a programmer's tool, the end users didn't know this and Apple didn't want to admit it. We had a couple of products that made HyperCard easier to use. And we had accessible telephone support.

The problem was, we weren't just getting support calls about our products. We were also getting lots of support calls about how to use HyperCard itself. While we wanted to help users (even those who weren't our customers), it just wasn't possible to help every Apple customer.

Our first solution was to try to get the customers to call Apple. This worked (sometimes). But we'd still get callbacks saying we were easier to reach (we were smaller and there wasn't nearly the hold time for us as there was for Apple), and we were giving them real answers instead of the Apple doctrine. It was really difficult getting rid of these parasite callers without souring a relationship with a potential purchaser.

Finally, though, we hit on an idea. Here we had customers calling for a clearly definable "product"—help with HyperCard. Customers. Need. What more can you possibly want for sales to take place? That's right. The way to fill their need. There's more than one way to skin that cat.

Instead of talking to them on the phone for hours, we secured the rights to remarket a line of videotape training courses for HyperCard. We did nothing but buy them from the tape producer and sell to our customers. But we managed to turn a problem into a profitable opportunity.

THE GREAT-AMERICAN-MASS-MARKET BUNDLE

Another tried-and-true product tactic is the bundle. A bundle (or a suite, or a set, or a collection) is a group of freestanding, separate products packaged together as one larger product, sold for one, usually lower, price.

I love bundles. Customers who wouldn't consider buying a single unit of a product will flock to purchase a bunch of titles packaged together for a single, unreasonably low price.

The software industry has been moving toward bundles in a big way. If you use a computer at all, you've heard of Microsoft Office, a bundle of Word (word processor), Excel (spreadsheet), PowerPoint (presentations), Mail client, and sometimes Access (database). Another example, fighting it out with Microsoft, is Lotus SmartSuite, a bundle of Ami Pro (word processor), 1-2-3 (spreadsheet), Freelance (presentation graphics), and sometimes Approach (database). It used to cost $495 just to buy Microsoft Word. Now you can get the whole bundle (what would have been a few thousand bucks) for $249. It's a heck of a deal from the consumer's perspective.

I love bundles.

It's also a heck of a deal from the bundler's perspective, especially in the software business. Take a bunch of disks, throw their contents on one CD-ROM, bind all the manuals together (or cheaply bind them individually), and stick them in one package. Cost of goods for the whole thing is about what it was for an individual product. But the perceived value is so high sales just go through the roof.

I love bundles.

The Saga of HyperBundle

I've had a couple of wonderful bundle experiences. My favorite is HyperBundle. In 1988, I introduced Icon Factory and Script Expert (for $49 and $79 respectively). After a few revisions, they eventually wound up with a suggested retail price of $99. Both Icon Factory and Script Expert sold into the HyperCard market exceptionally well for about two years, and with mediocre success for another year. In 1988, I also introduced StepAhead and Script Library. These two were duds. I think we sold five copies. Maybe six.

By 1991, even the stronger two of the four products had died. The HyperCard market had been decimated. These products were old. They deserved to die.

Even so, I didn't formally remove them from the product line. They still worked nicely. Just no one wanted them.

Problem: I didn't have anything really good to replace them.

Solution: Bundle.

I love bundles.

I repackaged Icon Factory, Script Expert, Script Library, and StepAhead into a bundle. To that we added SuperPalette (the only product not at least 3½ years old). Finally, I added a "free promotion." I'd acquired another once-popular product called 101 Scripts and Buttons for a very low price. It had died on its manufacturer's vine as well. I combined all these HyperCard developer tools into one package called HyperBundle. Separately, these products would have cost over $500 (if anyone wanted them). Together, I list-priced HyperBundle at $249, but sold it at a "discounted" price of $134.50 via direct mail.

HyperBundle sold like hotcakes. For the first year, we made more off of HyperBundle than we had earned from Icon Factory and Script Expert combined when they were at their hottest. This was after the HyperCard market had crashed. By the end of 1993, while not a super seller, HyperBundle was still moving units. This was a bundle containing six-year-old products, and it was still selling.

It wasn't until 1994 that sales of HyperBundle faded away. Of course, I stopped promoting it at the end of 1992 in favor of more prestigious products like FileFlex. Nonetheless, HyperBundle (consisting of a pile of old, has-been products) was one of our best sellers, ever.

I guess I must have gotten emotionally (checkbook emotionally) attached to HyperBundle. I just dusted it off and offered it to our installed base as a $49 special "while supplies last."

Hint: If you're ever in desperate need of sales, a boost, a midlife kick, or need to recycle some old products, consider making a bundle. You'll make a bundle.

MORE IDEAS

Having spent a large part of my professional career in product marketing, I could go on for pages and pages with product/service/ marketing strategies and tactics. But this book is intended for the whole business, not just for those areas that happen to be among the most fun. So rather than turning this chapter into its own book (OK, so that may happen someday . . . stay tuned), I'm going to wrap up by giving you a taste of some other things you can do to transform your product offerings:

- *Reposition Products.* Consider taking an existing product and positioning it differently, with either a new audience or a new benefit.

- *Branding Issues.* If you're fortunate enough to have created a branded product, make use of it as an asset. Always be conscious of the value of a brand itself, separate from the return on product investment.

- *Brand Extensions.* Brand extensions are great ways to expand your customer base from a central starting point. But beware of damaging the brand. For example, A&W always meant "root beer." In fact, A&W was just about the only brand associated with root beer. Yet, when A&W (the company) extended A&W (the brand) to cream soda, they damaged the market-dominating power of the brand.

- *Market Extension.* Never forget to look for other audiences who might need your product. FileFlex was originally intended for HyperCard developers. But more and more producers of multimedia needed database support. FileFlex was modified to work inside Macromedia Director, a leading multimedia production tool. Now the potential market for FileFlex is substantially larger.

- *Alternate Uses.* Try finding new things you can do with an existing product and see if that opens new doors. For instance, I have this great nonelectric heating pad (actually a tube) that you put into the microwave, zap, and it stays warm and cozy for about an hour. It's great for sore backs. I recently saw it in an APS Technologies catalog used as a wrist-rest for typing at a keyboard. Nice alternate use benefit.

- *Upgrade Marketing.* Consider turning a one-time sale type of product into a continuing annuity by offering regular upgrades or even a subscription to new releases. While this practice has been common with software, where a new version is released every six months to a year (and can be purchased for a fraction of the original price), industries as unexpected as automobiles are getting into the act. I'm not talking about a new model every year—that's not an upgrade. But at least one company, Ford, is experimenting with a program to literally turn customers into subscription buyers. Ford is now offering a 10-year lease, where every two years, as part of the term of your lease, you just drop off your old car and pick up a new one. Granted, you can get out of closed-end leases without Ford's program, but this is the first I've seen designed to generate upgrade business for at least four upgrades.

- *Cross-Selling.* Don't forget to sell and market related products together. A good place to consider cross-selling is a service program on the purchase of a product.

RECAP

As we move onward into chapters on marketing and sales, keep these product concepts and ideas in mind:

- To your customers, you're only as good as your current offerings.
- Products and services are often tightly related and sometimes indistinguishable.

- Poor products are often symptoms of other, serious problems in your organization. Don't stop with just dumping or fixing the products. Investigate and repair the root cause.
- Products require substantial investment both prior to customer shipment and afterward. Every product is both a revenue and cost generator.
- Products exist only to make profits, to secure a potential profit, and to support the profit-generation of other products.
- Dump bad products. There are lots of rationalizations for keeping the losers. Ignore the rationalizations. Dump the dogs.
- The growth-share matrix can help you see a product's potential and flag problem products. Go for rising stars, cherish your cash cows, use considerable caution with question marks, and dump your dogs.
- Adding products is often good, but make sure you add them in the right place. You can often use new products to open new, more viable markets.
- Acquiring products from outside is often a good deal. But make sure you watch out carefully for pitfalls that may result from even a slight loss of control.
- You can often acquire products for free. Remember, there are a lots of folks out there just dying to meet *you*.
- An easy way to add a product is to remarket someone else's.
- Bundling is good. I love bundling. (Bet you didn't know that!)

Unlike the stock market, the economy, your investors, your vendors, and your customers, you *can* control your products to a substantial degree. Tweaking product strategy and tactics, dumping a few bad products and adding a few potential winners can be a great first step. You'll often get disproportionately more out of the effort than you put in.

In the next chapter, we'll put some favorite marketing tactics under the microscope. See you there.

CHAPTER 10

The Collected Crimes of Marketing

Propaganda, to be effective, must be believed. To be believed, it must be credible. To be credible, it must be true.

—*Hubert H. Humphrey, 1965*

Get your facts first, and then you can distort them as much as you please.

—*Mark Twain, 1899*

During the reinventing process, you'll be presenting (sometimes widely) different views of your company to your customers at different times. It's critical that you be conscious of how your company appears to customers at *all* times. This is as much a matter of positioning and communication skills as it is tangible product and business strategy.

CHANGE WITH PRIDE

It's phenomenally important to infuse your marketing pieces, sales literature, and every single staff member with the following, almost religious, belief system:

- Be honest about change. If your company is changing, there's nothing to be ashamed of. Don't hide the fact. And don't act as if change is a sign of failure—it's not. Change is a sign of growth.

- For competitive reasons, you may not want to fully tip your hand about *what* you're changing, *how* things will be changed, and *when* the various steps of change will occur. But be sure to be clear and up front that it's happening.

- Present the *fait accompli* of change with pride, with excitement, even with some glee. If you act as though your company had been beaten into submission and was changing because it has no choice, you'll lose some of the intangible benefits of the process. But if you act as though change is exciting, wonderful, and something to be greeted openly, you'll appear far more successful to your customers.

I call this belief system *Change with Pride*. Not only will it have a positive impact on your customers, it will also have a positive impact on your employees. Employees fear change that's corrective or punitive. They will worry about any change, but they often approach change characterized as "Change with Pride" as change with hope.

Implementing Change with Pride is surprisingly simple. The key is to avoid being downbeat. Here are some tips:

- When your employees speak on the phone, their tone of voice is a powerful marketing message. Train your employees to be warm, friendly, and confident.

- When asked a question about change, and you don't know the answer, don't look down at your shoes and say, "I'm sorry, we don't know." That's depressing. Instead, be positive and confident and even if you still say, "Hey, it beats the heck out of me. Stay tuned," you're presenting excitement and anticipation. Not defeat.

- Use exciting marketing words such as "Introducing," "Coming Soon," "Stay Tuned," "Under Construction," "New," "New and Improved" instead of downer words such as "Revised," "Upgraded," and "Reworked."

- Consider giving marketing materials a face-lift by changing your logo, using bright colors, and keeping everything vibrant.

High technology companies think of change as a constant. As a result, everything they do is oriented around the new product and the new technology. But companies that haven't been steeped in the culture of change tend to approach it from a less positive frame of mind. The less-than-upbeat presentation becomes a self-fulfilling prophecy as potential change leads to worry and loss of confidence.

It may seem silly, but your reinvention process will be far more successful if let yourself have fun with it. Market change to your constituents (customers, investors, employees, press, etc.) just as you would any other great product.

THE THREE CRIMES OF MARKETING

Marketing can have a seductive pull. It's incredibly easy to "go off the deep end" in marketing directions that are easy and feel good, but do your company little good. I call these *marketing crimes*. The three most common are:

1. Marketing on image without substance.
2. Marketing on features without benefits.
3. Marketing on meaningless claims and bravado.

None of these will work. Image marketing, while it may vastly increase the "warm and fuzzies," won't do anything for your customer's understanding of your products. If your competitor does substance marketing while you're marketing on image, you'll lose. Feature marketing will tell your customers about your product functionality, but won't actually explain to them why they should want to buy. And, frankly, there's absolutely no credibility in making meaningless claims like "world's greatest" or "world's best."

IMAGE MARKETING VERSUS SUBSTANCE MARKETING

Even in the best of circumstances, corporate image advertising feeds your ego far more than it feeds your wallet. While you are reinventing, you must always avoid the temptation to market on image. Instead, your marketing must focus strictly on messages that tell customers clearly about your products and services and how customers can benefit from using them. Never do any marketing that does not have a measurable, bottom-line sales benefit. Leave the fluff to the fabric softener companies. (Even if you *are* a fabric softener company, you still wouldn't want to market on image. Market on benefits.)

A classic example of these two marketing approaches was the television advertising of Lexus versus Infiniti in the year the two cars came out. Both were high-end brands of existing car companies (Lexus from Toyota, Infiniti from Nissan). But the Infiniti marketers decided to market on image.

You may remember the marketing. Lots of trees and rocks. That's right, a car company that didn't show any pictures of the cars. No features. No benefits. Just trees and rocks. I'm sure the agency that produced these ads intended to give customers some sort of feeling about Infiniti, but instead it inspired a simple "huh?"

By contrast, Lexus marketing concentrated each advertisement on a specific feature/benefit premise. They took one aspect of the Lexus experience and put it under a microscope. One advertisement focused on the satellite communications network linking dealers. The benefit was that customer repair records would be available wherever your car was going to be repaired. This feature was tangible; it spoke of quality; it was solid enough that customers could grasp the benefit. Not a single rock or tree in evidence.

Both cars were well made. But Lexus beat the pants off Infiniti through good, solid benefit marketing.

WHY SHOULD YOUR CUSTOMER CARE?

Few high-tech companies are regularly guilty of the crime of image marketing. But like their industrial cousins, high-tech marketers consistently forget a founding premise of successful marketing: Sell benefits.

Almost every company has blown it once in a while. Many companies, however, constantly forget to tell customers the benefits of their products and services. These feature felons are sacrificing a huge percentage of their marketing firepower by turning real marketing expenses into a series of costly duds.

It's definition time. If you're in an engineering, scientific, technical, or industrial company, you must read the next few paragraphs carefully.

Simply stated, a feature is something your product does. A benefit is why the feature is important to your customer. Table 10.1 lists some features and their associated benefits.

Table 10.1. Marketing with the use of benefits.

Feature	Benefit
18-gallon gas tank (most cars have 12-gallon tanks)	You can go an extra 120 miles on a single tank of gas, so if you're ever on a long trip in wide open spaces, your car won't let you down.
Single-button mouse (for your computer)	Much easier to use because you don't have to remember what each button does.
Two-button mouse (for your computer)	Provides you with easier access to many more functions on your computer. Much more powerful. [Here's an example of a feature that presents two sides to the same argument—DG]
Four individual ink cartridges (cyan, magenta, yellow, and black) for your personal computer color printer	More cost-effective. You'll probably run out of one color before the others. With this printer, you just replace the color you need. Other printers have a single cartridge mechanism and you have to replace all the colors when one is empty—wasting the ink from the other three colors and wasting money.
Clear, plastic shampoo bottle	The clear bottle lets you see how much is left. The plastic bottle won't break if you drop it on the floor. This makes it much safer for you and your children.

Benefits explain the value your customers will get from your products. Fundamentally, customers buy something because of what they get out of the deal. The benefits are what they get.

Warning! Make sure the benefit is presented from your customers' viewpoint, not your own. One manufacturer actually promoted his circuit board as having fewer components (features), making it less costly to manufacture (benefit). But as a customer, I don't care if it's less costly to manufacture. I only care if he's passing those savings on to me. He'd have done much better if he'd promoted his benefits as:

Reduced part count makes it less costly to manufacture, allowing us to price the device at 20 percent less than what most other manufacturers charge. Further, less parts means higher reliability because there are fewer connections and less things that could go wrong. And fewer parts means reduced maintenance cost because it's much easier to diagnose a problem on a machine with 10 ICs than on a machine with 35.

Exercise: Pick a popular product or service. It can be one of yours or something by another company. Make a list of features. Then write down every benefit you can think of for each feature.

KEEPING CREDIBILITY IN YOUR CLAIMS

The third most heinous crime of marketing is making meaningless claims. You know the type: World's greatest. Largest. Best. Biggest. They don't say anything. They don't have credibility. And they don't help explain to customers why they should be interested. Here's a bunch of meaningless headlines culled from the top layer of magazines on my desk (my comments in italics):

- OK, Here's the Deal. *[Why do I care about a deal if I don't know what you're selling?]*
- Reach for the Stars. *[What does this tell me about you? Why should I care?]*

- Our New Software Company Has a Few Simple Announcements. [So what?]
- Reality Check. [You want reality? I got reality. The reality is I have no real idea what you do.]
- Unlock Your Potential. [An ad for a computer printer, it even had a picture of a lock. There are no features in the printer related to locks. And no clear meaning about potential.]
- Reach for the Stars. [Again, same magazine, different company, different product. Must have been a slow week at the ad agency.]
- Take the Next Step. [From where? To where?]
- Does It All, for Less. [All? Will it do my laundry? Will it put gas in my car? What all?]
- What's the Big Idea? [I don't know. What IS the big idea?]
- Smart Solutions. [Dumb ad.]
- ITI Delivers. [This seems to be a trend. There are a bunch of ads, in the same magazine, that all promise that they deliver. And none of them are a freight company.]
- Metromail Delivers. [Another one. At least see if anyone else in the magazine you're planning to advertise in has the same headline. Do some homework.]
- Val•pak Delivers. [Not only does Val•pak have the same headline as the other guys, but there were three Val•pak ads in the one issue of the magazine, all with the same headline. It's sad.]
- The Fastest Word Processor. [Oh really? On what computer? Do you have any data to back up your claims.]

Marketing is incredibly expensive. If you're going to invest heavily in buying ads or doing mailings, you really should do everything you can to make it work.

MORE MARKETING CRIMES

Marketing is a pretty complex topic, with lots of wonderful tricks. When I set out to write this chapter, I tried to select my favorite neat tricks to help you transform your marketing efforts. But the more I thought about it, and the more I reviewed the work I'd done with clients, the more it became clear that the key to marketing transformation isn't in doing new, cool things. The real key is avoiding blunders.

Most companies have a pretty good idea of what they need to produce. You know you need brochures, datasheets, advertisements, and so forth. You know you're selling through various channels, and you know what you produce.

The problem isn't what you know. The problem is the ease with which seemingly innocuous mistakes can creep into your marketing programs. Marketing is enormously expensive. It is also inexact. For every dollar you spend on marketing, you waste a good 80 to 90 cents on reaching people who don't care. This is the natural order of things. While disturbing, there's no real harm as long as you use the remaining 10 to 20 cents of the marketing dollar effectively.

The problem is, most of us chip away at the effectiveness of our 20 useful cents of marketing by making simple, easy-to-correct mistakes. The easiest and fastest way for you to boost your marketing effectiveness is to know and avoid these common mistakes.

POSITIONING MISTAKES

We'll start off with mistakes that send your message outward to be received by folks who either don't care or who can't buy.

- *Marketing to the Wrong Audience.* If you're not a programmer, not using a Macintosh or a PC, and not interested in managing data, no matter how great my FileFlex marketing, you're still not going to buy. All marketing is like a radio transmission: It must have a receiver to be heard. If your message is going out to people who aren't likely customers, it's as if they don't have a receiver. They just won't hear your marketing. Since it costs real dollars to send every single message, you want to make sure you're getting it to people who care. Make sure you *target* your marketing.

- *Marketing for Too Broad an Audience.* This is another symptom of poorly targeted marketing. If you have an accounting service aimed at CFOs, you're far better off buying an ad in *CFO* magazine than an ad in *BusinessWeek*. Generally, the more targeted the publication, the fewer subscribers. The fewer subscribers, the lower the marketing cost. The higher the degree of targeting and the lower the cost, the higher the return on investment. The higher the ROI, the happier you'll be.

- *Marketing for Too Narrow an Audience.* It is also possible to choose a market niche that's just too small. You need to make sure there are enough people out there to justify your marketing expenses.

- *Using the Wrong Medium.* Many business people dream of doing mass media (i.e., television, radio) marketing. Those in larger businesses even can afford to do so. But marketing dollars are often wasted here. Make sure your product is suited for mass media consumption before booking ad time.

ADVERTISING/COLLATERAL MISTAKES

Much of your marketing budget is likely to be made up of advertising and paper-based marketing. Here are some doozies to avoid:

- *No Call to Action.* Marketing is a form of PsyOps (Psychological Operations—propaganda and mind games used during war). Before winning access to the wallets of your prospects, you must win their hearts and minds. While effective substance marketing must present clear, understandable, supportable information, don't forget that everything also has subtle and not-so-subtle psychological impact. One of the most powerful is the *call to action.* You've seen these often. They're the coupons at the end of an ad. An instruction to call an 800-number for more information. A statement that says "order now." Simply put, a call to action tells consumers what to do once they've read the ad. Always, *always* include a call to action.

Exercise: That last sentence of mine was a call to action.

1. Watch television and read some magazines. See if you can identify the calls to action.

2. Are they suggestions to buy or to ask for more information?

- *Wrong Use of One-, Two-, or More-Step Closes.* You can't always close a sale in the advertisement. Many sales take repeated contacts and discussions. Some can take an incredibly long time.

  I finally closed a deal to start a newsletter that would be funded and managed by another company. The *sales cycle* for the deal took nine months, with one or two sales contacts per week, one physical on-site visit and about one customized package of information sent to them each month. This turned out to be something like a 40-step close.

  By contrast, my Icon Gallery product is marketed with the intent of a one-step close. We expect someone who sees our ad to pick up the phone, dial our 800-number, and give us a credit card number without the need for further contact. This works because Icon Gallery (a collection of pretty color images for computers) can be successfully and completely described in one advertisement.

  Often, you'll find that your ad budget doesn't permit you to buy enough ad space to completely explain and present your product in the space of the small ad. In this case, you should design your ad so the call to action isn't a suggestion to buy, but rather a suggestion to call for more information. The information you send out then goes for the actual close. This is two-step marketing and is often very successful as long as you don't commit the following felony.

- *Failure to Follow Up.* I can't believe how often companies are guilty of this. They spend zillions of dollars on marketing aimed at getting people to call in for more information, for a datasheet or for a catalog. Often the first stage is nicely successful; lots of people call in for more information. But the companies blow it on the second step by taking weeks or months to send out the requested information. Stupidly, some even forget to send any information out at all.

  A prospect who calls for more information has declared him- or herself to be an enthusiastic participant in the sales process, open to your marketing efforts. But if you delay, you run the risk of turning that enthusiastic prospect into a disinterested consumer, or worse: an unhappy prospect, disgusted with your lack of responsiveness.

Exercise: How many leads are sitting in your marketing department's hands? How often are they turned over to sales? How regularly is information sent out to requesters? Has your marketing department become a gaping black hole?

- *Failure to Train Phone Employees.* If you're going to do marketing, don't be a fool. Actually have a clue what you mailed so that when someone calls who's interested, you don't lose the sale. These are pretty brutal words, but true.

  I recently received a mailing in a plain white envelope with just a return address. It'd been sitting in my in-box all week. Eventually, I opened it and read the letter inside. While the letter was poorly written (the English was clear, but the message wasn't), there seemed to be the germ of something I'd been seeking. So I called the number in the letter. I asked for more information. When I did, the receptionist had no idea what I was calling about, so I was asked to spell the name of *their product.* She said she didn't know much about it, but someone would call. No one ever did. I threw the letter away. No sale.

- *Overly Fancy Design.* Ad agencies just love to create pretty ads. Art directors live for the advertising awards. But your reward isn't a pretty ad. Your reward is *sales.* Nothing less. So don't let your agency get carried away with making slick ads that don't sell.

Exercise: Find 10 really pretty ads. What the heck are they selling?

- *Too Ugly.* On the other hand, make sure you put some design quality into your marketing. Not only do poorly designed ads reduce advertising effectiveness, they can help consumers make negative value judgments about the quality of your products. Design clean, effective ads. Just don't get too carried away.

- *Humor or Inside Jokes.* Humor has its value in marketing (and in book writing). But make sure your ads aren't just funny. They have to sell. Humor is dangerous in advertising because not everyone will get the joke. Make sure your ads sell.

- *Giving Up on a Campaign Too Early.* When you design an ad, you live with it for quite a while—all the months before the ad comes out, then the time the ad's on the market. Eventually, you'll get sick of it and want to do a new ad. Make sure you only pull an ad after it's been given time to perform and you can prove it isn't doing its job. Remember that while you've got an intense impression of your ad campaign, your prospects don't. Also remember that repeated exposure is good. Besides, new ads cost money, so if an existing ad is working, keep it going.

- *Not Proofread.* Here's a simple way to improve quality. Proofread your ads. Quality is perceived significantly lower if there are misteaks in your ads. Actually, the same applies to books. That's why I count on the editors to make sure everything is spelt correctly.

- *No Pictures or Screen Shots.* Pictures sell. Make sure your ad includes photographs (preferred) or drawings (if photos are not available). If you happen to sell software, make sure you include screen shots (pictures of how the computer screen works). A screen shot is the best way to show what a program actually looks like.

- *Not Enough Copy.* There are huge debates about this, but rest assured, long copy *does sell.* Prospects who are truly interested in what you're selling will read every word of your copy. If they're not interested, it doesn't matter if the ad only has three words. The value of long copy is that you can fully explain your product, answer questions, overcome objections, and occasionally turn a two-step process into a one-step slam-dunk sale.

DIRECT MAIL MISTAKES

Direct mail is one of the most powerful marketing vehicles available to you. For the cost of a stamp, you can get one-on-one with your prospects. Plus, you're not limited to a quarter of a page (or even a full page) for a print ad or the typical 30 seconds allotted to a commercial. If your mailings are sent out bulk rate, you've got a full three ounces to get your message across. Use it all. The following are common direct mail mistakes:

- *No Headline on Outside of Envelope.* Before a prospect can buy, he or she must read your mailing. If the mailing is to be read, the unopened envelope *must not be thrown away.* To ensure the envelope is opened and read, put your most compelling sales message on the outside. Too many companies spend huge dollars on great brochures but nothing on the envelope. When the envelope arrives, the prospect doesn't bother to open it and so never even sees the all-powerful brochure inside. Too bad.

- *Folding Paper Wrong.* This is another winner. One of my clients recently had us produce a great, full-color brochure. He mailed it, along with an article-reprint, a mini-newsletter, and a cover letter. Prospects who opened the envelope (which had nothing on it but the return address), saw plain, white paper. He'd folded the contents of the mailing so the article-reprint (which was printed on only one side) showed blank, empty whiteness when the envelope was opened. Remember to do everything you can to make your direct mail package interesting. This includes showing the fun stuff inside, not hiding it.

- *No Discount Price.* Direct mail thrives on promotions. Make sure you've discounted your product's price by at least 50 percent to get the attention of the buyer. Make it seem like a great deal. In fact, to get the best response, make it *actually be* a great deal.

- *No Premium.* Customers also love to get free premiums (giveaways) with their orders. Make sure you've got something you give away "free" with a purchase. We did this with HyperBundle. If you bought HyperBundle, you'd get a "free" copy of 101 Scripts and Buttons. We'd actually designed the product to automatically include 101 Scripts and Buttons during manufacture. Even so, we got lots of purchase orders (from companies large and small) where customers had written "Free 101 Scripts and Buttons" under the HyperBundle line item.

- *Forgetting Magic Words.* Certain words affect the brain almost with chemical intensity. Among the most powerful are "free," "save," and "new." Make sure your marketing is liberally sprinkled with these magic words. I did a postcard recently that used the word "free" no less than 12 times. Response was enormous.

- *No Lift Letter.* Did you ever get a mailing containing a little insert with the headline: "Don't open unless you've decided not to buy"? This document, in its various forms, is called a *lift letter.* Unlike popular myth, it's not called a lift letter because you have to lift open the cover. In reality, it's called a lift letter because it lifts response rates. A lift letter can add as much as a quarter percent to your response rate.

- *Too Many Alternatives or Too Hard to Configure.* Some direct mail offers are just too hard to understand. Make sure that you don't offer too many choices or require the prospect to make too many decisions. Avoid the trap of requiring complex math or feature configuration. Each step will reduce your response rate measurably.

- *No Involvement Device.* The involvement device is another Psy-Ops tool for boosting response rates. You've seen them in Publisher's Clearinghouse sweepstakes, where you must peel off a sticker and affix it to an order form. This act of involving prospects also boosts response rate.

  Here's another example from HyperBundle. On the order form, we added a simple involvement device: a box where a customer could put a check mark. Next to the box was the phrase "Yes, I want to order HyperBundle."

  Think this through. We'd get a check or a credit card number, accompanied by a filled-out order form. It's not like we'd send the money back if the "Yes, I want to order HyperBundle" box wasn't checked off. Yet almost every single order came back with that box checked off!

MARKETING MANAGEMENT MISTAKES

You must manage your marketing operation to the same degree that you manage every other element of your company. Yet many executives seem to feel overwhelmed by marketing and either pilot their marketing operations by the seat of their pants or delegate complete decision-making authority to someone else. This is plain dumb. Marketing is a huge cost center in your organization and you should make sure you have a solid handle on everything that goes on.

***

Note: This isn't to say you should micromanage. Let your designers design, your copywriters write copy, and your salespeople sell. But make sure you oversee the operation as much as you would your factory or your R&D operation.

***

What follows is a list of costly marketing management bloopers you can and should avoid:

- *Forgetting to Do Public Relations.* Public relations (PR) provides great, credible marketing to your prospects. And, compared with buying space for ads, it's free. Yet many companies regularly forget to contact writers and editors to get their message out. Don't make this mistake and you'll increase your marketing output without measurably increasing your costs.

- *Ignoring Incremental Marketing Opportunities.* Like PR, there is another wonderful, virtually free source of marketing: the incremental marketing opportunity. In any organization, there's what you could call "big" marketing: ads, marketing literature, PR, direct mail, and the like. But there's usually a constant stream of incremental opportunities for exposure outside the mainstream (an ad in the back of a related book, a catalog listing, etc.). You shouldn't let these go. Take advantage of them. While you'll never be able to directly measure their results, the cost is negligible and the return, over time, significant.

- *Delegating Too Much Responsibility to Your Ad Agency.* Marketing is often a discipline foreign to company managers. To be effective, they often hire an advertising agency. Agencies are valuable; they can help design and write ads, give a different perspective on strategy, and buy media.

  But even though an agency may have your best interests at heart (many actually do), they aren't *inside* your company.

They don't sit in your big chair. So don't delegate all the decisions. Certainly don't give them the unchecked ability to spend your marketing dollars. It's your money. Let's try it again so it settles into your brain: *It's your money.* And again, just to make sure you heard:

It's *your* money.

Since its your money, you should take full responsibility for how it is spent. Ask questions. Investigate. Force your agency to justify recommendations. If you don't understand what they're saying, it isn't their fault. Make them teach you. It's your money!

- *Not Paying Attention to Each Penny of Cost.* It's easy to blow lots of cash when marketing. Some of it just has to be spent. But many times, money is simply wasted because of a lack of attention to detail.

  A classic place where most businesses pour cash down the drain is printing. Take something as simple as a color flyer. Most of us would simply call up our local printer and ask them to print up a couple of thousand flyers.

  But that's where money's being wasted. At Component, Denise Amrich recently did some comparison shopping. She surveyed about 15 different printers, asking for quotes on a short color run. She found prices ranging from $250 all the way up to $1,400 for the same job. Plus, some printers charged extra for film and plates, while others didn't. Arguably, the difference between $250 and $1,400 isn't all that much. But it's our money. Besides, we do this kind of printing regularly. It adds up quickly—why shouldn't we pocket the savings instead of squandering it out of laziness?

- *Overprinting to Get a Discount.* Another way to waste money on printing is to print more than you need to get a discount. Because of the time needed to set up printing presses, the larger the run, the less costly each final printed page costs. So a run of 1,000 sheets might cost, say, $250, whereas 2,500 sheets cost $500 and a 5,000-piece run costs $750. The cost per printed sheet works out to this:

Size of Run	Cost per Run	Cost per Sheet
1,000	$250	$0.25
2,500	$500	$0.20
5,000	$750	$0.15

At 15 cents a page, it certainly costs less per unit to print 5,000 units. But what if you really only need a few thousand pieces? While printing five thousand may cost you less per page, you've still wound up wasting $250 (not to mention the extra storage space needed to keep 2,500 unused flyers).

The urge to print larger runs is really strong. I've felt it myself. But, in the interests of clearing more space in the office, we've had to clear out old flyers. If you once, just once, accompany all those cartons of wasted cash out to the dumpster, you'll cure yourself of the urge to overprint.

- *Overspending When Not Warranted.* It's incredibly easy to discount the importance of controlling spending on such small issues as the cost of a flyer. That would be a big mistake. The savings that you'll gain from careful expense diligence on all the small items adds up, sometimes to thousands upon thousands of dollars.

Think of it this way. Even the smallest company has a bunch of products. Assume you have, say, 10 products. And if you overprint flyers for all 10 (using the preceding rates), you've wasted $2,500. OK, so maybe $2,500 isn't all that much money. But wouldn't you rather have an extra computer or . . . six more executive chairs or . . . the down payment on a car or . . . 10 more print runs (at the right run-rate) . . . than a bunch of cartons destined for the dumpster? Who's money is it anyway? It's your money.

RECAP

While there are many subtle tricks to marketing, you can do a great deal to increase your marketing effectiveness simply by being practical, clear, confident, and honest:

- Be confident about change. Market change with pride.
- Avoid the three most heinous crimes of marketing: marketing on image without substance, marketing on features without benefits, and marketing on meaningless claims and bravado.
- Corollary: Market on substance; market from the customer's perspective; and market credibly by limiting yourself to claims you not only can support but can prove clearly, quickly, and easily.
- You can substantially increase your marketing effectiveness simply by avoiding stupid mistakes.
- Market to the right audience, make sure your message counts, keep track of what's spent, don't overly delegate, follow up on leads, and don't get carried away.

CHAPTER 11

The Science of Selling

He's a man way out there in the blue, riding on a smile and a shoeshine . . . A salesman is got to dream, boy. It comes with the territory.
—Arthur Miller **Death of a Salesman, 1949**

The reinvention process takes a different turn when it comes to your selling methodologies. Many businesses suffer from some serious weaknesses in lead generation and prospecting rather than deficiencies in their closing techniques. The fundamental reinvention strategy for sales is to put some "science" into the process, to get you away from adversarial selling techniques and turn sales into an element of the overall customer relationship process. The premise is this: If you provide valuable products and services your prospects want, if you can get the message out to them, and if you can make the relationship with your company pleasant and productive, sales will improve.

THE PERCEPTION OF SALES

Sales is perhaps the most misunderstood and reviled discipline in a corporation. Yet sales (**S**ales—with a capital "S") is one of the most important. It's sales that connects the buyers with your goods and services. You're not a real enterprise until you deliver products or services to customers. More importantly, without sales, you don't have money. And without money, you don't get to do all the fun stuff that makes a business tick: make payroll, design products, manufacture products, pay the phone bill, contract for outside services, and print up pretty brochures.

Some companies believe that sales is practiced only by salespeople. I don't believe in this narrow view. That's because a sales relationship is more than the transaction. A sales relationship can encompass many tangible and emotional characteristics:

- Interaction
- Judgment
- Desire
- Relationship
- Observation
- Entertainment
- Excitement
- Lust
- Friendship
- Respect
- Trust
- Empathy
- And more . . .

If you buy into the premise that every time a customer or prospect encounters your company, he or she is forming an opinion, creating a perspective, and tuning a relationship, then you'll accept that every encounter with your company is a sales encounter. Therefore, whenever a receptionist answers the phone with a sunny, friendly, and helpful voice, a positive sales encounter is taking place. Whenever a customer service representative calls the customer back within the hour, a positive sales encounter is taking place. Whenever a person in your credit department calls to remind a customer of a bill that is a few days overdue, a sales encounter is taking place.

By this definition then, every employee in your company has sales encounters and is, in some way, a salesperson.

Yet, there are also the sales professionals. These are the folks who put themselves on the line, call on prospects, pound the pavement for leads, and take the slings and arrows of rejection day in and day out.

Sales is not an easy job. If you're a key player in your company (even if you're not, by trade, a salesperson), you're going to be selling. Whether you're an engineer, an artist, an accountant, or a salesperson is of not consequence. What matters is that you're relating with prospects and customers in a particularly complex dance designed to transfer your goods or services to them in return for payment.

PARTNERING WITH CUSTOMERS

Quantum Learning president Fred Marshall talks of "Building equity in the relationship with customers." This is an amazingly powerful concept because it reflects the tangible value both now *and in the future* of a customer relationship. The idea is that you're not just conducting a transaction between two parties but rather that the relationship between the two parties has value potentially greater than the transaction.

To many managers, the entire value of the selling relationship is the dollar amount paid when a customer buys a product. This tunnel-vision approach to sales is wrong, wrong, wrong. You get numerous tangible benefits from a customer relationship beyond the transaction (assuming you build equity in the relationship). Here are just a few:

- *Samples (or proof-of-service).* If you're an advertising agency, each ad you produce for a client is one more item to add to your portfolio. Often, you wouldn't have taken the time to produce ads of such caliber without the funding of a client. Therefore, you wouldn't have portfolio elements to use in proving your quality of service without the client relationship.
- *References.* Often, customers want independent verification of quality of product or service you provide. Satisfied customers are often thrilled to provide good references to prospective clients.
- *Referrals.* Many businesses (mine included) gain a majority of their new clients from referrals by existing clients. Referrals should be a potent component of your sales and marketing

strategy. It goes without saying that you won't get referrals if your current customers aren't happy.

- *Leads.* Leads are a bit different from referrals. Referrals are when a client tells a friend or associate to call your company because you'll be able to help. Leads are when your customer sends you a name of someone who might make a good customer. Generally, leads are less qualified (see following section) than referrals.

- *Repeat Business.* It's much, much harder (and therefore, more costly) to reach new customers than it is to sell again to existing customers. There's nothing more wonderful than when an existing client calls up out of the blue and gives you a new assignment. Of course, you wouldn't get this out-of-the-blue business if your relationship hadn't been solid in previous projects.

- *Partnering/Teaming.* Often, you and your customers can work together to solve a problem that wouldn't be possible for either of you on your own. Partnering takes many forms. In some cases, the client hires the service provider to do some work and contributes valuable input and capabilities. In other cases, partnering takes on a joint-venture flavor with both parties contributing money and talent in an attempt to solve a problem, open a market, or take advantage of an opportunity.

- *The Relationship Itself.* I really value my relationships with my clients, above and beyond the benefits described earlier. I like talking with them, sharing ideas, and brainstorming with other business owners, managers, and investors about all sorts of issues. I've gotten feedback for my books, ideas for products, critiques of plans, and good, old-fashioned friendship from those I work with. The relationships with many of my clients are often as valuable to me as the business revenue they provide.

QUALIFYING PROSPECTS

One of the biggest errors salespeople (and their managers) make is attempting to sell to a nonqualified prospect. In fact, a prospect who hasn't been *qualified* isn't a prospect at all.

Like marketers who don't carefully target their advertising, a huge amount of energy is wasted going after people who just aren't going to buy. While the old school of selling respected and applauded anyone who could sell ice to Eskimos, we can no longer afford brute-force sales techniques.

Sales requires finesse, relationship building, and some degree of accuracy. There's just no good excuse for spending all the extra time to battle your way through the natural and righteous defenses of someone who's not qualified (in a sales sense) to buy your product or service. Your time is better spent working with the qualified prospects and prospecting for new prospects whom you'll qualify.

A qualified prospect has these five characteristics (again, I'm using the word "product" to refer to both products and services):

1. *Desire for Your Product.* A prospect really isn't going to be worth your sales time investment if he or she doesn't actually want your goods. When my old car was breaking down, I had to make the decision whether to buy a new one or fix the old one. The fact was, I really didn't want to go through the process of fixing the old car—I really wanted a new vehicle. I had a desire for the product.

2. *Motivated to Buy Now.* A prospect who doesn't need your product today (or now) may want it later. Likewise, a prospect who wants your product now may not have an interest in it later. If I'm hungry and looking for someplace to eat, I've got a desire for lunch. I might wander into the local Burger King and be a qualified prospect—at that moment. But, 30 minutes later, after consuming an Ultimate Whopper Combo, I'd probably not be hungry. Therefore, I'd no longer have a desire for lunch and I'd no longer be a prospect.

3. *Genuine Need for Product.* Of the five characteristics of qualified prospects, this is the most debated. Sales purists ask, "Why do we care if they need it? Wanting it is good enough." I usually disagree. In most transactions, a sale isn't finished when you accept payment and deliver the product or service. In most transactions, a sale is only finished when the consumer decides not to return the product for a refund. Consumers often experience "buyer's remorse." After buying something, they take it home, play with it awhile, and decide they didn't really need it after all. The product is returned. So, while you may want to appeal to a prospect's prurient interests and drive

the "wanna" urge more than the need urge, keep in mind the risk of returns and canceled orders.

4. *Money to Pay for the Product.* I can't count the number of times I've asked, "Do you have money in the budget allocated for this now?" It's amazingly simple, yet even the most experienced salespeople will forget that in order to buy, you've got to have the green. Prospects aren't prospects if they don't have the money, don't have a budget to spend, don't have credit available, or any of the other myriad options that boil down to being able to plunk down good ol' fashioned cash money on the table.

5. *Authority to Purchase Your Product.* Selling is complex. Often, you have to make your case to someone who doesn't sign the purchase order. Yet, eventually, you'll need to make sure you've located the person who has the authority to make a purchase. Because even if money's been allocated, there's a need, a desire, and a motivation, someone still has to have the authority to purchase.

   I often break complex accounts into banks of *influencers, recommenders,* and *decision makers.* Often, the decision maker isn't familiar with the technical merits of the product or service being sold. Yet, the decision maker is the person who approves the sale. He or she relies on advice from influencers and recommenders. Sometimes, it's pretty hard to tell the difference. Generally, an influencer is someone with no direct authority, whose opinion carries some weight on a purchase or deal (usually an individual contributor who may actually need what your selling). The recommender is usually the person who evaluates the options, chooses the best (based on known tradeoffs), and tells the decision maker what should be bought (offers a recommendation). The decision maker reviews the recommendation, perhaps does some additional research, and then makes the decision to buy.

THE SALES PROCESS

Selling is an enormously complicated process. Not only are there the issues pertaining to the sale itself, but there are organizational issues, interpersonal issues, and political issues that accompany every large sales situation. Even so, there is a process, a "science," a set of steps that most selling situations pass through.

Warning: Don't even consider beginning the sales process unless you have a fully qualified prospect.

Here's a summary of the typical sales process:

1. *Plan.* Make sure you know what you're doing in the selling process. Understand each of the steps involved and plan out your actions for each of the steps. Do your homework.

2. *Pre-approach.* Prior to actually making a sales call (approaching the prospect), make sure you've fully considered how you're going to make the approach. Are you going to cold-call? By phone? In person? What are you going to say? How are you going to open up discussion? Prepare yourself, but don't memorize a fixed script. You need to be yourself and be comfortable.

3. *Approach.* This is the actual call itself, where you open up the discussion to what you're selling. A typical phone approach might be:

   Hi! My name is John Harris with the Fontana Company. Bill Donnely of Heavy Industries gave me your name. I understand you're in the market for some high-performance, low-cost industrial processors.

   Notice the use of the lead (Bill Donnely of Heavy Industries). This is a classic case of the value of maintaining a good relationship with your customers.

4. *Build Rapport.* It is said that first impressions take only seconds. Likewise, you've only got one to three minutes to build a degree of rapport with your prospect. Obviously, you're not going to mutually decide to be friends for life. But those first few minutes will be when your prospect decides whether to listen to what you've got to say or to chase you out of his office.

5. *Interview.* I consider the interview the most important part of any sales process. The interview is the stage where you try to get to know your customer's needs, concerns, issues, objections, and desires. It's from the interview that you have enough information to determine how to present your products and services.

   While I'm not a salesperson by profession, being the head of a company has required me to do much deal making and selling. I tend to lean heavily on the interview process, conducting extremely detailed and intense Q&A sessions with prospects. While there have been a few instances where the interview was somewhat off-putting (I ask very personal, probing questions about the businesses I'm trying to help), I've found that most react very positively when I explain that the more I know, the more I can help. Since much of my client services business revolves around using my expertise to help other companies, the more I know, the more effective (and credible) I can be.

6. *Sales Pitch.* The sales pitch is your presentation. Whether your presentation is verbal, accompanied by slides, overheads, or video, or is a complete product demonstration, it is during the pitch that you're actually communicating what you can do and *how it fits with the prospect's needs.* Your presentation must take into account all that's been learned during the interview and must address all the objections and concerns raised by the prospect in a clear, credible, honest light.

7. *Trial Close.* A sales close is when the deal is done. A trial close is like a trial balloon; you attempt a low-key close to see if the prospect is ready.

   This is where some salespeople try to play tricks. You know the kind: Keep asking questions that the prospect will answer with yes until you've asked if the prospect wants the product; ask whether the prospect wants a blue or a green product to try to establish a purchase desire in the prospect's mind; and so forth. Tricks are a waste of time.

   Instead, a trial close is almost like part of the interview. Honest questioning to determine whether the prospect is ready to buy is warranted. Gamesmanship is not.

8. *Learn Objections.* Often the trial close will lead to objections. You might say, "So, how's this all look to you?" (That's a soft form of the trial close.) Your customer will probably respond with objections (e.g., price, features, delivery, effort). During this step, don't try to counter the objections. Continue the interview and learn all you can about the dimensions of the objections. Try to learn whether the objections are honest (e.g., it really is too expensive for the budget) or manufactured because the prospect isn't interested in buying.

9. *Handle Objections.* Sometimes you can handle objections right away. You can either explain your way through an objection, change your offer, or provide other incentives. But sometimes you won't be able to immediately handle objections. Sometimes you'll need to do some homework away from the sales encounter. This is fine. But make sure you do the homework and actually follow up with the customer. Occasionally, you'll find an objection is legitimate and you really can't meet the prospect's needs. Be honest, shake hands, and wish him luck. Then walk away.

   If your prospect has been qualified, you've got a motivated, interested prospect. I've had a number of instances where my prospect has identified his objections and then we've gone off together to research how to overcome them. In these cases, the objections were legitimate; they weren't gambits on the part of the prospect to manipulate the deal, but were real issues that simply needed to be resolved.

10. *Loop to Sales Pitch.* Usually after you've met the set of objections presented to you by the prospect, it's time to go back to the sales presentation, modify it to discuss the objections, go through the attempt at the trial close, learn about new objections, meet those objections, and continue to work through the issues until the prospect indicates a willingness to move forward on the deal. This looping cycle can go quickly. Other times, it can take months. I just completed a deal where I looped through these steps for nearly a full year until we'd managed to handle (or reduce the perceived risk) of the prospect's objections.

11. *Trial Close* (again). Another way to think of the *trial close* is as a checkpoint in the deal-making process. It's the point at

which both you and your prospect determine together whether all the elements of the deal have been worked out and it's time to get down to business. As the deal gets closer to completion, you may find yourself doing trial closes on various elements of the deal, rather than the deal in its entirety.

12. *Symbolic Close.* I'm a big proponent of the symbolic close. Often, even after all the parties have come to agreement on terms, the actual paperwork that makes the deal legal takes some time. This period of time can often get in the way of the enthusiasm of the moment. So, even though the actual deal isn't closed until the purchase order is cut or the contract signed, I like to close the deal symbolically. Shaking hands, opening champagne, going out to lunch or dinner, having a party, or even doing a handshake over the phone are all symbolic ways to celebrate the completion of a deal.

   With the symbolic close, the rapport dynamic changes from salesperson/prospect to provider/customer and is critical as you build an entirely new style of rapport for the long-term business relationship.

13. *Real Close.* Of course, the real close is nice too. This is when the deal actually is done.

14. *Follow-Up.* You should never consider a deal complete when you get paid. Customers are valued source of new business (in themselves) as well as wonderful sources of referrals. Therefore (and for your own peace of mind and self-respect), you want satisfied customers. The follow-up stage is really a life cycle all its own. Follow-up means staying in touch with your customer and continuing the relationship.

15. *Analysis* (Debriefing). Whether a deal closed successfully, closed (but with effort), or failed, you need to debrief. Make sure you (and all the other members of your sales team) understand what worked and what didn't. Communicate to other departments any lessons learned from the selling process and any needs you have based on prospect feedback. Learn from the process.

Most companies approach sales like a visit to a casino in Las Vegas; just toss the dice and see what happens. But selling, like every other part of your business, can have a process methodology that makes it effective. Selling is so incredibly important to the success of your business. Don't treat it like a carnival sideshow act.

CHANNEL EXPANSION STRATEGIES

Where do you sell your products? How do you reach your customers? Where do you look for more customers? When you go beyond the "what" of what your enterprise produces and get into the "where" of where you sell your wares, you've moved into the realm of the *sales channel*.

Creative channel strategy can help you grow and transform your business. It can also help you get around barriers of entry and competitive pressures from more traditional players. Channel management (where you find your customers) is a secret weapon ignored or misunderstood by many businesses, large or small.

> *Note:* If you have a small or troubled company, creative channel strategy is one of the very few weapons you can deploy with a high probability of success and relatively low cost.

Traditional Channels

Each industry has its traditional channels. For example, cars are often sold by auto manufacturers to dealers, which are purchased franchises permitted to sell and service the vehicles. A nontraditional channel for selling cars is the auto broker. Most of us buy our cars from the dealer; only a few contact a broker who has partnered with a bunch of dealers.

The relationship between a traditional channel and a barrier of entry (how hard it is to get into a market) is fundamental. The established players always want to protect their turf from young upstarts, so they do their darndest to erect formal (or informal) barriers of entry. In the case of the car dealers, you need to have a lot of money to be a dealer—to have a building, service facilities, an inventory of cars, an approved location, support of the manufacturer, and more. The barrier of entry is millions of dollars.

But what if you wanted to sell cars, legitimately, but didn't have any way of breaking through the established barrier of entry? One highly successful method is the auto-broker. Brokering cars has a very low (in terms of capital) barrier of entry compared with opening a dealership. Brokering requires some advertising, a phone line or two, a computer or two, and good relationships with a bunch of dealers. Where it might take $5 million to open a dealership, $20,000 might be enough to open an auto brokerage. The product is the same, the channel has been changed.

While your alternative channel opportunities are limited solely by your creativity, five alternate channels regularly seem to hold a lot of promise: alternative resellers, international marketing, direct marketing, infomercials, and Internet/on-line marketing. In the next few sections, we'll look at each of these. But remember, the best alternate channel is one you devise yourself!

Alternative Resellers

Many industries sell their products through a traditional set of resellers or dealers. For example, auto manufacturers sell through car dealers, clothing manufacturers often sell through department and specialty stores, and fast-food companies often sell their concoctions through franchisees.

There are two fundamental forces to be factored into your planning. First, a traditional reseller today may be history tomorrow. In the early 1980s, the small chain computer store (e.g., Computer-Land, BusinessLand) was *de rigueuer.* Now, however, the computer superstore (e.g., CompUSA, ComputerCity) reigns supreme and the small, independent or chain computer store is virtually gone.

Second, wherever there's a traditional reseller pattern, there's at least one (often many more) alternative reseller options. Put simply, when you sell through an alternative reseller, you sell through a nontraditional channel. Alternative resellers can take many forms:

- *A Totally Different Kind of Reseller.* The auto-broker is a good example. This is a reseller that shares few, if any characteristics of the traditional reseller.

- *A Similar Reseller in a Totally Different Type Location.* Both Taco Bell and Dunkin' Donuts traditionally sell their products through self-contained storefronts. Yet both have expanded into alternative locations. Here in Princeton, within the Wawa (a kinder, gentler 7-11) store, there are miniature Dunkin' Donuts and Taco Bell kiosks. Within the past few years, there have been numerous instances of franchises locating inside large department stores and school cafeterias.

- *Dedicated or Semi-exclusive Resellers.* Software is often sold through dealers and mail-order companies (e.g., PC Connection, MacWarehouse, Egghead, CompUSA). For a smaller company like mine, the cost of maintaining the reseller relationships (especially since we're competing for shelf space with the likes of Sony, Paramount, Microsoft, and Disney) is prohibitive. Instead, we've established semi-exclusive relationships with one or two resellers for each of our products.

  These resellers take on a larger portion of the marketing and sales responsibility in return for a bigger share of the profits. In this way, we gain access to the marketing strength of companies with multimillion-(or multibillion) dollar revenue streams. Plus, since we partner with different companies for each of our products, we gain access to a much broader distribution spectrum than we ever could alone. Yet we still maintain our autonomy as an independent company.

International Marketing

Compared with our overseas cousins, American businesses are colonial in the extreme. This is no surprise, since our domestic market is among the world's largest. By contrast, companies outside the United States do international marketing as a matter of course—especially if they want to sell here in the United States!

It's often easy for us to ignore marketing outside U.S. borders. There are export rules, paperwork, and the logistical effort of simply *reaching* customers so far away.

Even so, if you need to broaden your markets, going international is a good idea. You can do this by opening your own subsidiaries—expensive, but for larger companies (and larger ticket items), often worth the investment. Or you can partner with resellers in each country—more costly, but you get the help of a local expert. Or, you can simply market to customers directly in those countries. Admittedly, the third option is costly. It's also a bit harder for customers outside the United States to work with a company based solely in the states. But for products that are in demand and are only available from U.S. companies (this fits for our software products), direct marketing is powerful.

We even do direct mailings to customers outside the United States—but only for upgrades. We've found that we have an unusually high response rate. When we got a fax from one of our overseas customers, we finally understood why our international customers were buying at such a high rate. We were one of the only U.S. companies that ever bothered to send upgrade notices to those outside our borders. Our customers were so grateful to be remembered that they bought in record numbers. Sad, but true. We now always send notices overseas at the same time that we send them to our domestic customers. It's well worth the added postage costs.

Direct Marketing

The cost and competition for shelf space is considerable. Smaller companies (or even larger companies with new products) often find the cost of achieving and maintaining shelf space higher than the profits from distributing in this manner.

In other cases, the demographics (or psychographics) of a particular customer segment are not reachable via traditional retail. The products being sold are so specialized that demand wouldn't be enough to sustain sales through stores (a great example of this is our technically oriented FileFlex).

In each of these cases, direct marketing (often through direct mail) is the way to go. Establishing a direct connection between the customer and the manufacturer, with no middlemen, is catching on throughout the country. There are substantial benefits to marketing direct:

- *No Middleman.* You get the full amount paid. Even if you choose to discount your price (and you should to get response rates up!), the customer may end up paying less and you'll still make more money.
- *No Distribution Fees.* Whether it's called a slotting fee or a marketing fund, there's no need to pay "grease money" to the middlemen for access to their customers.
- *Increased Data.* When you sell direct, you know your sell-through rates and your customer breakdowns immediately. This is information often not available when selling through intermediaries.
- *Less Waste.* If you take out an advertisement in a magazine, or buy shelf space in a store, your product will only appeal to a small percentage of buyers. If only 1 in 10 buyers is interested in your sort of product, you've wasted 90 percent of your marketing dollars. But if you can find a mailing list *specifically targeted* to people who want and use your type of product, all your marketing dollars will be used effectively.
- *Quicker to Market.* Whenever you have to rely on an intermediary, you increase the time to market. But, when selling direct, you can get your message to your customers at your own pace. There's no waiting for phone calls to be returned from store buyers, no waiting for evaluation committees to meet, no waiting for shelf space to free up. Instead, when you decide to go, you go. Boom. You have instant access to customers.
- *No Dilution of Message.* When you fully control what you say to customers, as you do when you use direct mail, there's no opportunity for an intermediary to dilute your message. However, were you to rely on intermediaries, they might, at best, put their own spin on your message and (at worst) completely get it wrong, reducing your chance to make sales and recoup your investment.

Notice I didn't claim an increase in profit. Going direct won't necessarily increase your profit per se. Even so, by gaining the considerable benefits of getting directly connected to your customers, reducing marketing waste, increasing time to market, and fully controlling your message, you should be able to sell more effectively. That should lead to higher profits.

Infomercials

Let's acknowledge that much of the opportunity presented by the early infomercials is gone. The original key to infomercials was the incredibly cheap airtime available on funky cable channels at 3 A.M. Well, that airtime's no longer all that cheap, so the chance to create your own 30-minute show and make a mint off nearly free advertising is over.

Be that as it may, the infomercial phenomenon is an excellent example of alternate channel strategies and deserves to be studied. The infomercial concept broke with marketing traditions in two tangible ways. First, the airtime was incredibly cheap since the early advertisers bought up space no one else wanted or thought was of any value. Yet, according to a recent report on CNN, nearly 60 percent of Americans are still awake at midnight, and a statistically huge number (especially if measured in purchasing power) are insomniacs, willing to do almost anything for self-gratification at two, three, or four in the morning. The infomercial pioneers discovered an alternate location for selling their products.

The second pioneering change from tradition was program length. While direct mail works well with long, detailed sales pitches, television had always pretty well maxed out at about a minute, with most spots averaging 30 seconds and some as short as 15 seconds. While it is possible to pack a surprising amount of persuasion power in a 30-second spot, there's really not enough time to either (a) provide a complete explanation of complex products or (b) attempt a one-step sell of such products. In 30 minutes, it's possible to do both.

That's where infomercials were brilliant. They made it possible to sell complex products (as well as not-so-complex products that just took a while to demonstrate value), they made it possible to do the sale in one step (instead of calling a number for more information and losing the buying impulse), and they reached customers at a very low cost.

Infomercials are still effective because the first two benefits, the selling of complex products and the one-step possibilities, are still valid. But like any successful channel, the more successful, the higher the cost.

If you're going to be a truly flexible manager, you'll look at infomercials not only as a possible business option, but as an example of truly brilliant selling. With inspiration like that, you might just invent the next killer sales channel. Hey, you never know.

Internet/On-line Marketing

One new sales channel that's growing almost as fast as the infomercial is on-line computer marketing. With audiences in the millions and demographics of relatively affluent users, this is definitely a market opportunity that will turn into a gold rush.

We do a lot of marketing on-line. Recently, we posted a collection of sample Halloween icons (to help push our Icon Gallery collections of icons) on CompuServe, America Online (AOL), and the Internet. It cost us nothing (well, actual on-line time was probably about three bucks) to post these samples. Over the weekend, we know that almost 400 people on CompuServe and more than 500 people on America Online downloaded our samples. There's no tracking facility on the Internet sites, but experience would indicate two to four times the combined downloads of CompuServe and AOL. So, conservatively, we had about 2,500 people (highly qualified, interested prospects) get free product samples in the space of three days at virtually no cost to us. That's 2,500 people who not only may have seen our print advertising, but who have had the option to play with a subset of our product. The return on investment (ROI) is amazing.

I mentioned earlier the story of our new product announcement and the purchases that started arriving minutes after posting.

There are enormous options when it comes to on-line and Internet marketing. In this new domain, even being a user takes some degree of expertise, not to mention providing advertising and sales services. But as other companies gain the experience we have and learn to do on-line postings and Web pages (detailed, linked, highly graphical dynamic computer displays), there will be huge targeted market opportunities.

Admittedly, we've invested very heavily in on-line and Internet marketing, developing substantial network mailing lists and promotional programs of a wide variety of presentation media. But as these opportunities grow, more and more marketing and technology-savvy firms like Component will be able to provide this expertise to other companies. Then, you'll simply approach such a company with your marketing needs and they'll get you up and running on the Internet with the same degree of effort it now takes to produce a mailing or a display ad.

Once again, by looking for new techniques for reaching customers, you'll be able to blast through barriers of entry and move your products and services to a wider and wider group of customers. That, after all, is what good selling is all about.

RECAP

A good sales organization is one that can do more than convince a group of Eskimos to buy ice cream. Rather, a good sales organization leverages off the environment created by marketing to reach out to customers and develop strong and lasting relationships.

- Selling is as much the building of a relationship of honor and trust as it is an attempt to move goods and services.
- Partnering with customers helps build current sales and a future value—in terms of sales and other relationship benefits.
- The value of a relationship with customers is more than bookings. Benefits of a strong relationship include samples, referrals, leads, references, and friendship.
- Prospects need to be qualified. While they may need to meet certain unique requirements for your market, they also have to evidence a desire for your product, a motivation to buy now, a genuine need, the money to pay for it, and the authority to make the purchase.
- Selling isn't just knocking on doors and sharing a cup of coffee. Selling should follow a defined process from planning through presentation to objection handling, all the way through a variety of closing styles, and ending up with the all-important debriefing.
- Where you sell is as important as how you sell. Most industries sell through traditional channels. But alternative channel strategies can help boost sales and help do an end run around the barriers of entry erected by your competitors.

In this and the preceding two chapters, we've looked outward at what we provide customers, how to get their attention, and how to build our relationship with them for the long haul. In the next chapter, we'll look inward at managing the deepest core of any business—cash itself.

CHAPTER 12

Cash Is Life

*The depth and strength of a human character are
defined by its moral reserves. People reveal
themselves completely only when they are thrown
out of the customary conditions of their life, for only
then do they have to fall back on their reserves.*

— Leon Trotsky, 1935

*A man who has never lost himself in a cause bigger
than himself has missed one of life's mountaintop
experiences. Only in losing himself does he find
himself. Only then does he discover all the latent
strengths he never knew he had and which
otherwise would have remained dormant.*

— Richard M. Nixon, 1962

There was a time when everything revolved around the daily cash
report. We'd made the mistake of relying heavily on one large contract. When that customer decided, as part of its own cash management strategy to delay paying all its vendors, we felt it like a
sucker punch to the kidneys.

We had bulked up (in staffing, facilities, equipment, and outside
contractors) to meet the needs of this contract to the tune of almost
500 percent more than our normal expense level. When the company who shall remain nameless in this book (but not in my night-
mares) decided to withhold payments for an extra 90 days, we were
faced with Armageddon. We just didn't have an extra 90 days of
cash flow. We'd bid the contract tightly, so we really didn't have

more than a few weeks of safety margin if payments didn't arrive like clockwork.

That all happened years ago, and I hope we've learned enough lessons to prevent it from occurring again. Cash management and ruthless expense prioritization have proven key in making our rebirth successful and could also be your most powerful weapons. If your financial position is sound today, cash management will ensure that your business remains sound in the future. If your business is on the rocks, cash management may be the only "funding" tool you have to drive a turnaround.

If you run a small to medium-size business (any business that can't get away with throwing good money away), cash is your lifeblood. Everything comes to a screeching halt without cash. Without cash, your employees walk, your suppliers don't supply, your customers lose faith, your investors become your enemies, and your life, frankly, becomes highly unpleasant.

If you've never been in a situation where your business was de facto bankrupt (whether anyone else knew it or not), you won't really, deeply, understand the intensity of this chapter. Thank your lucky stars. Then read this chapter again, over and over, until you do understand. You see, this chapter is as much for those who've never experienced fiscal disaster as for those who are trying to live through it. That's because, if you follow many of the simple guidelines described in the next few pages, you'll substantially reduce your chances of having a cash crisis. Just as loss of control when driving a car causes a collision, losing control of your cash can cause you to crash.

KNOW YOUR NUMBERS

If you get nothing else out of this book—in fact if you get nothing else out of all the business training courses, outside consultants, management team members, coaches, and others who try to educate you on the vagaries of business—get this:

Know Your Numbers

A very good analogy for cash is the fuel in your gas tank. When you run low, you need to get more. Alternatively, when fuel is low, you make sure you don't take long trips because you might get stranded on the side of the road. Instead, you're very conscious of exactly how far it is to the next filling station.

Likewise with cash. You can run your business on little cash. I had to do it for years (not fun, but possible). But you cannot run your business on no cash. You'll be stranded on the side of the road. If you must run your business on low cash, you need to watch the fuel gauge constantly. You need to *always* know your numbers.

The same is true of companies with a full tank of cash. You need to watch your gauge so that the tank never gets too low. I believe that the single biggest failure in presumably cash-rich successful companies is not watching the cash meter. Suddenly, cash runs low (it could be for a variety of reasons) and the company, unused to any adversity, is totally unprepared to deal with it.

Note: In the next few paragraphs, I'm going to speak directly to the owner, the CEO, the president, the COO, the person in the big chair. If you're not directly, totally responsible for the *operation* of your business, just listen in. But if you're in charge, listen up, pay attention, and *learn.*

Cash is life. You must constantly know your numbers. In Chapter 3, I listed a whole bunch of things I keep track of on a daily basis. I'm going to repeat that list here, but this time I'm going to annotate it for the purpose of cash management:

- Employee count, problem employees, and employees I can trust in an emergency. [*The number of employees is a key indicator of where the company is financially. The problem employees are those you can either let go in a short-cash situation or those who will require a disproportionate amount of management time. The most trusted employees are those you consider key (they're absolutely not all management). They're those who'd be kept in a scorched-earth cash disaster and would be the principal members of any turnaround team.*]
- Approximate cash balances in each of our bank accounts. [*This is perhaps the most important thing you should know. I*

normally track this daily, but I've occasionally had to track it hourly to meet a payroll. You MUST KNOW YOUR CASH BALANCES!]

Exercise:

1. Do you know your cash balances right now?
2. Wait a week. Have you kept up with your daily cash balances?
3. If you sit in the big chair and you haven't kept up with your balances, fire yourself. It's for your own good.

- Current clients, key customers and projects, and potential problems pertaining to each. [*Who are your most important customers? What is going well? What isn't? Is there anything you need to be aware of that could affect your lifeblood? Anything that could affect your reputation or the satisfaction of your customers as they experience your services?*]

- Next items due for each project, their due dates, and the fallback strategy if a due date is missed. [*What's due now? What's coming soon? What do you do if you miss a deadline? In this way, you won't have to fumble when faced with a problem. Be prepared to manage the problem through to conclusion. Give the fallback strategies some consideration before problems come crashing down on your head.*]

- Relative priorities for each project so I know which projects I can stall and which I can't. [*Constant prioritization is something we'll talk about in a few pages. But it's important to know—at all times—what's top priority and can push on other projects and what's lower priority and can be made to slip, if necessary.*]

- Any supplier who might be slow in shipping critical supplies and backup plans for getting materials when needed. [*Since we don't usually get paid (or can't deposit payments) until the products ship, we want to make sure everything ships in a timely manner. From a customer satisfaction perspective, we also want things to ship in a timely manner. So if we rely on a particular material (in our case, floppy disks are our biggest commodity consumed), we*] *need to have backup plans when our primary suppliers run into shortages. And yes, there have been shortages of floppies.*]

- Threats from potential creditors and which companies we're late paying. [*There was a time when I spent the majority of my day dealing with angry and dangerous creditors. Thankfully, that time is far past (and I hope it will stay there). But I always need to be aware of companies that we might be late with. We typically delay payment slightly beyond some due dates simply out of the logistics of cutting checks on certain days and certain weeks. Even so, and even now when business is good and most of our vendors are paid pretty much on time, we must watch this carefully. Delay payment by even a day or so and a critical magazine ad might not run. We'll talk about creditors in considerable depth later in this chapter.*]

- Problems with any receivables due us and the backup plans for making sure we get paid. [*Ah yes, the other side of the coin. Our customers aren't always as responsible as we'd like when it comes to paying us. Unlike the early years, we're now completely ruthless about getting paid. We've got programs in place to move payments up voluntarily as well as a whole host of collection options when necessary. But I need to know, daily, when any money expected in doesn't arrive and so do you. Incoming receivables are a very important part of the cash flow challenge.*]

- Status of sales efforts with critical prospects and a good idea whom we should call on if we run into snags. [*It's always nice to have a few tricks up your sleeve and if we're having a poor month (or, worse, we need a cash infusion right-this-minute-now), it's good to know which clients and customers you can call on to finagle a deal with a faster payment (these are often the same customers I've allowed to slip a bit during their dry spells). It's also important just to have a general handle on what's in the sales cycle so you can predict potential rough months well ahead of the potential crisis.*]

- Backup plans for a whole host of potential emergencies. [*Stuff happens. There's a whole pile of things that can go wrong (here, in the horrible northeast winters—any place where the temperature goes below 50 degrees Fahrenheit is horrible—we have snowstorms that make travel difficult to impossible). We've set up remote access to our phones, so on bad snow days, we can remotely reroute our phones to our homes. We have complete remote access to all our computers and networks so timely information and activities won't get dropped through the cracks in the ice. Make sure you plan for problems (whether snow, earthquake, or something more benign), and make sure you know how to keep your business running even in the face of trouble.]*

BANKS AND BILLS

When it comes to cash management, never operate with your head in the sand. A one-page report with the following items should be on your desk every morning: (a) cash in bank, (b) previous day's bookings, (c) previous day's deposits, (d) current accounts receivable balance, (e) current accounts payable balance, and (f) any immediate bills that must be paid for services you need to operate (e.g., phone bill, raw materials).

I talked earlier about situational awareness. Cash management (actually, corporate management) is an exercise in situational awareness. It doesn't take all that long to keep track of your numbers. But you need to be aware of where you stand. Here's a list of what you should know (at minimum) and how often you should update yourself:

1. *Bank Balances.* This is exactly how much money is in each of your corporation's accounts, to some degree of granularity. If you're a very small company, it might be important to know that you have $2,400 in the bank; if you're a much larger company, the pennies aren't important, but you should know your balances to a few hundred or a few hundred thousand dollars. In any case, this number should be on your desk every morning.

2. *High Probability Incoming Accounts Receivable.* This is the money you have a high degree of confidence will be coming in to your firm when you expect it. As part of your daily numbers, you should have a breakdown of what's expected in the next week and the next month.

3. *Cash to Be Deposited.* If you run an actual cash business (like a restaurant or a store), you should also know what's going to be deposited today. For noncash businesses, this would be the checks and credit card slips that are going into the bank today.

4. *Near-Term Accounts Payable.* You should break your A/P into two parts, the critical payments and the noncritical payments. A critical payment is any payment involving on important service or relationship that would be damaged or unavailable if payment is withheld. Less critical are those bills you owe, but for which the fallout won't be immediately damaging. You should know what needs to be paid today, this week, and this month, as well as your total A/P balance.

5. *Money to Be Spent.* This is the money you expect to spend today and this week. In the case of non-cash businesses, this is not the PO's you expect to cut. Rather it's the checks you expect to be writing.

I call the preceding five indicators "Banks and Bills." During the more difficult periods of our turnaround, I made sure I got an e-mail message with the updated banks and bills once *(or twice!)* a day. Now, I usually have a general idea of the balances on a daily basis and update my actual banks and bills numbers each week.

Figure 12.1 shows what a typical banks and bills e-mail message might look like (the numbers are totally made up).

At a glance, you'd be able to see the status of the company. This work usually takes a bookkeeper (with good computer support) about an hour to prepare. In a turnaround situation, it's well worth the time.

Knowing your numbers, though, is more than your daily banks and bills. Knowing your numbers is having a good understanding of your business's health. Most large businesses are good at tracking numbers and reporting progress, yet they manage to let accountants mold the results into something that looks good to outside agencies rather than report the raw information you need to run your business. So don't let your accountants play games when they recast your numbers. Make sure you know *exactly* what's going on inside your business.

Bank Balances:

First Federal	18231	
American National	9240	
Freedom First	11302	
Total	38773	(I would remember 38-7)
AR Expected	2300	
Deposits	3400	
Total	5700	(I'd remember 5-7)
AP Critical		
Phone	1000	
Rent	3400	
Total (must go today)	4400	
AP Other		
This week	6300	
This month	8340	
Today's Checks		
Phone	1000	(same as above)
Rent	3400	(same as above)
Mailing House	5200	(for big mailing)

Figure 12.1.   Banks and bills list.

Smaller businesses (in particularly sole proprietors) commit a different sort of crime. They just go through business as usual, these happy-go-lucky entrepreneurs who often have no real clue whether their business is making money, losing money, or what. Worse, they also don't know *where* their business is strong and where it has problems. You *must* keep track of your cash flow, you *must* look at your monthly numbers with some degree of detail, and you must make decisions based on financial performance, not just gut instinct.

Note: You must micro-manage your cash as if there's no to-morrow. If you don't, there may not be a tomorrow!

ACCOUNTS PAYABLE

This is the time in this book where we look at paying the piper. Accounts payable. That oh-so-innocuous phrase. But business wouldn't be business without buying and selling. When you buy, you have to pay for things. And sometimes, you wind up getting trade credit, meaning what you get today, you have to pay for tomorrow. Eventually, tomorrow arrives. When it does, that so-nice salesperson is often replaced by a not-as-nice person with his hand out. The implied threat: Pay up or else.

Note: If your business is healthy, you won't need to worry about creditors as much. But you should read this section just so you can be prepared in case you run into trouble.

How to Manage Payables

There are two things we need to get clear when talking about money. The first is that *your business must come first.* While it's important and honorable to be nice to other people and companies, the ultimate survival of your business must be your top priority.

That said, the second thing to keep in mind is that money transactions are ultimately *transactions with people.* These aren't just numbers moving around in their own world. Decisions you make about who to pay and who to delay impact other people, their companies, and sometimes their families.

This is true whether your business is large or small. If you're a small company buying a service from another small company, the payment you delay may be the rent check your vendor doesn't get to mail to her landlord. If you're a large company, the corporate policy decision you make to delay payments by a few weeks or months could cause serious harm to an untold number of companies and families. Certainly when our huge client decided to delay payments by 90 days, it severely damaged the lives of a significant number of people in our company.

So, while your business must come first, keep in mind that you're part of an economic system that's fundamentally people. Try not to damage other companies and guard against getting into situations where you might eventually have to cause such damage. Having good relationships with other companies isn't only good business, it's good karma.

If you do find yourself in a cash crunch, you should begin to actively manage your payables. Here are some useful techniques:

- *Prioritization.* You must always (even when you're doing well) prioritize your payables. As a corporation, you should make sure that you know which creditors are high priorities, which are moderate, and which aren't all that important. The highest priority payables are those services you rely on and cannot replace: your local phone company, your key suppliers, and so forth. The moderate priority payables are those companies you deal with regularly. I categorize low priority payables as two groups: those I deal with very rarely and don't rely on, and those who've been unnecessarily rude or vicious. Those who were unfairly abusive (you know who you are!) just didn't get paid until the nicer creditors were paid in full. Funny how that happens!

- *Honesty about Your Situation.* I've found that when you factor in the people component, honesty goes a long way. When we were in deep trouble, I went to my creditors and let them know the truth. While it wasn't a truth they wanted to hear, and while most still took hard lines (after all, they needed payment as much as we did), the relationship was cordial rather than rabid. By being honest, it allowed us to . . .

- *Negotiate Payment Schedules.* It's often not possible to pay an entire bill at once. But you'll go a long way to reconcile accounts if you negotiate a payment schedule with regular payments that'll chip away the balance. Almost all your creditors will accept a payment schedule. The place where you'll disagree is in the size and frequency of payments. Again, honesty (and a certain amount of inflexibility) will go a long way. Once you negotiate a payment schedule you think you can live with . . .

- *Keep to Your Payment Schedules.* There's nothing worse than negotiating a schedule for payments and then blowing it off. You lose total credibility and your creditor's willingness to negotiate goes right out the window. So keep to your payment schedules. If, for some reason, you find you're unable to keep to your schedules, don't ignore the problem. Get on the phone with your creditors and renegotiate.

Here are a few other tips for reducing payables:

- *No Interest.* Often, payables accrue interest. The creditor will decide that being a creditor is like being a bank. Interest should accrue. Legally, creditors in most states have the right to charge interest. However, I don't recommend you ever pay interest on your payables. Virtually all your creditors will be so thrilled to get paid anything at all that they'll waive the interest charges. So, always, always, always negotiate so that interest is out of the picture.
- *Pay $50.* Some creditors are irrational. Fact of life. They want to be paid the entire amount due now, period. These creditors rightly believe they have a moral right to be paid in full. Unfortunately, these creditors don't always have the maturity to recognize the realities of life; sometimes it's just not possible to pay them. If you run into one of these hard cases, send them a check for fifty bucks each week or each month. In this way, you're demonstrating your regular willingness to make some payment. Eventually, if the creditor assigns the account to a collection agency or a lawyer, you can try to negotiate afresh.

How to Make Your Creditors Feel Warm and Fuzzy

Every company has creditors, companies they owe money to. If you're currently in serious cash trouble, you definitely have a bunch of creditors. At some point, if you don't want to go down in flames, you'll have to agree to payment schedules with certain key creditors.

These folks may be creditors you need continuing services from, like the phone company; creditors who you want to avoid going to court with; and creditors you've already gone to court with and have to pay off. You may even have established a payment schedule with some creditors just because they've been decent with you and you want to be honorable with them.

In any case, the creditors with whom you've already established payment schedules are the ones you want to keep feeling warm and confident. After all, you've already had your confrontation and presumably negotiated the best deal possible with them. One way to maintain their continued feeling of comfort is to let them know you intend to keep your part of the bargain. If they're comfortable with you, they're less likely to become threats again.

Tip: A Phone Call a Payment Keeps the Lawyers Away

If it's a month, a week, or even a day or two late, when you finally do mail your payment, call up the creditor in question and explain that you've dropped the check in the mail. Add to your credibility by offering to supply the check number (have it available before you call). If your creditor is still unhappy, offer to fax a copy of the check before you mail it. While you might not make a friend, you will stand a better chance of defusing the situation.

Put yourself in the creditor's shoes. Imagine you've got a deadbeat account who's promised to pay you. The due date arrives and there's no check in the mail. You went out of your way to establish a reasonable schedule and he wasn't reliable enough to do his part. The guy either isn't going to pay or is so irresponsible he forgot. You begin to contemplate taking more serious action.

Then the phone rings. It's your deadbeat customer. He's nice and polite and says he just mailed your check. If you'd like, says he, he'll be happy to read you the check number over the phone. You can expect it in your hands by Friday.

You feel a heck of a lot better about this guy. OK, the check didn't arrive today. But it will. And the guy was decent enough to call. He's an honorable businessperson and you'll continue to cut him slack as long as he continues to be reasonable.

Turn the situation around. You're the deadbeat and your creditor isn't sure about your intentions. You can begin to see that a little attention to detail goes a long way in keeping a relationship smooth and threats diffused.

GETTING YOUR MONEY

Now let's look at accounts receivable. By any estimation, A/R is a much more pleasant topic than A/P because it deals with bringing all that lovely cash into your enterprise. It's all a matter of perspective. That's why we think of taxes as taxes and hate 'em and our fine Congress thinks of taxes as revenue and seems to love them. The key though, when your perspective is attuned to bringing payments into the organization, is to let no payment remain uncollected.

Net Terms Can Be Terminal

Back when I was but a naive pup, I did a business plan. The goal of the plan was to convince some venture capitalist to give us a load of cash that we'd then go off and waste on some economically unsound idea—in this case, $149 robots built from Radio Shack parts (no kidding, I've still got the plan). In any case, we discovered that we had to do pro forma financials (a spreadsheet) showing what we expected to spend, what we expected to sell, and what our cash flow would look like.

So, like good wet-behind-the-ears, would-be entrepreneurs worldwide, we made up the numbers:

> *"Gee Jim, whaddya think? Think we'll sell three thousand in March, four thousand in April, five thousand in May and be up to twelve thousand units in December?"*
>
> *"Sure Dave, sounds reasonable."*
>
> *"So if we're selling five thousand units in May, and we get half of the $149 list price, we should have about $375,000 to spend in June. I don't see what all this cash flow fuss is all about."*

What I didn't understand was that while we might *ship* some number of product in May (and just cranking the numbers up an arbitrary count was pure fantasy), there was no guarantee we'd be *paid* the next month (or, for that matter, the month after, or the month after that).

When a kindly (and highly amused) accountant pointed this out, we factored a receivables delay into our spreadsheet. Ohmygod! All of a sudden, a pristine spreadsheet showing amazing profitability wound up showing us deep, deep in the cash flow hole. Needless to say, we had to make up a whole new set of fantasy numbers.

Lessons Learned

I never forgot that little exercise in creative accounting. Years later, when I was actually running my own business on all-too-real numbers, I noticed that our receivables averaged about 75 days out. I also noticed we were about to enter a cash crunch. Playing the reverse game on the spreadsheet, I recast our next six months' numbers assuming receivables at 45 days instead of 75. Wow! Not only would our cash crunch pretty well dissipate, but I'd gain enough money to hire another complete body.

The challenge, of course, was pulling receivables in. To do so, I hired another staffer, whose primary responsibility was collections (prior to this, we didn't have anyone doing collections, we just sent out statements). By hiring this person to constantly follow up on overdue bills, we managed to bring in our receivables by a full 30 days—and it took us less than a month to make it happen.

Here's a tip: When we hired the person in this job, I was emphatic in letting her know that we were a struggling small company. If she wasn't successful in bringing in the cash, we might not be able to make payroll and our other expenses. There is no more motivated collection person than a mother who's convinced that every non-paying debtor is keeping food out of the mouths of her babies!

MORE TIPS FOR IMPROVING YOUR CASH FLOW

Certainly, hiring someone to manage receivables and make sure we got paid was a fabulous way to improve cash flow. But other tricks I've used over the past years have also achieved substantial success:

- *All Deals Must Be the Best Deal.* Be ruthless about cash management. All expenditures must be justified and "smart." All large purchases must include some measure of bargaining or looking for the best deal.

- *When Not Buying Can Cost More.* Always evaluate whether a purchase is important now or later. Look at "opportunity cost," that is, the cash cost of making a purchase now versus the pain and suffering incurred by making a purchase later. For example, stationery and business cards can suffer this ruthlessness: get them when you can no longer put them off.

- *The Silver Bullet Theory of Purchasing.* Always evaluate a purchase based on the "silver bullet" theory. The theory is, you only have so many silver bullets, meaning if you don't buy one thing, you can get something else. For example, a powerful computer for an engineer is a more important purchase than fancy chairs in your lobby. Use your silver bullets wisely.

- *Discounting.* In direct mail, you'll boost response rate substantially if you offer a 50 percent or more discount off list price. We discovered that if we offered the 50 percent discount but denied the discount to anyone who insisted on net terms, we were able to convert about 99 percent (literally!) of our sales to prepayments. This included colleges and government agencies who "never prepay." After all, it was pretty hard telling your boss that you paid $249 for something that's available from the same company for $134.50! For those customers who were concerned about this policy (or who didn't know how to do a check request), we provided a form that completely explained our policy.

- *Discounting (revisited).* After using mail-order discounting as a tool for forcing prepayment for a year or so, I decided to try it on my consulting customers. After all, if mail-order buyers couldn't pass up a good deal, maybe consulting customers couldn't either. However, I wanted to preserve my consulting fee structure, so I only offered the prepayment discount to my smallest clients (under $2M in revenue and less than 20 employees). We accomplished a few things: We got more deals from cash-starved smaller clients; we were able to provide services to smaller, credit-risky clients (because we were being paid up front); and we saved substantial costs on collection expense.

- *Simply Denying Credit.* Now, as a practice, we simply deny credit (in other words, we don't accept purchase orders) on smaller orders. Period. We're willing to lose some customers to make sure we get fully paid. Want to know something? We've lost fewer customers than the number of customers who became bad debts when we accepted POs.

SHOULD COLLECTIONS BE UNAVOIDABLE

When facing the issue of collecting from a deadbeat customer, feel no guilt. Ask yourself this question:

Whose Money Is It Anyway?

After thinking long and hard, there's only one answer:

It's Your Money!

Let's make sure you get this firmly implanted in your psyche. Whenever faced with the issue of chasing down payment, ask yourself, "Whose money is it anyway?" Stand up. Raise your fist in the air. And yell, "It's my money!"

It's your money. It belongs to you. Go get it.

Remember that this game is played for keeps. No matter how strong your God-given right to payment, there will be companies that don't want to pay. Our policy: Anything over 60 days goes to collection. We use the most obnoxious, nasty, horrible, annoying collection agency on the planet. We love them. We've actually gotten paid by companies who told us they don't pay anyone, but our agency was so unbelievably annoying (well within the law, but annoying just the same), they paid us anyway—just to get these guys to go away.

Camping on the Doorstep Tactic

You can often get what you want by just not leaving the other guy's office till you get it. If you have some stamina, you can use this tactic to incredible advantage. What follows are two "war stories" on how it's worked for us.

In 1990, we got a custom software development contract from one of the premier trade publications in the Macintosh industry. Our job was to develop the software for a CD-ROM they were publishing. Physically, a CD-ROM looks exactly like a compact disc (or CD) you'd play in your stereo, except a CD-ROM stores lots of computer data instead of audio.

The CD-ROM technology of 1990 had three unique attributes that made development of the software less than a cakewalk. First, CD-ROMs were *big*. You could put almost 500 megabytes of data on a single CD-ROM. Second, CD-ROMs are optical, meaning that, at least in 1990, they were much slower than normal computer hard disks. This could make complex timing for animations and sound difficult. And third, they were write-only at the factory, meaning your software couldn't count on storing and retrieving temporary data from the CD-ROM.

These factors posed unique problems for us. To master a CD-ROM, you had to place all the data onto large computer hard disks. You also had to test it all before you went to the expense of mastering the disk. We just didn't have 500 megabytes of hard disk space and we couldn't afford to go out and buy it.

Note: Today, 500 megabytes of hard disk space costs less than $279. Back then, it cost thousands of dollars.

You need to understand that while we weren't shy about telling the magazine about the technical hurdles of the project (because, after all, that could raise the price we got paid), we were absolutely unwilling to tell them we were so poor we couldn't afford the computer equipment necessary to do the job (which, in the height of George Bush's recession, was the absolute fact).

The other thing you should know is that mastering a CD-ROM was costly, so even creating one or two for testing could cost a bundle. Since a typical program requires many thousands of tiny tests and revisions, it would be impossible to test the software by continually cutting new CDs.

Fortunately the client had a wonderful fix for all these problems—if we were smart enough to make it work. At the same time they'd been talking to us about creating the CD-ROM, they'd also been approached by a hardware manufacturer in Scotts Valley. This company had just announced a $19,000 CD-ROM simulator and wanted some publicity. This simulator was the answer to our prayers. It had all the data storage capacity we needed, and it also allowed us to test our software as if it had already been mastered onto a CD-ROM. All we had to do was go down to the manufacturer and take the machine off the company's hands.

So, after a couple of weeks of phone tag, we managed to set up a meeting at their site to get a quick overview of their equipment and pick the simulator up. At this point, we had three parties in the mix, all of whom had different agendas:

1. The magazine, the client, wanted a CD-ROM created. They had a fixed budget and weren't going to spend a penny more. They also had some passing curiosity about the manufacturer's simulator. The magazine did not attend the meeting.

2. The hardware manufacturer wanted press about the simulator. Remembering that ad space in the trade magazines could cost up to $20,000 a page, some free publicity could have some serious value. If they could talk about how a product was created using their machine, they'd get a much-needed credibility boost. So their agenda at our meeting was to get us all hyped up about the simulator and try to get us to generate press for them.

3. We wanted the cash that would come from the consulting contract. That meant we had to finish it to the satisfaction of the magazine, and we couldn't do that until we got the simulator into our hot little hands and trucked it back to our offices.

When we got to the meeting, it was a classic scene. The hardware manufacturer had a band of marketing and sales types spouting marketing hype. They even hauled in their engineering VP to provide a dash of engineering credibility. We were sitting in this plush conference room (they had to be spending someone else's money!), and they were trying to feed us "The Hardware Manufacturer's Story."

Attending this meeting were me, Jim (fellow deal maker, old buddy, and VP Business Development), Ben (test engineer . . . actually, he was along because he had a Chevy Suburban that could hold the machine), and Patrick (the engineer we had subcontracted the development to). We had absolutely no interest in the marketing hype. All we really wanted was the machine. (I'm leaving out Ben and Patrick's last names because they still have a reputation to uphold. You've already met Jim.)

In any case, we all sat in this too-fancy conference room making polite marketing and sales noises to each other for about an hour and heard their pitch. Then we asked about taking a machine back with us. The sound of silence isn't a song. It was a real-life tangible fog that suddenly invaded the conference room.

It seemed that they didn't have all that many simulators. Oops. And it seemed that they didn't actually have one configured with all the proper components we'd need to do the job. Oops. Perhaps we could call back in a few days and schedule a time to pick it up. Big Oops.

This would not do. First of all, it took us weeks to get through the phone tag to set this meeting up—ostensibly to pick up the machine. We didn't have the time to waste just listening to mindless marketing hype. Second, they were a good two-hour drive from the office. Third, we had suckered Ben into taking his Suburban (which already had many, many miles), and he might not go for it a second time. Besides, we were on an already tight deadline from the client. Leaving without the machine could cause us all sorts of unpleasantness ranging from hassles to outright critical problems. And finally, who knew when the hardware manufacturer would actually get their act together and give us a machine?

It was pow-wow time. Jim and I instinctively understood the problem and the necessary tactics. We asked the manufacturer a series of questions: "Do you have a unit with most of the necessary components?" *Yes* (guarded). "Is it reasonably easily accessible?" *Yes* (turned out to be their conference room demo machine). "What do you need to make that machine suitable?" *A certain type of tape drive* (that's a critical component!). "Anything else?" *Yes, the integration time necessary to make the tape drive work with the machine's software* (apparently they were still at a preliminary technology stage for this product, and they hadn't yet figured out how to make it all work—not something they'd admitted to us or the magazine before now). "Oh, and what is the actual time, assuming all the components are available, to get the machine up and running?" *About three hours* (bingo!).

So these guys had all the parts, they just needed to make it work. No problem right? Wrong. In a larger company, requisitioning parts from one department of a company to another could take days. And taking the appropriate engineers off what they were working on to integrate a system like this is a political hot potato.

But that was OK. We were willing to wait. We told them that meeting our client's schedule was so important to us that we were willing to endure a few hours of waiting to ensure that the magazine was satisfied. This put the pressure on them, because they were afraid we'd report back to the client (remember: a big trade magazine) that they didn't have their act together.

In fact, we said, we were willing to go take a slow lunch and we'd be back in two hours to see how they were doing. See ya at 2 P.M.!

All four of us trooped out of their offices and went to find lunch. We came back at about 2 P.M. and got a progress report: some minimal progress. They had managed to get all the parts up to the conference room, but couldn't seem to get the machine to work quite right. They were sorry, but we'd be better off going home and checking with them in a day or so.

Polite refusal. We'd be happy to just chit-chat for a while. Maybe talk with their marketing people about what kind of message they'd like the magazine to hear, and check in with our office. And a tour of their facility would be nice also. By this time, we were tying up senior management, product managers (who were pretty embarrassed about having nonfunctional products), and lead engineers. The only way they'd all get back to work was to get us out of there. And the only way we'd leave (everything polite, of course) was if they gave us a working simulator.

Another hour went by. They still weren't sure they could get everything working, but were definitely getting closer. We knew this because we told Patrick (our engineer) to stick to their engineer like glue. So we had our own guy who was able to determine that it looked like a matter of hours, not days.

They tried to get rid of us again. We declined, but to get out of their hair, we'd go get a cup of coffee. We left for another half hour, had some very nice coffee and munchies at a local designer coffee shop, and came back. We were a little bored, but definitely well fed.

They were frazzled. But it looked like they were close to a break-through. About a half hour later (a total of nearly four hours of wait-ing), they finally got it working.

We loaded the machine onto Ben's Chevy and headed for home. We'd managed to secure the free use of a $19,000 piece of capital equipment (the most expensive piece of capital equipment we had access to at that time) just by waiting them out and not yielding.

You Can Sometimes Score by Camping on Their Doorstep

Sometimes you can get what you want simply by not leaving some-one's office. And the longer you wait and the longer *they let you wait,* the harder it is for them to get rid of you and the more likely they are to give in. This works for everything from getting equip-ment to getting paid.

We've used this tactic a bunch of times for collections on ac-counts receivable. It can get pretty embarrassing for a company to have someone waiting forever in their lobby to get paid.

We had a nasty distributor in Los Angeles that just wouldn't pay their bill. So we sent Jim's brother (a big tall guy who just happens to live near L.A.) to camp out in their lobby each morning until we got paid. Because we were willing to go to this extreme, they paid us, and we made that week's payroll.

Corollary: If Camping Out Doesn't Work, Try Showing Up Every Day

If you can't get paid (or whatever) on the day you show up, try showing up every single day first thing and staying until they kick you out. Often, they'll just get tired of seeing you and literally pay you to go away.

You don't want to use this tactic on a customer you intend to keep forever. Or at least, make yourself scarce after you score until they forget (or at least are no longer angry at you) for pulling this rude tactic on them.

The key is simply a willingness to get the job done. If you're willing to endure a little pain, you'll often succeed.

RECAP

Cash is the lifeblood of any business. While dealing with money issues often isn't pleasant, it is absolutely the most important thing you can do to make your business succeed. Hmm . . . that's actually not true. Rather, dealing regularly and intimately with money issues is on the critical path to making your business succeed—without good cash flow, you won't be able to do all the other important things your business does well. Remember:

- Cash management can actually increase your available cash. As a result, aggressive cash management may be the only funding tool available to you if your business is in trouble.
- Know your numbers. Make sure you know your balances, your bills, your expected receivables, and your cash flow from previous months. If you don't, you may find yourself out of a job.
- Manage receivables so that you don't have too many people owing your business money for too long. Make it a corporate priority to pull payables in to no more than 45 days (preferably, 30 days or less). Whenever possible, try to avoid granting terms on accounts.
- When dealing with creditors, be honest. Negotiate payment schedules and stick with them.

This chapter has been more hard-nosed than some of the others. Cash management is critically important. In the next chapter, we'll get into a topic as important, but perhaps a bit more fun: Operations. See you there!

CHAPTER 13

Maximizing Operations Effectiveness

There are two things to be considered with regard to any scheme. In the first place, "Is it good in itself?" In the second, "Can it be easily put into practice?"

—Jean-Jacques Rousseau, 1762

Major battles have been lost because soldiers on the front ran out of supplies, food, or ammunition. Likewise, your battle for success can be lost if facilities, manufacturing, shipping, fulfilling, and customer service operations aren't working at both peak efficiency and peak creativity. Many company owners assume there's only one way to manufacture their goods. After all, maximizing operations effectiveness isn't nearly as sexy as designing a new ad campaign. They couldn't be more wrong: If you can't ship products or can't deliver services, or if they cost too much or take too long to deliver, your customers will go elsewhere. And redesigning operations to be effective is fun—after all, it's the heart of your business.

You must manage manufacturing (and the rest of operations) as if your business depends on it. Constantly balance what's best to manufacture in-house versus what can best be manufactured by outside suppliers. If any process is subject to boom and idle times, it is an ideal candidate for shipping outside. Also constantly look for

204

new ways to improve your productivity, reliability, and output. Maximize inventory turns, keep minimum materials on hand, reduce material purchase investments, and maximize your ability to be flexible and make midstream product and production changes based on market and customer demands.

If cash is the lifeblood of your organization, operations is the heart.

EVERYTHING IS A "FACTORY"

Organizations are so different from each other, it would be ludicrous for me to try to describe how to transform your production line. Even so, virtually every organization has some form of manufacturing—whether you think of it that way or not.

I was recently in a small restaurant. It had new owners, but much of the staff had stayed over from the previous regime. I had the opportunity to overhear Lynn, a young waitress, lecturing the new owners about manufacturing processes. She explained to her new manager (a man much older than she) that at least three discrete systems had to be maintained simultaneously. First, there was seating. She pointed out that if two tables were dirty, one with a customer seated at it, he should make sure the table with the customer was cleaned first (demand allocation). Then she went on to explain that when orders were taken by the waitress, they had to be delivered back to the kitchen (the factory) for cooking (manufacturing). Once the cooking was complete, it was essential to get the hot dishes to the customers rapidly (shipment). She pointed out to him that even if the food was still hot, if the plate was warm to the touch (having had the time to acquire some thermal warmth from the food), the customer would know it had been waiting (quality control).

As you look at your organization, seeking out ways to make it better, make sure to give your manufacturing processes detailed examination. If you don't think you have a factory, think again.

In today's world, the factory doesn't have to be a large set of buildings belching carcinogens out a smokestack. Instead, consider a factory to be any group of processes where you take one set of materials, add value, and produce something else. Even if you're in a purely service-oriented business, you can have a factory. Here are some examples:

- *Advertising Agency.* Projects come into the firm. They're assigned to teams to develop concepts, then on to creative direction and copywriting, and then final production. That path is your production line and ads are what your ad factory produces (creates).

- *Cleaning Services.* Large companies contract to bring a team of people into their offices to clean up after they go home. Assembling the team, gathering the equipment into trucks or cars, traveling to the site, fanning out, each person doing assigned tasks in his or her area of the premises: That's the procedure. This factory produces clean offices.

- *Hospital Emergency Room.* Patients in pain come in under their own power or on an ambulance stretcher (receiving). They're logged in based on degree of seriousness and insurance coverage (hopefully in that order!). The process of logging in new patients and characterizing their degree of seriousness is the hospital analogue to order processing. Then (again hopefully) in order of seriousness, patients are examined, with temporary curative work done right in the ER (manufacturing). Eventually, patients are either sent home or checked into the hospital itself for further work (shipping).

- *Sales Rep Firm.* Leads are generated or acquired (think of this as the input stage to the factory). Salespeople are assigned and call on leads. Salespeople also continually call on and maintain their preexisting accounts, demonstrate products, handle objections, and overall do a great job to sell products and services. The process is how sales are managed and the product (the output of the sales factory) is actual orders.

Each of these examples is notable because of the existence of a process. Process is the essence of manufacturing and production and wherever there's a process (or should be a process) throughout your organization, you've got yourself a factory.

This is a very powerful tool. Like the microbusiness and the company-within-a-company, the concept of a "spot factory" (like a "spot weld" or a "spot color"—a tightly focused area of production) can help you transform your entire enterprise. Let's look at the key elements of spot factories:

- They may not be perceived as traditional factories. Rather, they're probably normal elements of your business that you do every day.
- They have some form of input (e.g., patients, leads, dirty offices, ad specs).
- They have some form of output (e.g., better patients, orders, clean offices, and finished ads).
- They can have (or should have) a tangible process through which work should pass.

Consider applying the spot factory concept anywhere where it would make sense. You may find yourself looking at how you get work done a whole different way.

> *Note:* Those of you with "real" factories, pay attention. While the preceding section was intended to get those who might not know they were in the manufacturing business up to speed, the rest of this chapter applies to everyone.

OPTIMIZING WORK FLOW

If you remember your government courses, you may be familiar with the term "pocket veto." It refers to a situation whereby a bill informally gets blocked or passed because of the President's inaction. Normally, if the President fails to act within 10 days of receiving the legislation, the bill automatically becomes law *except* if Congress adjourns before the 10 days have passed. In this case the bill gets killed.

Relating this to business operations, inaction ostensibly gets the bill either passed or killed; the analogy is it sits in the in-box until it's too late. Two process management components at work are *signoff* (where the President's expected to approve or veto), and *time delay* (failure to act in 10 days makes the issue moot).

Signoff and time delay are two prevalent factors in organizational life that can benefit from a reevaluation of how work flows (*workflow*). Another is *added value,* which results when an individual builds on the work of preceding individuals. All are tied together by a *process.*

MAPPING THE PROCESS

It is said that the production line represents one of Henry Ford's biggest contributions to modern manufacturing. Students of contemporary management theory will know that there's much debate on weaknesses of the hard-core production line concept (my own company has gone back to on-demand production for much of its products), but for the purpose of this discussion, let's just focus on the benefits Ford derived by using his production line.

The automotive industry has made active use of Ford's production line concept (which the Germans called "Fordismus") from the early 1900s up through present-day manufacturing. However, the process flow on the production line has changed considerably from the absolute rigid uniformity that controlled building the Model T Ford to the current process where a wide variety of options and choices can direct the flow according to the needs of the individual item being manufactured or the resource flow into the factory.

Saturn runs a television advertisement where a worker refers to a special day. He vividly recalls that day because it's "The day I stopped the line." He goes on to say that he saw a problem, a fix that needed to be made to a retaining clip. He had the power to stop the entire factory to make one small repair. Earlier views of process flow insisted that nothing should stop the process. Over time, we've learned that while the general goal is to keep the line moving, to produce output, we also have to factor in other influences. As important as it is to keep the line moving, it's equally important to design the line to be flexible enough to support stopping the line, reconfiguring it, or solving intermittent problems.

Likewise, corporate information (mostly paperwork) flows through an organization. Paper moves from office to office, desk to desk, getting delayed at each point, disappearing in an in-box here, being dropped in priority in favor of something else there.

When there's no production line for the information/paper flow, everything takes far longer and the costs are much higher.

The potential savings in making information flow rather than dribble and spew is enormous. At the Royal Bank of Canada, there are 9,000 different forms, of which 2,500 are being used internally. Disregarding the forms that are used to communicate with outside organizations, the internal forms are used mostly to communicate something specific from one group to another. Filling out the forms is time consuming and the delay time as the receiving groups wait (even just for internal "Sneakernet" mail delivery) can add up. At the Royal Bank, the cost for managing the internal forms runs in the millions of dollars.

If you could eliminate some of the internal paperwork because you've made the information available through more efficient means (e.g., using workflow automation software; one example: Lotus Notes), you could save big bucks.

That, in fact, is what's been happening at the Royal Bank. The Royal Bank is putting Notes software to work to improve their efficiency in many different areas.

We've established, then, that if you can improve the efficiency of flow (whether it's the flow of vehicles on a line or information throughout your offices), you can positively impact your organization.

Of course, to improve flow, you've got to have a flow. Another word for flow, more pedantically accurate, is *process.* How much your enterprise will benefit from process flow optimization depends on four aspects of process: *process clarity, process complexity, process variability,* and *process concurrency.*

PROCESS CLARITY

Simply stated, process clarity asks this: How well do you understand what needs to happen? Is the process clearly understood or are you pretty much clueless about how things need to be done?

Clearly if the process is well understood, it stands a chance of being described and automated. If the process is poorly understood, then any effort at automation will be more like chasing your tail than process optimization.

Let's use processing reimbursements for relocation expenses as an example. Normally, we wouldn't think of processing reimbursements as part of a production line. Yet this is clearly an instance of a spot factory. Since there's a "goes-in" (the requests for reimbursement), and there's a "goes-out" (the approval or denial of the reimbursement), it's a spot factory. How clearly understood is this process?

We certainly know a few immediate facts about the process:

- An employee (or new hire) moves from one town to another.
- Said employee wants to get reimbursed for costs.
- Someone (maybe more than one person) needs to approve the expenses.
- Once approved, a check needs to be cut and delivered to the employee.

The place where process automation would be involved would be:

- Tracking the requests so we know who's made a request.
- Tracking the status of requests (paid, unpaid, declined, etc.).
- Tracking the details of the expenses themselves.
- Making sure the right people sign off on the expenses.

While we might not be precisely sure who are in the sign-off loop and the immediate requirements, we can find that information out. The *degree of process clarity* for this application is quite high.

So far, it looks as if relocation expense reimbursement would be a good candidate for process optimization.

PROCESS COMPLEXITY

Process complexity refers to—you guessed it!—how complex the process is to define. In other words, even if you know how everything is done, is it a set of pretty straightforward steps or is the process nasty and messy?

The *degree of process complexity* refers to the number of steps involved and how interrelated and interdependent they are. The more steps, the more possible actions. The more actions, the more dependencies. One company that's studied process optimization, Lotus Development Corporation, says that as the number of stages in a business process increases, "The number of possible actions rises *exponentially* [my italics]."

You can infer then, that if the process is hellishly complex, it will be very difficult to optimize the process *based on the existing set of steps*. You may need to throw out much of the existing process and reengineer something new.

Note: Classical reengineering discussion recommends wholesale slaughter of existing processes. As I've stated before, this is dangerous. However, there is one specific time when completely reworking a process makes sense: when the degree of process complexity is so overwhelming that it's simply impossible to optimize what currently exists. Use this as a gauge and you won't bet the company on needless reengineering projects.

Conversely (maybe perversely), once you've optimized the process and have it under continual maintenance, you should be able to save big by not having to rely on an internal person who's the living embodiment of *process expertise*. Nor will everyone have to relearn the process each time it needs to be accomplished.

In the case of the expense reimbursement application, we know that it's not going to be terribly complex. We know:

- One or more people will have to approve the request.
- Once approved, the request goes to the next higher approver until all have signed off.
- If the expense is rejected, a message goes back to the original requester.
- All the approvals or rejections get stored in a computer database.

The degree of process complexity for this situation is manageable.

PROCESS VARIABILITY

We know the process is repeated or we wouldn't be thinking about optimizing it. But is the process rigidly unchanging like Henry

Ford's original Model T production line? Or do many variants have to be engineered into the *process map?* If the process has few variations, the *degree of process variability* is relatively low.

So how variable is the moving expense reimbursement application? There are only a few conditions:

- If the expense is approved, it goes on to the next approving manager or is filed as approved. If it's declined, it's mailed back to the requester.
- Depending on who the employee is, different managers need to sign off.
- If the expense is over $10,000, a vice president needs to sign off. If the expense is over $50,000, a senior VP needs to sign off.

There are a few, manageable variations in the process flow. These variables can be easily calculated in a computer's workflow database.

PROCESS CONCURRENCY

In project management, there is something known as a *critical path.* If a task needs to be completed before another task (or tasks) can be started, the first task is said to be *on the critical path.* Often, PERT (Program Evaluation and Review Technique) charts are used to track the tasks and to determine what tasks have *dependent subsequent tasks.*

Likewise, information flow can be on or off the critical path. For example, if the immediate supervisor must first sign off on the expense reimbursement before the group manager gets to see it, then the immediate supervisor is on the critical path for this employee's reimbursement.

The problem in organizations today is that too many people are on too many others' critical paths.

Those people who are on the critical path often don't know or care. Sure, they care when they have a tangible task that must be done as part of a larger project, like the editing task for a book or the cement-pouring task in building a house. But they don't care much when hundreds of slips of paper cross their desks and hide in the in-box.

Let's assume you need six approvals. If each approval needs to go before the next one, and each languishes for an average of a month on the desk before being signed and sent out, that means the job will take six months for completion.

Even if the managers still take a month each to sign off, but they all receive the approval request simultaneously, completing the job will take only a month.

By taking sequential steps and making them concurrent, the job can be completed in a sixth of the time.

Sometimes politics won't allow you to make a task concurrent. For example, you probably don't want to ask everyone involved with the expense reimbursement to sign off at once. Senior managers should only be asked to approve expenses that their subordinate managers have already deemed valid. Therefore, the expense reimbursement application would have a *low degree of process concurrency.*

By looking carefully at how you perform certain tasks, do your best to take things off the critical path and set them up to run concurrently. Each contributor will still have the same time to get the job done as before, but the overall operation may get completed days, weeks, months, or even years sooner.

Aside: I've met many business owners who suffer from what I call "Creeping Pre-itis." This is the disease where everything must wait until one minor, presumably critical, action has been completed before anything else can be done. Sufferers of Creeping Pre-itis insist that all other activities *must* come to a halt until said critical task has been completed. Three particularly damaging elements of this delusional behavior are (a) the critical task is rarely actually critical, (b) the critical task is rarely truly on the critical path, and (c) the critical task rarely gets completed because of the fear of all that will need to be finished once the then-completed task opens the floodgates for all that's been held back.

ON-DEMAND PRODUCTION

The magnitude of your production operation is downwardly independent of the size of your enterprise. In other words, just because you have a huge company, this doesn't automatically imply you have a huge factory—particularly if you have lots of spot factories throughout your organization.

While there's certainly much to be said for economies of scale in manufacturing, far less has been said about the "economies of small" in the same manufacturing operations. Face it. Not all manufacturing is (or should be) large runs. Large production runs of any sort, unless fully utilized and consumed, can be wasteful (both economically and ecologically).

We use a form of on-demand production throughout our software factory here at Component Software. While there are numerous ancillary benefits, the primary one in our fast-to-market technical arena is that we're able to print new products to market in *a third the time and a tenth the cost* of our competitors. Even outside the realm of manufacturing, this a real strategic advantage.

Benefits of on-demand manufacturing include the following:

- You can test a questionable product without making a substantial dollar investment.
- You reduce the amount of unused inventory when discontinuing or changing a product.
- You can decrease time-to-market lead times drastically.
- You can continue selling marginal products at a profit.

Let's take a moment to look at the value of product testing with on-demand production. Rarely will you know if a product is going to be a winner before you build. How often have you wanted to try out a questionable product, but passed on the opportunity because dollar risk inherent in the build costs was so relatively high? On-demand production gives you the chance to try out products that may (or may not be) big hits.

When we use on-demand production, we can test out a new product acquisition in the marketplace at virtually no cost. If it's a hit and generates suitable sales volume, we might then turn to traditional manufacturing techniques. If it's a marginal performer (but still generating a profit as long as we build on demand) we might continue to sell it just for that incremental profit. And—importantly—if it's a dud, we haven't lost much.

There's also a real value in continued sales of marginal performers. In a traditional manufacturing operation, marginal performers are normally discontinued (especially when the current inventory build runs out). But what if the marginal performers have a limited support overhead and each individual sale is profitable? Do you trash the product? You would if you had to justify tooling up for an entire new production run. Manufacturing cost is the only thing that prevents continued order taking and incremental profits.

On-demand production allows marginal products to stay around, generating incremental revenue. But there are other benefits in addition to dollars:

- It fills out product line in areas needed by customers.
- Interesting product categories might bear further investment later. The marginal product becomes a place holder or shelf-space holder.
- Good deal-making opportunities may come up (e.g., selling rights to use in a bundle).
- In our market, all development tools are marginal performers. Yet the sum total of their incremental revenue has created a nicely profitable company.

Don't assume that on-demand production will be cheaper than doing it the old-fashioned, bulk way. Two key driving factors keep actual cash expenditures somewhat higher. The first is the cost of setting up the on-demand production facility, including any specialized production equipment you might need. Second, it will usually be cheaper at the high end to produce items in volume, so your per unit cost will be lower. This is a sliding scale, again depending on the volume to be produced.

On-Demand Case Study: Icon Gallery

What follows is an example from one of our products here at Component. This is a consumer product, shipped in a full-color package and aimed at the retail channel. First, the traditional costs (for producing 1,000 units):

Color separations	$ 100
Prepress	$ 500
Print run	$2,550

Using on-demand production techniques, it doesn't make sense to judge costs based on a full production run. Here's a quick run-down:

Color master (generated in-house)	$ 5 once
Printed color sleeve (on color Xerox)	$ 1 each
Plastic clamshell	$1.50 each

The net of all this: On-demand per unit cost is $2.50, whereas while the higher volume production per unit cost is $1.24 (about half the cost per unit). If all you're managing is cost of goods, it always makes sense to go the traditional route. But if you're managing cash out of pocket (especially if want to take advantage of some of the benefits described earlier), on-demand production will work up to a certain point.

Here's what we calculated for Icon Gallery:

50 units	$ 125
200 units	$ 500
500 units	$1,250
750 units	$1,875
1,000 units	$2,500

Based on the preceding table, on-demand production of Icon Gallery made sense unless we expected to produce more than 750 or 1,000 units. But since we (a) never know whether a product's going to be a hit or a dud, and (b) often have to make changes to update the product before we sell out the production run, it makes sense to do the first few runs on-demand.

We average about 45 inventory turns a year. Because we build less units at once, we need less floor space and inventory. All the money that we'd normally tie up in extra floor space and inventory is available to be applied to boosting our marketing and advertising budgets. On-demand production also eliminates the waste from what's almost always some leftover inventory at end-of-life (or new version) when building product the traditional way.

ENVIRONMENTAL BENEFITS

Each production operation is going to be different. But for software at least, we've found that on-demand production has tangible environmental benefits. Generally, software production involves buying and duplicating floppy disks, buying and printing labels for the disks, printing and assembling some form of colorful consumer packaging, printing and binding a manual, assembling them all together, and (when unavoidable) shrink-wrapping.

Dangers of Traditional Production

We can all picture dirty factories belching black smoke into gray skies. But not all industries pollute in such a visible manner. The software industry is one such industry. On the surface, it seems that software is relatively environmentally benign. But that couldn't be further from the truth. Software production, unless carefully controlled, can be environmentally devastating.

Software consumes an enormous amount of paper:

- *Excess Waste Paper from Oversized Manuals.* Some manuals are produced in odd paper sizes. To get those paper sizes, larger paper has to be cut down. The excess paper from millions of manuals is pure waste.
- *Packaging.* Product packaging is also pure waste. Most is not reusable. Many packages are much larger than they need to be to actually hold what's inside. Plus, all those toxins are released from melting plastic to produce shrink-wrap.
- *Overprintings.* We've talked about overprintings before, but since there's such a huge difference between cost and selling price—FileFlex costs $6 for material and sells for $119—there's a tendency to print extra at each print run. The extra printings

are often wasted, especially when new product versions make the old versions obsolete.

Upgrades generate waste paper:

- *Excess Waste for Landfills.* A typical product generates two or three upgrades worth of waste. This is waste not only at the manufacturer's level, but at the consumer's as well. Each time a product is upgraded, the old product is often thrown out (whether from the manufacturer's warehouse or from millions of consumers' shelves).
- *Damage to Forests.* Entire forests are wasted when a major upgrade obsoletes old documentation.

Worse, all this printing generates dangerous toxins. A recent study showed that silver iodides from printers' waste is one the most dangerous (and hidden) wastes from small industrial companies.

The "Greening" of Production

In the software business, on-demand production is environmentally sound. It may be for your industry as well. When software is produced on demand, there's no wasted paper. There's no packaging waste because it's all consumed. And when coupled with direct sales campaigns, packaging doesn't need to be as wasteful as it does when it needs to catch the eye from a retail shelf. On all but retail sales, shrink-wrapping is unnecessary, reducing or eliminating non-biodegradable plastics. And, using the clamshell approach (reusable packaging), the product packaging (made from recycled materials) can be reused, providing storage for disks and other media.

Here are some other ways software can be more environmentally friendly:

- On-line demos generate no waste.
- On-line documentation generates no waste.
- Printing on demand virtually eliminates waste by-products.
- Direct imaging for color printing eliminates setup wastes generated in creating color printer plates.

Exercise: Software's not the only industry that can be "green." Can you think of three easy steps you can take today to make your company more friendly to the environment?

RECAP

Operations is fun. When I started my company, I never expected the operations part of the business to be fun. It was just the necessary evil between designing the products and marketing the products. But when necessity required that I find ways to make the company more effective (and profitable), I was forced to "dirty" my hands in production and manufacturing. While the proper execution of the operations part of any enterprise is deadly serious, I was pleasantly surprised to find out how fascinating and engaging operations could be. And yes, how much creativity could be applied to an area I had presumed to be boring and unchanging in its regularity:

- There are many ways to maximize the productivity of operations. You must be creative and look for new techniques and methods to make your enterprise more effective.
- Manage manufacturing as if your livelihood depends on it. It does.
- Even if you don't think of yourself as a manufacturing organization, you probably are.
- Treat every aspect of your business that is subject to process as a "spot factory." Think in terms of what goes in, what comes out, and how to create the most effective process in the middle.
- How much your enterprise will benefit from process flow optimization depends on four aspects of process: process clarity, process complexity, process variability, and process concurrency.
- Look to on-demand production as a way to test new products, cost-justify questionable new products, keep marginal products generating revenue, reduce waste, and be good to the environment.

No matter how good your business is on paper, it's people who make it all work. In the next chapter, we'll be looking at the people of your organization and how you can make them both happier and more effective at their jobs. We'll also look at the implied contract of honor between employer and employee; there are certain standards of behavior you, an employer in the 1990s, are expected to live up to.

CHAPTER 14

The Flexible
Workforce

*No matter what time it is, wake me, even if it's in
the middle of a Cabinet meeting.*

—*Ronald Reagan, 1984*

*Surround yourself with the best people you can
find, delegate authority, and don't interfere.*

—*Ronald Reagan, 1986*

The relationship between an employer and employees is complex.
The employer is the "customer" of the employees, and so must
make sure he receives value for his money. Yet, employees have a
strong influence on the employer and also receive services back
from employers (from their paychecks to their insurance benefits).
As such, they too must be treated as "customers," this time by the
employer.

Management/labor conflicts result when one or both parties
become more concerned about receiving service than providing
service. As an employer, you must make sure you get the best results from employees, which involves managing your relationship
with them.

There's been tremendous change (not all good) in our relationships with employees. The implied contract between employer and
employee has changed. As companies weathering difficult economic times find themselves in a struggle for their very existence,
they can no longer even make pretensions that employee welfare

221

comes before that of the corporation. First and foremost comes survival of the enterprise. Period. Once survival is assured, then and only then can compassion for the employees enter into the equation.

Employees, keenly aware of the changing corporate realities, are finding themselves required to put their own interests first with an aggressiveness that's new to all concerned. This isn't the age-old labor/management conflict. Instead this is a new reality faced by all employees (whether they hold a VP's title or that of a mere stock clerk). There's an element of fear as well; not all employees are prepared to fend for themselves in the event of a layoff or the closing of their company.

When you reinvent your company to be more competitive and effective, you will probably be forced to make substantial changes to worker composition and responsibility. This often results in fear and uncertainty in the minds of your workers. We've talked earlier about how credible honesty can help temper the panic of workers experiencing fear and change. Honesty goes a long way toward coping with the evolving relationships between employees and their current and future employers.

THE FLEXIBLE WORKFORCE

If you think about the nature of change, you'll surely recognize that it has to affect your relationship to your workforce. Certain skills will suddenly be needed; others will be of little value. When business slumps, you'd like to have a lower payroll. When business booms, you'll need access to more labor, management, and skilled professional resources. While each business is different, and not all the techniques shown here may be appropriate or acceptable to you, here are some ideas other businesses are using:

- *Core Contributors.* Rather than the traditional division of labor and management, consider rating your employees as "critical" and "noncritical." Your critical employees make up the core of your business; the boiled-down essence of what you do. Your noncritical employees, while still valuable, represent those who might be recast as contractors, outside service providers, part-timers, or temporary workers.

- *Avoid Long-Term Commitments.* For all but your core contributors, you may want to avoid long-term employee commitments that you may have to break if business slows. By avoiding long-term commitments for noncore people, you may also reduce your costs, including health insurance, worker's compensation, and the like.

- *Permanent Part-Timers.* Many businesses have natural peaks and valleys in their business cycles. Rather than trying to weather the valleys with full-timers, many companies are seeking out long-term part-timers. These are people who may have other life commitments (like kids or other nonincome goals) or people who split their work hours between more than one job. We've been highly successful with permanent part-timers here at Component, although it occasionally takes some extra management effort and benign flexibility to make sure we can synchronize the part-timers' interests with our own. One important tip: Don't forget that certain permanent part-timers can also be valuable core contributors.

- *Professional Temporaries.* Temps have traditionally been non-professional (secretaries, bookkeepers, and the like). But more and more professionals (some recently laid off) are choosing temporary work as a fill-in for freelance careers or as a stop-gap while searching for new permanent positions. These temps with degrees are available to provide services such as programming, accounting, and engineering on a short-term basis.

- *Testing through Temps.* Ever wary of the interview process weeding out nondesirables, many employers have turned to the temporary labor pool as a proving ground for future employees. According to *The Kiplinger Washington Letter,* approximately 40 percent of temporary employees are offered full-time jobs.

EMPLOYEE AS ENTREPRENEUR

From an operational sense, there's a blurring of identity between employee and employer. The role of the employee continues to change, which is causing fits at the IRS. Many employees are really becoming hired guns—ranging anywhere from temps to contract workers to employees of other corporations. This makes it tough even to identify when an employee is an employee (from a manager's perspective rather than that of a tax accountant) and continues to evolve the relationship from employer-as-employer to employer-as-customer.

Bosses are becoming clients. This is transforming the entire management dynamic. At the same time, it puts both more and less emphasis on the relationship. Good working relationships become critically important for the worker who wants more work while managerial discipline is wielded by payment schedules and contracts rather than by notes in some HR docket.

In a very real sense, migrant workers are back—and they're in your corporation. Rather than moving from farm to farm, migrant workers (often highly skilled professionals) are moving from contract to contract, company to company, performing their services and then moving on. This has tangible advantages to the corporation (especially weathering the ups and downs of business income), but it also has some disadvantages. The expertise developed by workers isn't sustained or retained within the company. Not only can it (the expertise) leave your company without impunity (you can enforce nondisclosures, but not expertise), it may next migrate to your competitor. Even access to critical company data may depend on whether you have access to a particular worker.

For example, when the Product Power Group prepares an advertisement for a client, we may use a given desktop publishing program on a specific very high-end computer configuration. While we always give the resulting computer files to our clients, they often don't have access to the computer power or configuration necessary to read or modify the documents. So while we never purposely trap them into using our services, it often happens by default. Customers sometimes must come back to us for edits and changes because they don't have the necessary capital equipment to read their own files (because they outsourced all that cost to us, and we've amortized it among a bunch of clients). Of course, they also often become repeat customers because they like the results. It's an interesting Catch-22: They hire us because of our expertise *and* because of our investment in various technologies. By the same token, they're often tied to us for the very same reasons.

Outsourcing is growing. As you stick to your core business (especially as you optimize around your strengths and jettison your weaknesses), you'll let others handle previously internal tasks such as information systems, accounting, marketing, human resources administration, benefit programs, and even professional services normally performed by senior management.

In fact, we have a number of Product Power clients for whom I act as an on-call marketing VP, CEO, or COO. This relationship (that of senior management outsourcing) can take many forms. I know a number of executives who split their weeks among five companies. They're officially COO, CFO, or even CEO at each of them one day per week. I work differently. Because much of my time is dedicated to managing my own enterprise, I most often take on the senior management role in an advisory role, often on a project basis, and because of the very real limits of my time, often for a well-defined, relatively short time period.

While individual projects may be relatively short term, clients benefit from a long-term relationship. I've known many of my client companies and their ups and downs for years. When companies use outside management advice, they often get the benefit of an executive who, by virtue of personal experience and a diverse client base, has expertise across industry lines. Client companies are able to benefit from a much broader perspective from these part-time executives than they might obtain by hiring, say, a marketing VP who'd been in their industry forever.

I've found this part of my job to be very professionally gratifying. It's not my primary business and certainly not the source of the bulk of either Component's or Product Power's income. But I get to see deeply inside many more companies than I would either as a senior employee or as manager of just my own company. I meet interesting people with fascinating and diverse perspectives. The broad knowledge I derive from interaction with such a variety of enterprises has brought clear and tangible benefits not only to my clients, but also to my own business. Plus, it's a sure cure for boredom!

THE VIRTUAL EMPLOYEE

One measurable change in the traditional employer/employee formula is location. More and more employees (and certainly many of the outsourced virtual "pseudo-employees") no longer do their daily work at company-provided workspaces. In fact, many *contributors* (a good word when dealing with these new, blurry lines of demarcation) will, as a rule, work off-site.

Work off-site opens a whole host of new issues:

- *Communications.* When a contributor is primarily off-site, communication takes on a different form. There are far fewer chance meetings on the way to the restroom or in the hall outside the conference room. You'll need to develop the discipline of communicating and relating when not face-to-face.

- *Management Discipline.* Trust. It all boils down (from the manager's perspective) to being able to trust that contributors are actually working when they say they are. Generally, you'll be able to judge by output, but you may find you can only use off-site workers that you know possess the self-discipline to get the job done without constant management supervision.

- *Morale.* Working from home is both better and worse than working in the office. It's better because it's often more comfortable. It's always a blast for new home-workers to do a big business deal while in their undies. But it's also a big morale problem because working alone, at home, is lonely. People contact is going to be important.

  When I first started my business, I worked from home. I found it psychologically difficult to stay at home—I was desperately lonely and felt terribly trapped. I felt enormously better when I moved the business into separate offices. My office is now about 15 minutes from my house. I also have an office in my house that completely duplicates my workspace (including my specially designed "mission-control" computer desk and a full subset of our office computer systems). In this way, I can get work done at home when I need to (this is particularly important during winter storms), but I have a tangible office location to do business and meet customers. At the end of the workday, I can leave work behind and actually *go home.*

- *Relationships.* Remote work relationships form differently from those that develop among employees working together in an office. It's still very possible to develop strong relationships, only with fewer people. When working in the corporate office, an employee has a better chance of developing acquaintance relationships with many more people than when working away from the office.

- *Collaboration.* Collaboration is also possible when working remotely. However, it's much harder than having everyone gather around a table, hand around a new product, or crawl inside a particularly recalcitrant piece of factory equipment.

- *Technology.* Technology, along with overnight shipping services, is the glue that makes working remotely even (pardon the pun) remotely possible. Fax, computer mail, file transfer, teleconferencing, and other media make it possible to get the job done.

I've long advocated the "Network as Headquarters" paradigm for geographically dispersed enterprises. Component, for example, has many contributors and many clients. Virtually none of them work from our offices in Rocky Hill. Much of our daily business is coordinated over the networks, through dial-ins, file transfers, faxes, and other means. I really don't consider our office to be our headquarters. Rather, our operation is defined by the tentacles of network connections that stretch from California to New Jersey, from Minnesota to New York, from Washington State to Florida.

Is it actually possible to work remotely? Unquestionably. I've built many successful products—including a few *bona fide* award winners—with people I had never, *never* come in contact with, face to face. I have some great client relationships with people I've now known for years, again, whom I've never, ever seen. I've worked with these clients on major projects with great success. And, I've developed many good, solid, personal, wonderfully warm friendships with people I wouldn't recognize if we were in the same room together—because I've never actually seen them in person.

It does take some skill, some practice, and some *pacing* (learning how to balance the communications needs with the available mediums). Do a few projects this way and you'll realize how viable, cost-effective, empowering, and fun it can be to be able to work with people all over the world—without having to fight traffic, pay for overpriced plane tickets, wait forever for flights, waste time on airplanes, and sleep in places not of your choosing.

SOFTWARE FOR VIRTUAL EMPLOYEES

The coordination of geographically scattered contributors is often made far more effective through the use of computer software.

> *Note:* Even (especially) if you're not a computer person, *you must read this section.* Software for group coordination has generated major increases in productivity *and* satisfaction.

I'm going to discuss two of the more prevalent forms of collaboration software, electronic mail and workgroup software. I promise to limit my vocabulary to English, and I'll try not to get carried away with the technical terminology.

Electronic Mail

If you aren't currently using electronic mail in your office, you should. Period. No discussion. Even if you only have two people in your office, e-mail is valuable.

> *Aside:* When I installed e-mail into our office, we had only two people. In the first week, my assistant and I generated over 200 highly productive messages, just between ourselves.

If you haven't yet encountered e-mail, the premise is quite simple. You type a message on your computer, select a recipient, and click "Send." On the recipient's computer, a little bell sounds, informing the person that there is a message. A recipient who happens to be away from the computer can check for mail later, when he or she returns to that workstation. The person can review your message, respond to it quickly (at a touch of a button), and fire off a reply. When you return to your computer, the message is there for you to read and act on at your convenience.

There are all sorts of advanced "bells and whistles": You can send messages to groups, you can forward messages you get to other people, you can often include voice notes, you can attach computer files, you can have messages sent to others (and yourself—great for reminders) at specific times, and more.

To give you an idea of the value of e-mail, I'll share three messages I received today. The first I viewed from home. I dial into my office computer first thing every morning. I got a message from a customer in France who had a technical question about FileFlex (had it arrived by letter, it might have taken three weeks to travel and then languished in my two-tier in-box for a month). I needed more information from him to answer the question. Rather than typing a formal reply letter, I copied his question (with one swipe of the mouse) and pasted it into my message box. I then typed a three-sentence follow-up query, highlighting his original question, and sent it off. Later in the afternoon, I received a message back from the customer ecstatic that he'd gotten such a rapid response. He included his answer to my query. I again copied some of his question, answered his original question (which I still had sitting in my e-mail), and sent off the answer. No time zone troubles.

One big benefit of e-mail is that the unwritten laws of polite computer correspondence allow you to send very short messages. You don't need to go through all the labor involved in a formal letter.

The second message was from my assistant. She had read a message I'd left for her yesterday and provided me with the answers I needed. Since we hadn't been physically in the office at the same time for a while, this was a great way to stay in sync.

The third message was an urgent plea for a product upgrade. The customer discovered late last night that he needed an upgrade to FileFlex. Before he went to bed, he sent a note to me, asking for special handling, to make sure his upgrade got managed. I hit the reply button, sending a note back telling him to make sure he called my assistant with his ordering information and also told him how to reach her by e-mail. I then hit the forward button, sending a copy of his urgent request to my assistant, along with a note asking her to make a special effort to get the upgrade out to him immediately.

Yes, we could have handled his request through normal means. But I was able to help and respond immediately. From his perspective, he got great customer service. More importantly, it took me less than 30 seconds to handle his complete problem. That's an amazing increase in productivity.

Workgroup Software

Workgroup software (or "groupware") is a rather nebulous term encompassing tools like e-mail, shared calendars, and scheduling and collaboration software. The leading player in groupware, at least today, seems to be Lotus Notes.

I spent a year studying Notes in use at a variety of organizations—from government to banking to service and product companies. In my book *Lotus Notes Revealed!* (see Appendix B), I profiled nine organizations and their applications: the Vermont Department of Motor Vehicles; the U.S. Health Care Financing Administration; the Port of Libreville, Gabon, West Africa; the Royal Bank of Canada; Maryland National Bank; McGlinchey & Paul (a PR agency); Synetics (a systems integrator); Houghton Mifflin (a major publisher); and Cabletron (a networking hardware provider).

As part of my research, I examined Notes in actual use throughout the organizations. I was able to learn their reasons for choosing Notes, as well as their trials and triumphs installing, developing, and managing Notes applications. This was the first (and only) time anyone had been given this level of access into the operations of organizations that depend heavily on software support for collaboration and communication.

The common thread among all the interviews was high perceived value derived from using workgroup software. It seems that groupware plays a key role in helping to coordinate organizations and getting people to communicate effectively. The corporations I studied provided some very interesting observations about Notes use:

- *Clear Organizational "Reengineering" Benefits.* Each of the profiled organizations found it very difficult to quantify the dollar benefits derived from Notes. But while the return on investment was difficult to quantify, the organizations were unanimous in claiming substantial benefits. All the organizations showed tangible examples of increased productivity, time savings, and increases in overall quality of service to customers. These benefits were the direct result of Notes eliminating steps in processes, eliminating or reducing bottlenecks, and reducing the amount of information lost in transit from one person to another.

- *Reduced Paper Flow.* While Notes will never lead to the mythical paperless office, Notes has been seen to reduce overall paper flow. Reduced paper flow has numerous benefits: reduced paper demand; reduced need for photocopying; fewer worker hours for photocopying; fewer worker hours required for sorting and delivering documents; fewer worker hours required for opening and reading documents before sending them to their appropriate destinations; reduced filing costs; less time required to discard paper, carry it out of the facility, and pick up or recycle paper; and fewer trees destroyed. As I mentioned earlier, The Royal Bank of Canada has over 9,000 different forms. If Notes use eliminated even a fraction of these forms, a multimillion-dollar savings would result.

- *Staying Connected.* One trend was particularly promising: Notes users really like using Notes. Notes was often brought into an organization for one group to solve one small problem. Often Notes use grew as more and more people found that information could be presented in a way that wasn't possible before. In particular, Notes "replication" feature allows people in the field to stay comfortably connected into the corporate database—even from an airplane.

- *Downsizing.* Many organizations are using distributed Notes applications to replace tasks previously assigned to very expensive mainframe computers. They felt that whereas mainframes were capable of performing the needed services, Notes was much less expensive to implement and maintain. The modularity of Notes (particularly replication) made it possible to decentralize control of development, maintenance, and administration.

Although groupware software is generally received positively by users, it often takes quite a long time to penetrate the organization. Many of the users profiled expressed initial doubts about the benefits of Notes, often confusing it with more traditional electronic mail or database systems.

I found strong resistance to Notes from only one quarter: traditional database developers who were outside contractors. I was shocked. I dug deep enough and finally discovered that these guys didn't like Notes because building applications in it took a lot less time than with traditional systems. That meant less billable hours per project—a strong justification not only to examine your employees' productivity but to find out exactly how your outside contractors approach their jobs!

Workgroup software is not the universal panacea for inefficient organizations. But the companies profiled show that workgroup software products like Notes can generate a fundamental cultural change in an organization. Though workgroup software is useful, political factors can help determine the success or failure of a groupware installation. Upper management tends to be cautious about adopting it in one chunk. But the majority of those organizations who've implemented pilot projects have gone on to see much larger installations.

My research with experienced Notes users showed that workgroup software helps in informally flattening the organization chart which gives everyone easier access to others throughout the organization and makes the hierarchical structure less rigid. The kind of information flow capability provided through groupware empowers individuals to do their jobs better with higher satisfaction levels.

One more important note: Software like e-mail and Notes doesn't replace or obsolete real person-to-person communication. In fact, just the opposite is more likely. Electronic networks are just one more way we can all get together to make things happen. So don't be afraid that installing an e-mail system is going to turn all your employees into electronic zombies.

MANAGING THE PEOPLE DYNAMIC

People are interesting creatures. They react to their environment, and they influence their environment. A chain of reactions and influences causes a very fast ripple effect. You've certainly seen at least one manifestation of this ripple effect: the "rumor mill." Whether it's rumors racing through your company at warp speed or a change in how people relate to each other after a reorg, you can't help but be conscious of the effect. I've seen the people dynamic go haywire in many different areas. Here are some interesting war stories and tips.

The "D" Word

One of the most amazing examples of the people dynamic was my experience with what I now call the "D" word. When my business grew, I decided that I'd divide the employees into logical groups: sales, engineering, and production. Each department would have its own manager.

You need to understand the dynamic before this reorganization. We had grown rapidly. I doubled the size of the company in less than four months (not something I ever intend to repeat). We moved from an overcrowded house into a much larger office building. We were, to all appearances, "official."

Prior to the reorg, everyone worked well enough with everyone else. If a salesperson needed a product shipped for a critical customer, he'd ask a production person to make a critical build. Everyone worked together to make the business work.

Then, all of a sudden, we had Departments. Where days earlier, we had harmony, suddenly we had division. It was no longer Sherrie or Merrie or James. It was Sales (with a capital "S"), Production (with a capital "P"), and Engineering (with a capital "E"). Each Department (with a capital "D") had its own set of priorities and became insular. When the same salesperson would ask the same production person to do the same job as a week earlier, suddenly it became a question of whether Production (with that damnable capital "P") was required to accept a task from any old salesperson and where that task fit into Production's responsibility. This transformation rocketed throughout the company at about Warp 12.

This caught me totally by surprise. Nobody had been told to behave this way. None of the "Departments" had received any specific instructions on how to relate to each other. The reorg was accomplished to free me up from managing everyone (which was beginning to sap my time) and to give me the opportunity to give kudos and promotions to the folks who had long deserved it.

Where before there was limited politics (and always on an interpersonal basis), now there were turf battles and real company political strife. Again, let me stress that this transformation occurred almost instantly. I tried, in individual discussions, over lunches, in group meetings, in any way I could, to get these groups to play nice with each other. It just didn't work.

Finally, in a fit of desperation, I abolished the "D" word and the departments along with it. Those who were managers were to be considered senior (or more experienced) employees. Nothing more. Everyone reported to me. Period. And even the utterance of the "D" word was subject to punishment so terrible as to not have been specified.

No doubt, there was some degree of dissatisfaction among the displaced managers, but the political squabbles ceased within another very short time, and work continued to move forward with far more amity and far less strife.

Titles as Marketing Tools

In traditional corporate America, your job title reflects your rank in an organization. VPs are more important than managers, managers more important than supervisors, and down the line. In some sense, a title is important as a measuring tool. But positional authority goes only so far. Eventually, your importance to the organization must be factored in.

In my company, I've always treated employee titles as marketing tools. A job title reflects how we want someone outside the company to perceive the employee, not how one employee relates to another.

Here's a very good example. Since I started the company, I've hired only very, very effective personal assistants. They're keenly aware of how the business runs and are usually able to manage or troubleshoot many elements of the business and business relationships. But to outsiders, assistants are "secretaries," with all that title conveys. They're not respected or treated as people of significance. Yet my assistant is vitally important to the business and often serves as the chief operating officer—in span of authority and contribution, if not in title.

When setting appointments for me, she might just call herself a secretary. But when completely managing our trade show efforts, she'd never get a call returned by management companies if she used the secretary title. Now she's the "Trade Show Manager." When dealing with vendors, it's "Purchasing Manager" or "Production Manager." All are vital titles. Yet you can't fit them all on a business card. So the title is chosen to be appropriate to the people she talks to outside the company. We don't care about her title internally. We all know she runs the place. And that's all that matters.

Growing Your People

No matter how much I value a contributor, no matter how much I'd like to see that person with us forever, I know that everyone, some-day, may decide to leave the company. That's the natural order of things.

I believe this natural order mandates our obligation as managers to grow our employees so that they're more employable and more valuable to their next employer than they were when they started with our companies.

You saw it described first in the MediaLab Manifesto: We have the obligation to grow our employees by at least one job position or level during their tenure in the company. That means we must provide training, personal growth, counseling, and support. It also means not pigeonholing people because they happen to do one job well. When you make employee growth part of the fabric of your business, you'll see people grow, change, and eventually move on. This is the way it should be. And it should make you proud when you see a par-ticularly promising junior employee grow into a competent, sea-soned professional.

If you strip away everything else about running a company, that's what I think is the most important thing I, at least, strive constantly to give back: the simple dignity of growth.

RECAP

Your business is worthless without the people who make it run. Even so, the survival of your business must come before the interests of any specific employee. Ensuring the survival of the enterprise is a sacred contract not only with your investors, but with all the employ-ees and all their families throughout the future of your business.

Once that survival is ensured, your next obligation is to your employees. These are the people who have, literally, placed their livelihoods in your hands. Decisions you make will directly impact their lives, the lives of their families, and their futures. It's an awesome responsibility, but one that business leaders carry on their shoulders with pride every single day.

Your relationship with your employees should be based on honor, respect, and the fundamental nature of labor hours for payment. Any employee may trade you some time in return for dollars. But, if you want that employee's heart as well as mind or body, you must go beyond the business transaction into the world of the relationship. Treat all your employees, from the lowest to the highest, with respect. Understand and have concerns for their needs. Recognize the impact your actions and your decisions have on them and their families. Answer questions honestly. And take pride in the great social contract that's connected you with your workers:

- The nature of the business contract is that you are the customer of your workers and they are the customer of you. Be conscious of this relationship.

- Optimize your workforce to be flexible, to account for booms and slumps.

- Identify core contributors, avoid unnecessary long-term commitments, make use of permanent part-timers and professional temps, and test potential new hires by working with them as temps first.

- There's a blurring of the lines between employees and contributors. Employees must all now be part entrepreneur.

- Outsourcing is growing—from traditional clerical services to professional services. Even if you can't afford all full-time senior management, consider hiring a part-time VP, CFO, or COO.

- Many workers are working without walls, outside your organization. The growth of the virtual worker has opened issues of communication, management discipline, morale, relationships, collaboration, and technology.

- Your headquarters may no longer be a building. In many companies, the network is the headquarters.

- If you're not using it already, give serious consideration to adding electronic mail to your organization. Also look into workgroup software to help keep people connected.

As a business leader, you're the caretaker of your products, marketing, operations, cash flow, and employees. But if you don't take care of yourself, the rest won't matter. In our next and final chapter, we'll talk about taking care of the most important asset of your enterprise. You.

CHAPTER 15

Get a Life!

All animals, except man, know that the principal business of life is to enjoy it.

—Samuel Butler, 1903

Building, nurturing, and improving the fortunes of our businesses becomes an all-consuming activity for most of us who own or manage our companies. We work long hours and bring work home. When we're not actually working, we're worrying or planning or scheming or worrying some more. We often feel the weight of the entire enterprise on our shoulders and don't give ourselves enough opportunities to take a break.

Surprise! Your sanity is your company's business. If you can't think clearly, if you're overworked to the point of burnout, or if you work so hard you get sick, your company will suffer with you. You've got to learn to balance the stress of running a company with having an out-of-work lifestyle specifically designed to nurture you so that you can respond to the daily demands of your job.

This chapter will talk about the danger signs and how to avoid serious problems. It will also help you understand how the necessary intrusions of work into your hours outside the office can be made more tolerable. Finally, you'll learn how to reinvent, reposition, and refocus your lifestyle so you can have both a healthy company and a happy and healthy lifestyle.

I need to come clean here. I have a pretty good handle on the theory of life outside work, but the practice still sort of eludes me. My business consumes a vast percentage of my time and attention; most would say way too much. This chapter is the living embodiment of the age-old adage, "Do as I say, not as I do." Of course, there's always some hope that I'll go back and read what I've written and, along with you, learn how to reinvent parts of my life.

THE SEPARATION OF HOME AND WORK

As I discussed last chapter, I used to have the business in my house. This was a major drain on my sanity. There were nights I'd find myself driving around town, just around and around, because I wanted to get away from work. Since my office was at my house, being home meant being at work. This was not good.

My overall stress level went down considerably when I separated home from office. Even though there are many times I think of bringing them together again (particularly if I want to use resources that are in the office when I'm at home), I'm convinced it would be a bad idea. Your circumstances are probably different—most larger businesses could never fit in a house. Yet, it is still important to figure out tangible borderlines between work and home life.

One of the things I've learned in my quest to get something of a life is to simply try to make life easier and more pleasant. Here are some ideas (often obvious—but many of us have missed the obvious) about how to make things easier:

- *Optimal Commute.* Commuting is often a bear. If possible, try to live near work or (since it's your business!) move work closer to home. In any case, there isn't really a good excuse for you to be incurring a daily drive of more than a half hour each way. I've found some value in a short commute (mine's 15 minutes). It's long enough that I'm not (often) tempted at 4 A.M. to run back to the office for a paper I left on my desk. But it's short enough to be pleasant—I have some self-imposed isolation time to think, plan, or just "veg."

- *Telephone.* I used to give everyone (including customers) my home number. I used to get lots of calls at home. I thought this made me effective, but it really interrupted any small amount of relaxation I could find for myself. Now, I give far fewer people my home number. Business contacts can call me at the office, on my cellular phone, or via e-mail. I do check my e-mail from home, even on weekends (but only at my convenience). If there's an urgent customer problem, the wait isn't all weekend.

- *Private Line.* If you want people to be able to call at home, the other alternative (but one I would prefer to do without) is to have a private line for business calls. Put this on an answering machine so you don't have to talk unless you want to. This is a great way to selectively get business calls at home. Give out one number to business contacts and the other to family. If you don't want to be interrupted, don't pick up the business line.

WHEN WORK INTRUDES

If you run a successful business, work will always intrude on your private time. The key to success seems to be controlling how you allow it to intrude. It took me a long time to develop my own style for balancing how I work and what I'm working on. For example, I focus my time and attention very differently when I'm working on a book than when I'm doing a turnaround for a client or negotiating a big deal. Although all these activities may take up time outside the office, each one requires a different style.

Conventional wisdom would argue that allowing work to intrude on personal time is unacceptable. Were we to live in a conventional world, this might be true. I haven't found a way to confine my work time to a dedicated eight hours between 8 A.M. and 5 P.M. There are some "good" reasons for work to intrude:

- I often write from home (although as I write this, I'm sitting in my office). When I write from home, I often do it very, very late at night, when there are no phones ringing and no other distractions. Because I find writing physically tiring (wrists, arms, and shoulders), being at home means I can stretch out for a while when I start to feel discomfort.

- I often scope out projects alone over a meal at a local restaurant. For example, when I'm outlining a chapter or defining a feature set for a product, the pacing is such that it often takes a few hours of considering, thinking, brainstorming, and the like. When I'm away from home, away from the office, and in a neutral setting, I find I can think more clearly with no interruptions. It's also great having a regular supply of coffee delivered without having to interrupt the thinking process.

- I often need to be in contact with customers, clients, or constituents when I'm away from the office. I have a cellular phone where I can be reached and where I can reach out. While cellular phones are certainly not uncommon, active use can let you accomplish work that would otherwise chain you to your office desk. And, carrying a phone with me means I can leave the office even if I'm expecting an important call. In the pre-cellular phone days, I'd occasionally stay in the office all day, no breakfast or lunch break, waiting on a call. But having the phone has meant I can leave the office, and either be reached directly by a client or by my assistant if something heats up.

- We had horrible winter storms last winter. I think we lost 18 or 20 work days when it was virtually impossible to get into the office. A few times I was *trapped* at home when a three-foot wall of ice locked my car into its parking space. Even so, most deadlines just don't care about weather. The work still had to be done. By working from home, we were able to accomplish almost everything that had to be done.

SOME HOME (SECOND) OFFICE IDEAS

The key to surviving the storms revolved around that old Boy Scout motto: Be Prepared. We took pains to set up our systems so, should it be necessary, we could become a virtual company and all work away from the office. Here's how it works:

- *Remote Call Forwarding.* Normal call forwarding allows you, from the main phone, to forward calls to another number. This is a nice idea, unless you can't get to the main phone at the office. Remote call forwarding allows us, with a call to Bell Atlantic and a few codes, to retarget our main numbers so calls to the office ring at our homes (or wherever else we might be working. Customers calling the office don't feel like we're out of touch.

- *Multiple Home Phone Lines.* This is important so at least one line is open for voice communication and one line is open for fax or computer communication.
- *Capable Computers at Home.* Word processing and database access are essential. Having a capable computer system at home means that you can run the critical software necessary to keep your business running.
- *High-Speed Fax Modems.* High-speed fax modems are cheap. Having one in the home-based computer allows you to receive and send faxes from home. The fast modem also allows you to dial out from your computer into online services, the Internet, and into the office network.
- *Remote Access Software.* Our computer network is set up so that we can dial in remotely, assuming we have the correct security codes.
- *Remote File System.* Once connected into the network, we can access the hard disks on our server and on our personal office machines. This means that we're never without critical files from the office (unless, of course, the power goes down at the office).
- *Teleoperation.* Also, once connected into the network, we have specialized software that allows us to remotely operate the computers at the office.
- *Remote Database Access.* Much of our business's brain trust is stored in our centralized database system. Being out of touch with the system is like being cut off from the world. By being able to dial in and grab information out of the database, we're able to stay up to speed on everything of importance.

As you might imagine, I rely on technology to make my life easier, whenever possible. This may seem like a lot of trouble to weather a few weeks of snow. It is. But the benefits go way beyond snow survival in the suburbs. How many times have you forgotten a critical document at the office? I've done it a lot. Before this system was set up, I used to have to get into the car (usually at midnight or later) and do the half-hour round trip in the cold, dark night, just to get something I needed to work on. Now it takes less than a minute to dial the phone, grab the file, and get on with the work. All without having to go out in the cold.

> *Note:* Many states are starting to require larger companies to institute some form of telecommuting as part of compliance with the Clean Air Act.

RECREATION TIME

Think about the word "recreation." Look at it carefully—"re" and "creation." Together, they're "re-creation." Re-creation has a whole lot more powerful meaning than recreation. In fact, re-creation seems to be very much in the spirit of our quest for reinvention. At the core of reinvention must be re-creation.

Recreation is re-creation. It's the recharging of the system, the refreshing of the mind, body, and soul. It's the maintenance phase of life.

And for most of us who run businesses, it's what other people do.

I've come to believe that it's probably a good idea to get some recreation. I've never been really good at convincing myself to find the time (or figuring out what to do, or how not to feel guilty doing it), but it seems like a good idea.

Stealing Time from Work

If you operate on the assumption that your entire life is dedicated to work, then any time you allocate to recreation is time stolen from work—whether it's a Saturday afternoon or a Thursday evening. But there's an interesting flaw in this logic: You can't steal from yourself.

If you run the business, if you're the boss, the business has become you. So when you take time from work to have some recreation, you can't steal time from work. You're just reallocating some of your time. If you choose to take a Sunday off from work, you're not stealing it. If you choose to spend Thursday at a meeting of car buffs, you're not stealing time from work. And if you choose to take a Tuesday morning class in the literature of Jane Austin (or even Steve Austin), it's your time to take.

You're the boss. You can take whatever time (within reason) you want. One of the very few luxuries we really have as senior managers is the total authority to take control of our time. We may not exercise this authority often. But we have the capability. We can do it.

Let me share a secret with you. I know, you're saying you don't have time. I tell myself this all the time. But the fact is (here's the secret . . .), nothing's going to explode if you take a day off on the weekend. OK, there will be times that the realities of some project or other won't allow it, but most of the time, you can take the time and the world won't end. It really won't. Every day, in every way, you're getting better and better.

Breaking It Up

It's essential to break up your time, so that you're not spending it all on work. There are thousands of things (so I'm told) that people can do for recreation, from socializing with friends, to going to movies, to having a hobby. Make a list of activities you find are pleasant (if you can't think of any, ask a friend who's got a life). Then pick a time, actually make an appointment in your calendar, and do something from your pleasant activities list.

Vacations?

Most of us vaguely remember vacations from those times before we were managers. If you don't take vacations (and you know who you are!), listen up. Vacations are good things. But they don't always have to be the type where you take a long trip for a week or more. Let's talk minivacations:

- *Ten Minutes of Peace.* The easiest (and often highly effective) vacation is simply finding yourself 10 quiet minutes. Get up, stretch, take a walk around the parking lot. Find yourself a cozy little hiding place and give yourself 10 solid minutes of blissful freedom. It'll do you a world of good.
- *A Pleasant Lunch Hour.* Many executives work through lunch. Instead, consider staying (or getting) sane. Take a lunch

hour, go shopping, play a round of tennis, visit a park, get some air.

- *An Enjoyable Evening.* Make an appointment with yourself (or, preferably, with your spouse or a good friend) for an evening away from the office. You might just go out for a nice meal or combine it with a movie or show. Another pleasant excursion is booking a room at a local hotel—just for a pampered night away from the pressures of work, a nice meal, some time in a sauna or hot tub, and maybe even a good swim.

- *A Weekend Away.* Whether it's just a Friday night, or a long weekend, the weekend minivacation is an ideal way to recharge the system. Leave early Friday and return home Sunday. Or, even better, leave Saturday after a cozy morning sleeping in and return Monday evening—avoiding all the Monday office chaos.

- *Attach Vacation Time to a Business Trip.* This is my preferred trick for getting vacation time. Often, when I go on a business trip, I add as little as a day or as much as a week in the area I travel to. I get to play tourist, relax, and explore. And, because I'm traveling on business, I don't feel nearly as guilty about taking time off.

- *A Week or More.* Eventually, after taking time in shorter chunks, you may get yourself to the point where you can actually go away for a week. Do it.

- *Taking Work Along.* While you really never want to take work with you, if the choice is between staying home and working or taking work with you, take it with you. At least you'll get some time away. If you must take work along with you on a break, consider getting a fast laptop computer with a quick modem. You'll be able to stay in touch if you wish, and shut out the real world when you need quiet.

Get Physical

Exercise (you know, that pumping, sweating, grunting thing people do in health clubs) is good for you. Or so I've been told. You should get some kind of exercise every day. Granted, you may not work out in the health club, but exercise anywhere is possible.

> *Note:* Many businesses have health clubs or exercise facilities for the benefit of their employees. Hey, you're the boss. If you have one, use it. If you don't have one, consider adding it to your facility. It'll be a good investment for everyone.

THE QUEST FOR BALANCE

The essence of re-invention is the quest for balance, the bringing of elements of the enterprise into harmony with each other. Because you are a central, pivotal element of the company, your enterprise cannot exist in harmony unless you first are in balance. To achieve balance in your life, there is no question you must seek success in your chosen profession. As a manager, your success is the success of the enterprise. Yet you are more than your profession. You are your interests, your abilities, your needs, your desires, your family, your loves, your fears, and your physical self. To be a balanced human being, you must maintain and nurture all these aspects of yourself (your "self"). For without that balance, there cannot be harmony. And without harmony, change is merely another word for chaos.

Afterword

My hope is that during your reading of *The Flexible Enterprise* you have discovered new ways to transform your business that will benefit from your company's inherent strengths. Earlier, I was presumptive enough to request that you refrain from reducing your workforce until you finished reading this book. That time has come, and I hope that you have found sufficient strengths, not only in your products and processes, but in your people. It is my most fervent hope that you have found the heart and soul of your business in those workers—and that your transformation will leverage off the strengths they contribute, not off the payroll their unfortunate absence would reduce.

We've come to the end of the book and the beginning of a new way of life. Change can be tremendously empowering or unbearably horrifying. How you relate to change will play a big part in determining whether change will be your friend. Change can be an incredibly uplifting force within your organization, your life, and your world. Give it a chance. Don't fight it. Embrace it.

You have my very best wishes.

—David Gewirtz
Rocky Hill, NJ

247

APPENDIX A

Staying in Touch

Chances are, you've already transformed an important aspect of your organization as a direct result of an idea or discussion you learned in *The Flexible Enterprise*. Question: What happened? Did you get people previously at odds working together? Did you get a project back on track? Did you save time and money getting a product shipped? Did you replace an antiquated mechanical system? Did you take on a tough cultural challenge? Or did you go above and beyond the call of duty to make sure your employees felt like valued contributors to the organization?

Whatever the circumstances, if effective transformation played a part, I'd like to know about it and so would other readers. Your experience can be very helpful and could make the difference in the sanity, satisfaction, and happiness of thousands of people you may never meet. Tell me, in your own words, what happened, and if I think it will appeal to a wide range of readers, I'll rewrite it to reflect your personality while adding my own personal touch so it fits the message and format of the book or article it's included in. Final approval (within reason) will be yours.

Here's why I hope you'll respond: First and foremost, you'll get great satisfaction from helping other readers. Second, you'll get the chance to be just a bit better known, and that could really enhance your success. Third, I really love hearing from, exchanging e-mail with, and chatting with readers.

Of course, if you just want to chat—and you want to keep the contents of the discussion confidential—I will certainly respect your wishes.

AUTHOR CONTACT INFORMATION

Here's how to get in touch with me (or to add your name to our mailing list of readers interested in reinvention and transformation):

David Gewirtz
Component Software Corporation
P.O. Box 201
Rocky Hill, NJ 08553
609-497-4501
FAX: 609-497-4008
CompuServe: 76004,2162
Internet: david@component-net.com
World Wide Web: www.component-net.com

THE FLEXIBLE ENTERPRISE JOURNAL

If you just can't get enough of the Flexible Enterprise, consider subscribing to our new monthly newsletter *The Flexible Enterprise Journal*. To get more information and a free issue, call Component at 609-497-4501 or visit www.component-net.com.

FLEXIBLE ENTERPRISE INTERNET MAILING LISTS

If you'd like to stay in touch, you should sign up to the Flexible Enterprise Internet Mailing List. This free electronic mail service allows you to automatically get new Flexible Enterprise information and to talk with other readers. If you have an e-mail account within your company, or on any of the major online services, you can be part of this dynamic interactive readership.

To get information postings and interesting news about the Flexible Enterprise, you should subscribe to *flexible-enterprise-announce*. Whenever we have important information to announce, we'll post it through flexible-enterprise-announce.

To receive mail from flexible-enterprise-announce, send an e-mail message to the internet address listserv@netcom.com. In the first line of the message (not the subject!), include the following:

subscribe flexible-enterprise-announce

The flexible-enterprise-talk list is an "open" list that provides a mechanism for Flexible Enterprise readers to converse among themselves. This list is unmoderated and unedited. Anything you send to flexible-enterprise-talk will be replicated and mailed to all the subscribers on the list. In turn, anything any other subscriber mails to the list will be sent to you (assuming you've subscribed).

Flexible-enterprise-talk is intended to provide Flexible Enterprise readers with a way to share great ideas, get help on sticky problems, and work together to explore new ideas. So send messages and reply to messages. Get together and talk, have fun, and share great stuff!

To receive mail from flexible-enterprise-talk, send an e-mail message to the Internet address listserv@netcom.com. In the first line of the message (not the subject!), include the following:

subscribe flexible-enterprise-talk

See you on the Net!

Flexible Enterprise Resource Guide

Many of us learn by experience and by doing. But we also learn by reading. There are, as my editor has often reminded me, thousands upon thousands of business books available to any interested reader. But we all have favorites, and I certainly have mine. In this appendix (following a bit of self-congratulatory prose about my Lotus Notes-related writing pursuits), you will find brief descriptions of some of my favorite books on business change.

TO LEARN MORE ABOUT LOTUS NOTES

Lotus Notes is one of the most popular software tools for improving communications and organization effectiveness in large corporations. Since Notes has been such a contributor to helping people within an organization connect with each other, you might want to read more.

Lotus Notes 3 Revealed!
David Gewirtz
Rocklin, CA: Prima Publishing, 1994

In this book, I provide compelling, real-life examples of how Notes transformed some of the world's most successful corporations in areas such as customer service, sales management, telemarketing, product development, and human resources management. If you're curious about how a software product can impact organizational effectiveness, you should definitely read this book. Please forgive this small amount of gratuitous book promotion when I tell you that to order, you should see your local bookstore or call Prima at 916-786-0426.

Workspace for Lotus Notes
David Gewirtz, Editor-in-Chief
Louisville, KY: The Cobb Group

Following on the success of my Lotus Notes book, The Cobb Group (the nation's largest computer newsletter and journal publisher) is publishing a great monthly journal on Lotus Notes. Not only is it chock-full of interesting analysis, product tips, reviews, and more case studies on software-supported reinvention, it's got me as Editor-in-Chief! To find out more about *Workspace for Lotus Notes,* please contact The Cobb Group at 800-223-8720.

THE FLEXIBLE MANAGER'S LIBRARY

Reengineering the Corporation
Michael Hammer and James Champy
New York:HarperBusiness, 1993

This book has become the Bible of reengineering. Hammer and Champy do an excellent job of looking at the largest corporations and issues of process. While my recommendations are, in many ways, diametrically opposed to those within this book, it is nevertheless a seminal work and should be read by all serious students of positive change.

Working from Home
Making It on Your Own
Getting Business to Come to You (with Laura Clampitt Douglass)
Paul and Sarah Edwards
New York: Jeremy P. Tarcher, 1991

Paul and Sarah Edwards are two of the most down-to-earth business writers I've encountered. While their target reader seems to be the work-from-home entrepreneur, they have a great understanding of both the practical issues of running a small business and the personal trials and pressures that small business owners must withstand. Even if you don't work at home (in fact, even if you work in a much larger company), you owe it to yourself to read these books and benefit from Paul and Sarah's advice. They also operate the great Working from Home forum on CompuServe. Here you can dial in and chat with Paul, Sarah, and hundreds of other small business owners.

Downshifting
Amy Salzman
New York: HarperCollins, 1991

Downshifting puts the quest for a simpler life into a clear perspective. If you're wondering how to bring a sense of self back into your life and career, if you want to shift out of the fast lane, this is a book you should read. Downshifting is not what I'd call recommended reading for business transformation. Rather it's a great resource for those interested in truly getting a life.

Thriving on Chaos
Liberation Management
Crazy Times Call for Crazy Organizations
Tom Peters
New York: Alfred A. Knopf, 1992

Tom Peters has single-handedly screwed up my world view more than any other author (with the possible exception of Robert Heinlein when I was a teenager). Tom Peters has a great way of looking at complex business issues and just plain cutting through the garbage, to leave the real world in stark evidence. Every time I read one of Peters' books or listen to one of his seminars, I wind up going on a thinking spree for weeks, re-examining many of the presumed truths I had previously held dear. If you want to get fabulous inspiration, some real understanding, and actual, pleasant reading, get your hands on anything written by this guy.

Managing Brand Equity
David A. Aaker
New York: The Free Press, 1991

While product and brand marketing are critically important disciplines, they have historically gotten very little play in business texts. Aaker takes a critically important element of marketing, the maintenance and growth of a brand, and subjects it to microscopic examination. Excellent work.

Growing a Business
Paul Hawken
New York: Simon & Schuster, 1987

Paul Hawken's book has become a classic example of the New Age business manager. In *Growing a Business*, Hawken shows how a business is an expression of self. While many of us have struggled for years trying to extricate ourselves from identifying ourselves with our businesses, Hawken shows how your business can identify itself with you.

The Mind of the Strategist
Kenichi Ohmae
New York: Penguin Books, 1982

This book is old, but exceptionally valuable. I don't know if it's still in print, but if you ever get a chance—buy it. Ohmae helps to put strategy and planning into real perspective, with examples out of Japan's most successful businesses. This isn't just another book on Japanese business practices. Rather it's an excellent, understandable, and exceptionally well-considered guide to strategic thinking.

The Macintosh Way
Selling the Dream
Guy Kawasaki
New York: HarperBusiness, 1991

Guy's an interesting guy. Formerly head of Apple's evangelism group (where they tried to recruit independent software producers to write software for Macintosh computers) and the head of his own software company, Guy has an unmatched view of the high-tech culture surrounding Macintosh. While *The Macintosh Way* gives you another insight into the world of software companies, *Selling the Dream* is really a guide to marketing a vision, a dream. *Selling the Dream* makes an interesting counterpoint to *Managing Brand Equity*. In Aaker's book, the issue is very tangible—this is the product, this is its positioning, this is its brand. In *Selling the Dream,* Guy comes at the brand equity problem from the opposite direction—that of an evangelist.

Reinventing the Corporation
John Naisbitt and Patricia Aburdene
New York: Warner Books, 1985

A great book in its time, *Reinventing the Corporation* is now somewhat dated. Written by the author of *Megatrends*, *Reinventing the Corporation* describes how the business world was expected to change. They got some of it right and they got some of it wrong. If you filter out many of the predictions and read it for the practical "how-to" lessons, the book still holds value today.

Marketing Warfare
Positioning: The Battle for Your Mind
Al Ries and Jack Trout
New York: Warner Books, 1981

Ries and Trout put the strategic and tactical issues of marketing in clear perspective with Marketing Warfare, showing powerful similarity between marketing campaign and a military campaign. Positioning is another one of the truly classic marketing books. It'll help you understand how to use positioning to gain the upper hand.

The Handbook of Strategic Expertise
Catherine Hayden
New York: The Free Press, 1986

Organized almost like an encyclopedia, this book is a gold mine of concepts and techniques for the strategist. This book probably has more sticky-pad bookmarks in it than any other book in my library.

A Whack on the Side of the Head
Roger von Oech
New York: Warner Books, 1983

Back in the early 1980s, *A Whack on the Side of the Head* was all the rage in Corporate America. Still available on some bookstore shelves, *Whack* can help you start thinking "outside the box." It's a great coach for helping you break down mental locks and boosting innovation.

The Addictive Organization
Anne Wilson Schaef and Diane Fassel
New York: Harper & Row, 1990

When we think of our company, the last thing that comes to mind is any thought of addiction. Yet many of us, employees and managers alike, exhibit addictive behavior towards our company. This book is a fascinating look into a deeply buried corner of all our minds.

The Art of War
Sun Tzu
(Published in many translations, written more than 2,000 years ago)

If you have any strategic responsibility, you must read and ponder the sayings of this ancient Chinese general. Still valid after all these thousands of years, *The Art of War* is amazingly applicable to corporate and competitive strategy even today.

The Invisible Workforce
Beverly Lozano
New York: The Free Press, 1989

If you find yourself looking more and more toward implementing a Flexible Workforce as described in Chapter 15, consider reading *The Invisible Workforce*. Lozano describes, from almost a social scientist's perspective, how American business is changing to integrate outside and home-based workers.

The Design of Everyday Things
Donald A. Norman
New York: Doubleday, 1988

This is such an incredibly cool book. If you ever expect to market products—even if you're not an engineer or a product designer—you owe it to your customers to read this book. Through fascinating journeys into the design of objects we use every day, Norman helps us see how to design products that can be used and enjoyed.

Crossing the Chasm
Geoffrey A. Moore
New York: HarperBusiness, 1991

This book provides a new perspective into a critical transition phase for many companies: from niche to mainstream. More importantly, the book points out that such a transition exists and helps business owners understand the risks inherent in crossing the chasm.

Competitive Strategy
Competitive Advantage
Michael A. Porter
New York: The Free Press, 1980

If you have competition (and unless you're my cable company, you're facing competition every day), you should add Porter's books to your library. *Competitive Strategy* is *the* textbook for competitive analysis while *Competitive Advantage* is an excellent guide to applying that analysis to your benefit.

Index